Narrative of an Attempt to Reach the North Pole

Engraved by J. W. Finden.

NARRATIVE

OF

AN ATTEMPT TO REACH

THE

NORTH POLE,

IN BOATS FITTED FOR THE PURPOSE, AND ATTACHED TO
HIS MAJESTY'S SHIP HECLA,

IN THE YEAR MDCCCXXVII.,

UNDER THE COMMAND OF

CAPTAIN WILLIAM EDWARD PARRY, R.N., F.R.S.,

AND HONORARY MEMBER OF THE IMPERIAL ACADEMY OF SCIENCES AT
ST PETERSBURG

ILLUSTRATED BY PLATES AND CHARTS.

PUBLISHED BY AUTHORITY OF HIS ROYAL HIGHNESS
THE LORD HIGH ADMIRAL

LONDON:

JOHN MURRAY,

PUBLISHER TO THE ADMIRALTY, AND BOARD OF LONGITUDE.

MDCCCXXVIII

LONDON

Printed by WILLIAM CLOWES
Stamford-street

TO

SIR HUMPHRY DAVY, BART,

LATE PRESIDENT

AND TO

THE COUNCIL OF THE ROYAL SOCIETY,

BY WHOSE RECOMMENDATION

THE ATTEMPT TO REACH THE NORTH POLE, RECORDED IN THE FOLLOWING PAGES, WAS UNDERTAKEN

BY ORDER OF THE LATE LORDS COMMISSIONERS OF THE ADMIRALTY

THIS VOLUME

IS INSCRIBED

BY THEIR FAITHFUL AND OBEDIENT SERVANT

WILLIAM EDWARD PARRY

ADMIRALTY, *January*, 1828

CONTENTS.

CONTENTS.

APPENDIX

DIRECTIONS TO THE BINDER FOR PLACING THE PLATES

ERRATA

Page 37, bottom line, *for* ' affod," *read* ' afford '

    43, first line, *for* " three to four," *read* ' four to five '

    id , note, *dele* " subsequently "

    52, line 10 *for* 260, *read* 268

    60, line 20, *for* " In," *read* " It "

INTRODUCTION.

In April, 1826, I proposed to the Right Honourable Viscount Melville, First Lord Commissioner of the Admiralty, to attempt to reach the North Pole, by means of travelling with sledge-boats over the ice, or through any spaces of open water that might occur. My proposal was soon after referred to the President and Council of the Royal Society, who strongly recommended its adoption; and an Expedition being accordingly directed to be equipped for this purpose, I had the honor of being appointed to the command of it; and my commission for His Majesty's Ship the Hecla, which was intended to carry us to Spitzbergen, was dated the 11th of November, 1826.

The reports of several of our navigators who had visited Spitzbergen, and were well qualified to judge of the nature of the polar ice, concur in representing it as by no means unfavourable for this project. From one of the Seven Islands, and almost on the very spot from which we subsequently took our departure in the boats, Captain Lutwidge, the associate of Captain Phipps in the Expedition towards the North Pole in 1773, describes the ice to the north-eastward, to the distance of ten or twelve leagues, to have the appearance of " one continued plain of smooth unbroken ice, bounded only by the horizon." In Captain Phipps's chart of that voyage, the ice to the northward of the Seven Islands is represented as " flat and unbroken ;" and, in another situation, rather more to the westward, and about the same parallel, he describes the " main body of the ice to be lying in a line, nearly east and west, quite solid *."

The testimony of Mr. Scoresby, jun., a close and intelligent observer of nature in these regions, is entirely to the same effect. " I once saw," says he, " a field that was so free from either fissure or hummock, that I imagine, had it been free from snow, a coach might have been driven many leagues over it in a direct line, without obstruction or danger." Indeed, in a paper upon the subject of the Polar Ice, presented by Mr. Scoresby to the Wernerian Society of Edinburgh, and published in their Memoirs †, he enters at considerable length into the arguments in favour of the practicability of this enterprise, and in his subsequent work, above quoted, repeats his conviction to the same effect ‡. To the respectable authorities already mentioned I may also add the testimony of several intelligent and experienced whalers, whom I consulted as to the nature of

* Phipps's Voyage towards the North Pole, pp 59—60, 55.
† Vol ii. p 328.
‡ Scoresby's Account of the Arctic Regions, i. 54—61, 242.

the ice, with reference to this project; and who, without exception, agreed in considering it as highly favourable for the purpose.

But the hopes I had formed of being able to attain this object, and the plan now suggested for putting it into execution, were principally founded on a similar proposition formerly made by my friend and brother-officer, Captain Franklin, who, judging of this enterprise by his own experience, as well as by that of his associates, Captains Buchan and Beechey, though by no means thinking lightly of the labour and hazard attending it, had drawn up a plan for making the attempt, and himself volunteered to conduct it *. Following up, in the most essential particulars, the plan of this distinguished traveller, the principal features of which will best be understood by reference to my Official Instructions, two boats were constructed at Woolwich, under my superintendence, after an excellent model suggested by Mr. Peake, and nearly resembling what are called "troop-boats," having great flatness of floor, with the extreme breadth carried well forward and aft, and possessing the utmost buoyancy, as well as capacity for stowage. Their length was twenty feet, and their extreme breadth seven feet. The timbers were made of tough ash and hickory, one inch by half an inch square, and a foot apart, with a 'half-

* This plan, as originally proposed by Captain Franklin, was given to me by Mr Barrow, soon after my return from the Expedition of 1824-5.

timber " of smaller size between each two. On the outside of
the frame thus formed, was laid a covering of Mackintosh's
water-proof canvas, the outer part being coated with tar.
Over this was placed a plank of fir, only three-sixteenths of
an inch thick; then a sheet of stout felt; and, over all, an
oak plank of the same thickness as the fir; the whole of
these being firmly and closely secured to the timbers by
iron screws applied from without. This method of planking
the boats was proposed and executed by Mr. Lang, Master-
Shipwright of Woolwich dock-yard; and the following
Narrative will show how admirably the elasticity of this
mode of construction was adapted to withstand the constant
twisting and concussion to which the boats were subject *.
On each side of the keel, and projecting considerably below
it, was attached a strong " runner," shod with smooth steel,
in the manner of a sledge, upon which the boat entirely
rested while upon the ice; and to afford some additional
chance of making progress on hard and level fields, we also
applied to each boat two wheels, of five feet diameter, and a
small one abaft, having a swivel for steering by. like that of
a Bath chair; but these, owing to the irregularities of the
ice, did not prove of any service, and were subsequently

* The first travelling-boat, which was built by way of experiment, was
planked differently from these two, the planks, which were of half-inch oak,
being ingeniously " tongued" together with copper, according to a method
contrived by Mr Peake, in order to save the necessity of caulking, in case of
the wood shrinking This was the boat subsequently landed on Red Beach.

relinquished. A "span" of hide-rope was attached to the fore part of the runners, and to this were affixed two strong ropes of horse-hair, for dragging the boat; each individual being furnished with a broad leathern shoulder-belt, which could readily be fastened to or detached from the drag-ropes. The interior arrangement consisted only of two thwarts; a locker at each end for the nautical and other instruments, and for the smaller stores; and a very slight frame-work along the sides, for containing the bags of biscuit, and our spare clothes. A bamboo mast nineteen feet long, a tanned duck sail, answering also the purpose of an awning, a spreat, one boat-hook, fourteen paddles, and a steer-oar, completed each boat's equipment.

Two officers and twelve men (ten of the latter being seamen, and two marines) were selected for each boat's crew. It was proposed to take with us resources for ninety days; to set out from Spitzbergen, if possible, about the beginning of June, and to occupy the months of June, July, and August, in attempting to reach the pole, and returning to the ship; making an average journey of thirteen miles and a half per day. Our provisions consisted of biscuit, made by Mr. Le Mann, of the best wheaten flour; beef *pemmican* *; sweetened cocoa-powder, manufactured by

---

* For this article of our equipment, which contains a large proportion of nutriment in a small weight and compass, and is therefore invaluable on such occasions, we are much indebted to the kindness of Mr. J. P. Holmes,

Messrs. Fortnum and Mason; and a small proportion of rum, the latter concentrated to fifty-five per cent. above proof, in order to save weight and stowage. The proper instruments were provided, both by the Admiralty and the Board of Longitude, for making such observations as might be interesting in the higher latitudes, and as the nature of the enterprise would permit. Six pocket chronometers, the property of the public, were furnished for this service; and Messrs. Parkinson and Frodsham, with their usual liberality, entrusted to our care several other excellent watches, on trial, at their own expense *.

I have again to express my obligations to the Navy and Victualling Boards for their readiness in attending to my wishes, in the course of this equipment; as well as to Commissioner Hill, and to the Officers of Deptford and Woolwich Dock-yards, for the very obliging manner in which they executed the Instructions of their respective Boards in providing for our various wants.

Annexed is a list of the different articles composing the equipment of the boats, together with the actual weight of each.

Surgeon, of Old Fish Street, who had resided several years in the Hudson's Bay Establishments, and undertook to superintend the manufacture of it The process, which requires great attention, consists in drying large thin slices of the lean of the meat over the smoke of wood-fires, then pounding it, and lastly mixing it with about an equal weight of its own fat. In this state it is quite ready for use, without further cooking

* See Appendix, No. II.

	Enterprize	Endeavour
	lbs	lbs
Boat	1539	1542
Bamboo mast, one spreat, one boat-hook, one steel-oar .	46½	46¼
Fourteen paddles . . , . . .	41	41
Sail (or awning)	22	22
Spare rope and line	6	6
Small sounding-line (750 fathoms in all) . . .	8	10
Carpenters' tools, screws, nails, &c . . .	10	10
Copper and felt for repairs	19	19
Four fowling-pieces, with two bayonets . . .	15	15
Small articles for guns	—	4
Ammunition	17½	17½
Instruments	29	29
Books	7	5½
Spare Clothes. { Fur Suits for sleeping in (fourteen in each boat) .	162	162
Thicknailed boots (ditto ditto) . .	47	47
Esquimaux do, with spare soles, (ditto ditto) .	33	33
Flannel shirts (seven in each boat) . .	8¾	8¾
Guernsey frocks (ditto ditto) . .	11½	11½
Thick drawers (ditto ditto) . .	14	14
Mittens (twenty-eight in each boat) . .	5	5
Comforters (fourteen in each boat) .	1	1
Scotch caps (ditto ditto) .	4	4
A bag of small articles for the Officers, including soap, &c. &c .	4	4
Ditto ditto for the men ditto .	12	12
Biscuit	628	628
Pemmican	564	564
Rum	180	180
Cocoa-powder, sweetened	63	63
Salt	14	14
Spirits of wine	72	72
Cooking apparatus	—	20
Tobacco	20	20
Medicine chest	19	—
Pannikins, knife, fork, and spoon, (fourteen in each boat) .	5	5
Weighing-dials and measures . . .	2	2
Various small articles for repairs, &c., not mentioned above .	14	—
Packages for provisions, clothes, &c. . . .	110	116
	14)3753½	3753¾

Weight, per man . . . 268 lbs.

Exclusive of four sledges, weighing 26 lbs. each .

In drawing up my Journal for publication, I have, as before, thrown into an Appendix the details of such meteorological, magnetic, and other observations, as our situation and
circumstances enabled us to make; and these, I trust, will not
prove altogether unworthy the attention of men of science,
who are engaged in similar pursuits. For the description
of the specimens of Natural History, brought home by this
Expedition, I am once more indebted to the kind offices of
those gentlemen to whom I owe a similar obligation on
former occasions; and whose labours, so highly appreciated
by the scientific world, in the various branches of natural
knowledge, have imparted to our imperfect collections a
degree of value, which, without their assistance, they would
never have been found to possess.

I have not thought it necessary, in the course of this volume,
to enter into any examination of the question respecting the
approaches to the North Pole which had already been effected,
previously to our late attempt This question has, of late
years, been so fully discussed and brought into public notice,
in consequence of the strong and general interest excited by
the progress of Arctic Discovery, that I could not hope, by
any remarks of mine, to throw fresh light upon the subject.
I shall, therefore, only add that, after carefully weighing the
various authorities, from which every individual interested
in this matter is at liberty to form his own conclusions,
my own impartial conviction, at the time of our setting out

on this enterprize, coincided (with a single exception) with
the opinion expressed by the Commissioners of Longitude,
in their Memorial to the King, that " the progress of discovery had not arrived northwards, according to any well
authenticated accounts, so far as eighty-one degrees of North
Latitude *." The exception to which I allude, is in favour of
Mr Scoresby, who states his having, in the year 1806, reached
the latitude of 81° 12′ 42″, by actual observation, and 81° 30′,
by dead reckoning †. I therefore consider the latter parallel
as, in all probability, the highest which had ever been attained, prior to the attempt recorded in the following pages.

* See His Majesty's Order in Council of the 23d of February, 1821. Also
p. 13 of this Narrative

† Account of the Arctic Regions, vol. 1. p 212

c

OFFICIAL INSTRUCTIONS.

---

*By the Commissioners for executing the Office of
Lord High Admiral of the United Kingdom
of Great Britain and Ireland, &c.*

WHEREAS the President and Council of the Royal Society have expressed an opinion that an Expedition, for the purpose of attempting to reach the North Pole, " cannot fail to afford many valuable results and settle important matters of philosophical inquiry ;" and whereas, conformably therewith, We have thought fit, from your desire to be employed on this service, and your zeal and experience in prosecuting discoveries in the Arctic Regions, to entrust to your charge the conduct of the said Expedition, and to appoint you to the command of His Majesty's Sloop Hecla ; You are hereby required and directed, so soon as the said Vessel shall in all respects be ready for sea, to make the best of your way to the northern part of Spitzbergen , calling, however, at Hammerfest in Lapland, on your way, if you should think it expedient to take with you from thence a certain number of tame rein-deer to draw the boats over the ice.

On your arrival at the northern shores of Spitzbergen, you will fix upon some safe harbour or cove, in which the

Hecla may be placed; and having properly secured her, you are then to proceed with the Boats, whose equipments have, under your own directions, been furnished expressly for the service, directly to the Northward, and use your best endeavours to reach the North Pole , and having made such observations as are specified in the Instructions for your former Voyages in the Northern Regions, and such as will be pointed out to you by the Council of the Royal Society, added to those which your own experience will suggest, you will be careful to return to Spitzbergen before the winter sets in, and at such a period of the autumn as will ensure the Vessel you command not being frozen up, and thus obliged to winter there.

If, in proceeding towards the Pole, any difficulties should arise from the intervention of high and extensive land, or from the rugged surface of continuous ice, or other difficulty, the surmounting of which would evidently require a greater length of time than it would be prudent to consume, in order to secure your safe return, you are, in such case, to be careful not to risk your own life, and the lives of those who accompany you ; even though, by perseverance, you should be satisfied that such difficulty might be overcome, but at the expense of so much time as might put to hazard the certainty of returning to the Ship   You will, therefore, in such case, content yourself with the best examination of such land, should any be found, as time and other circumstances will allow.

Previous to your departure from the Hecla, you are to direct Lieutenant Foster to proceed, in a boat fitted for the purpose, as soon as the season shall be sufficiently advanced, to survey the Northern and Eastern Coast of

Spitzbergen, and to continue down the latter as far as may be practicable; with instructions to him to make observations on the dip, variation, and intensity of the Magnetic Needle, the temperature; the barometric pressure of the atmosphere; and such other meteorological phenomena, as he may be enabled to notice, the extent of open water; the quantity, the position and nature of the ice; the depth, temperature, and specific gravity of the sea; and you will also direct him to pay attention to the number of Whales he may meet with, in order that an opinion may be formed as to the expediency and practicability of extending the Whale Fishery on that Coast, and you will give him such directions, as to the time he is to remain on this Survey, as will ensure his return to the Vessel, so as not to endanger her being shut up in the Ice for the Winter.

While these two operations are carrying on by yourself and Lieutenant Foster, you are to instruct the Officer left in the Command of the Hecla, to employ the Officers and Men remaining on board in embracing every opportunity of making all such observations as may best contribute to the benefit of general Science, and collect and preserve all such specimens of Subjects of Natural History, whether Animals, Plants, or Minerals, as may be deemed new or curious.

When you have chosen the situation in which the Ship is to remain, and have become acquainted with the local circumstances of the Coast, you will be enabled to judge of the Instructions which it may be necessary to give the Officer who will remain in the Command of the Ship for ensuing your finding her on your return, and for facilitating her putting to sea as soon as the detached parties shall have rejoined : after which you are to make the best of your way to England ; and on your arrival, you are immediately to repair to this Office, in order to lay before us a full account of your proceedings, taking care, before you leave the Ship, to demand from the several Officers, Petty Officers, and all other Persons on board, the Logs and Journals they may have kept, together with any Drawings or Charts they may have made ; which are all to be sealed up, and to be thereafter disposed of as We may think proper.

Given under our Hands, the 24th March, 1827

(Signed)   MELVILLE,
                 WM. JOHNSTONE HOPE,
                 G. COCKBURN,
                 G. CLERK,   .
                 W. R K. DOUGLAS.

To
    Captain WILLIAM EDWARD PARRY,
    Commander of His Majesty's Sloop
    Hecla

            By Command of their Lordships,
                 (Signed)   J. W. CROKER.

EXPLANATION OF TECHNICAL TERMS,

MADE USE OF IN THE FOLLOWING NARRATIVE.

BAY-ICE—Ice newly formed on the surface of the sea. The expression is, however, applied also to ice a foot or two in thickness.

BESET—The situation of a ship when closely surrounded by ice.

BLINK—A brightness in the sky usually seen over large bodies of ice, and over land covered with snow.

CALF—A mass of ice lying under a floe, which, when disengaged, rises with violence to the surface of the water. See TONGUE.

FIELD—A sheet of ice generally of great thickness, and of an extent too great to be seen over from a ship's mast-head

FLOE—The same as a field, except that its extent is smaller, and can be distinguished from a ship's mast-head

FLOE-PIECE—An expression generally applied to small pieces of floes, not more than a furlong square

HOLE of Water (or Pool)—A small space of "clear water," when the rest of the sea is covered with ice

HUMMOCK—A mass of ice rising to a considerable height above the general level of a floe, and forming a part of it. Hummocks are originally raised by the pressure of floes against each other

LAND-ICE—Ice attached to land, either in floes or in heavy grounded masses.

LANE of Water—A narrow channel among the masses of ice, through which a boat or ship may pass.

NIPPED—The situation of a ship or boat when forcibly pressed by ice.

PACK—A large body of ice, consisting of separate masses lying close together, and the extent of which cannot be seen

SAILING-ICE—A body of ice, of which the masses are sufficiently separated to allow a ship to sail among them

STREAMS—A long and narrow collection of broken masses of ice

TONGUE—A mass of ice projecting under water from an ice-berg or floe, and generally distinguishable at a great depth. It differs from a "calf" in being fixed to, or a part of, the larger body

WATER-SKY—A dark appearance of the sky, indicating open water in that direction.

YOUNG ICE—Nearly the same as Bay-ice, except that it is only applied to ice very recently formed.

NARRATIVE,

&c.

THE Hecla being ready to proceed down the River, she was taken in tow, at ten, A.M, on the 25th of March, by the Lightning, steam-vessel; and having received and returned the cheers of the Greenwich pensioners, the children of the Naval Asylum, and of various ships in the river, she made fast to the moorings at Northfleet at three, P.M. The following day was occupied in swinging the ship round on the various points of the compass, in order to obtain the amount of the deviation of the magnetic needle, produced by the attraction of the ship's iron, and to fix Mr. Barlow's plate for correcting it *. On the 27th the Hecla was visited by the Right Hon. Viscount Melville, First Lord Commissioner of the Admiralty, who was pleased to express his

1827.
March
Sunday,
25th.

Monday.
26th

Tuesday.
27th.

---

* The merits of this simple but valuable invention being now too well known to require any detailed account of the experiments, it is only necessary for me to remark, in this place, that the compass having the plate attached to it gave, under all circumstances, the correct magnetic bearing.

B

approbation of our equipment; and the two succeeding days were employed in receiving the powder and other gunner's stores, and in making various magnetical experiments with the instruments intended for the voyage   These being completed, we were taken in tow by the Comet, steam-vessel, at eight, A.M, on the 30th, and anchored at the Little Nore, at one, P.M.   Here we were indebted to the well-known kindness of Vice-Admiral Sir Robert Moorsom for the supply of our few remaining wants ; and
on the 2nd of April that officer did us the honour of a personal visit on board the Hecla   On the 3rd the ship's company received three months' wages in advance, together
with their river-pay, and on the following morning, at half past four, we weighed and made sail from the Nore.   By the kindness of Sir Thomas Byam Martin, the Comptroller of His Majesty's navy, which we had experienced throughout this, as well as our former equipments, the Comet steamboat was ordered to tow us clear of the sands.   By her assistance we reached Orfordness before dark ; and at six, P.M., she parted company from us, giving us three hearty cheers, and receiving our pilot, together with our despatches and letters.   Being now fairly at sea, and favoured by a southerly breeze, we shaped our course, under all sail, to the northward.

We had at this time remarkably fine weather for the season of the year, and such a continuance of southerly winds, that we arrived off the island of Soroe, within which Hammerfest lies, on the 17th, without having had occasion to make a tack till we entered the Fiord which forms the northern entrance. In the course of our passage hitherto, we noticed, when to the northward of about the 58th parallel, a very decided north-easterly current, which has usually been understood to exist here, and is often the means of setting ships over towards the coast of Norway. Its direction appeared to vary between E.N.E. and N.N.E., and its amount from five to thirteen miles per day. Another circumstance struck us as well worthy of remark, though it has doubtless been often remarked before, which is, that, in proceeding from the Nore, a little to the eastward of the meridian of Greenwich, the whole way up to the latitude of 70°, the variation of the magnetic needle continues nearly the same, namely, from about 24° to 29° westerly, and, indeed, it undergoes very little alteration as far as 80°, where it is still 25°. But in the parallel of 70°, and, as we afterwards found in much higher ones, immediately on sailing to the eastward, the variation begins rapidly, though very regularly, to decrease, till at Hammerfest, in the longitude of 23¾° east, we find it only between 10° and 11°. These facts appear among the simplest, and yet the strongest, in favour of the theory of *two* magnetic poles in the northern hemisphere of the earth.

I may further remark that this change in the variation of the needle, coincident with a change of meridian only,

1827.
April
would afford, to those who are not furnished with better means, a very tolerable method of finding a ship's longitude, in any part of the North Atlantic, to the northward of the parallel of about 55°. This would be especially the case in ships having Mr. Barlow's plate attached to the compass; if not. observations with the ship's head north or south, and made in fine weather, will give very nearly the true variation; provided always that one fixed place has been selected for the azimuth compass, right amid-ships, and sufficiently high to be removed from the influence of *immediate* local attraction.

Wednesday,
18th
The wind becoming light from the southward, and very variable, we were occupied the whole of the 18th in beating up towards Hammerfest. In the evening a Lapland boat came on board, and one of the men undertook to pilot the ship to the anchorage, which, after beating all night against Thursday,
19th. an ebb tide, we reached at three, A.M, on the 19th. Soon after we had anchored, Mr. Crowe came on board, accompanied by Mr. Akermand, the Russian Consul, and also the Collector of Customs, all of whom offered their services in any way we might require. Finding that our rein-deer had not arrived, I immediately despatched Lieutenant Crozier, in one of our own boats, to Alten, from whence they were expected; a distance of about sixty English miles. At the same time we landed our observatories and instruments at Fugleness, near the establishment of Messrs. Crowe and Woodfall, the British merchants residing here; and Lieute-

nant Foster and myself immediately commenced our magnetic and other observations, which were continued during the
whole of our stay here.   We completed our supply of water,
and obtained a small quantity of venison, with abundance of
good fish, (principally tosk and cod,) and some milk.   We
also purchased a set of snow-shoes for our travelling party,
together with the Lapland shoes of leather, (called Kamooga*,)
which are the most convenient and comfortable for wearing
with them ; and we practised our people in the manner of
walking in them in deep snow, which afforded them fine
exercise and amusement.

On the 23d, being the day appointed to be kept as the
anniversary of His Majesty's birth-day, we dressed the ship in
colours, and fired a royal salute.   In the afternoon, Lieutenant Crozier returned in the boat from Alten, and was
followed the next day by Mr. Woodfall, who brought with
him eight rein-deer for our use, together with a supply of
moss for their provender (*Cenomyce Rangiferina*).   As,
however, the latter required a great deal of picking, so as
to render it fit to carry with us over the ice, and as it was
also necessary that we should be instructed in the manner
of managing the deer, I determined on remaining a day
or two longer for these purposes.   Nothing can be more
beautiful than the training of the Lapland rein-deer.   With

---

* It is remarkable that the Esquimaux word for boot is very like this—
Kameega.

a simple collar of skin round his neck, a single trace of the same material attached to the " pulk," or sledge, and passing between his legs, and one rein fastened like a halter about his neck, this intelligent and docile animal is perfectly under command of an experienced driver, and performs astonishing journeys over the softest snow. When the rein is thrown over on the off-side of the animal, he immediately sets off at full trot, and stops short the instant it is thrown back to the near side. Shaking the rein over his back is the only whip that is required. In a short time after setting off, they appear to be gasping for breath, as if quite exhausted; but, if not driven too fast at first, they soon recover this, and then go on without difficulty. The quantity of *clean* moss considered requisite for each deer per day is four pounds, but they will go five or six days without provender, and not suffer materially. As long as they can pick up snow as they go along, which they like to eat quite clean, they require no water; and ice is to them a comfortable bed. It may well be imagined, with such qualifications, how valuable these animals seemed likely to prove to us; and the more we became accustomed, and I may say attached to them, the more painful became the idea of the necessity which was likely to exist, of ultimately having recourse to them, as provision for ourselves.

Our preparations were completed on the 27th, but the wind continuing fresh from the north-western quarter in the

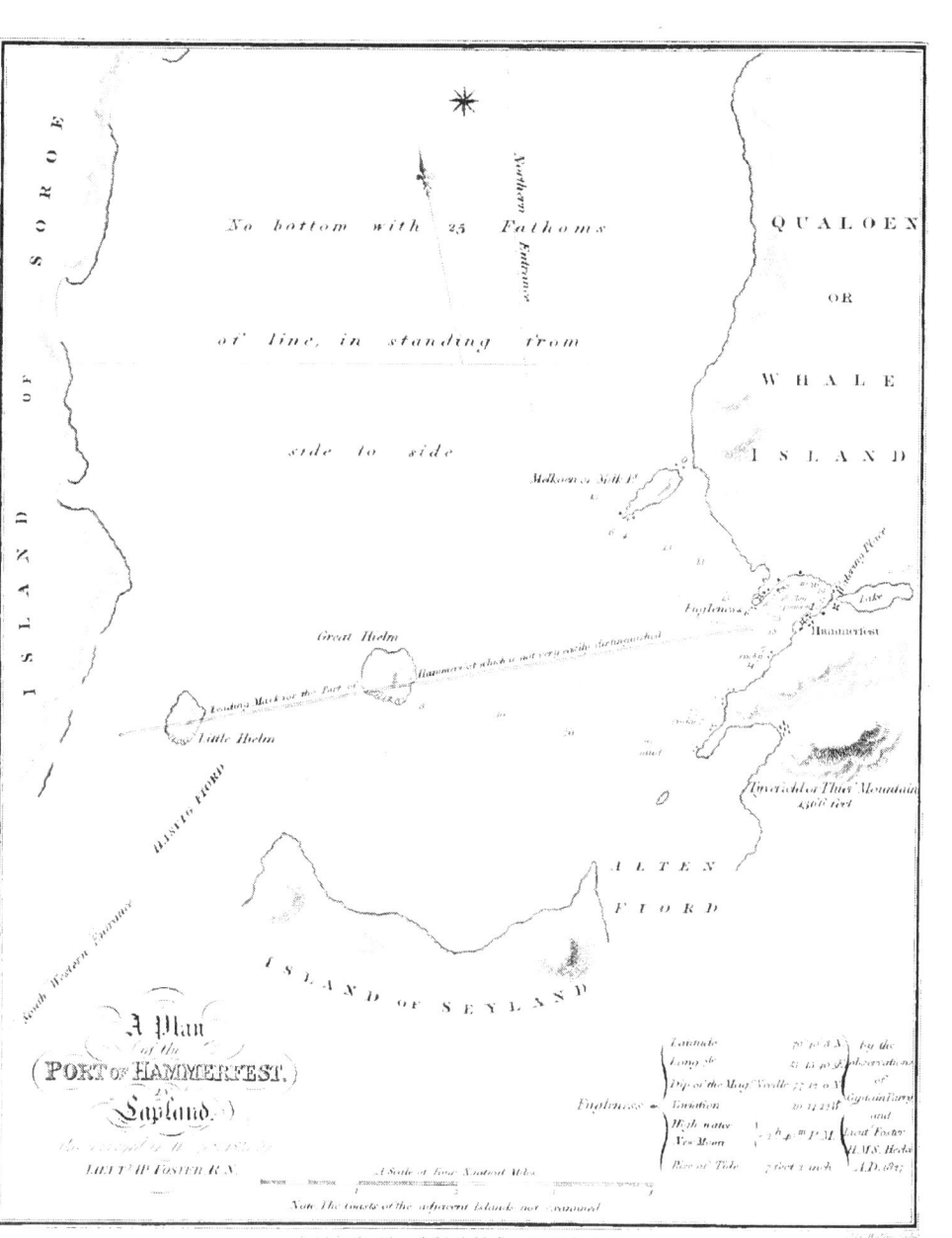

ISLAND OF SOROE

QUALOEN
OR
WHALE
ISLAND

Northern Entrance

No bottom with 25 Fathoms

of line, in standing from

side to side

Melkoen or Seal I.ᵈ

Fuglenæss

Hammerfest

Great Helm

Leading Mark for the Port of Hammerfest which is not very easily distinguished

Little Helm

HASVIG FIORD

Tyverichlet or Thief Mountain
4366 feet

ALTEN
FIORD

South Western Entrance

ISLAND OF SEYLAND

A Plan
of the
(PORT OF HAMMERFEST,)
in
Lapland.

LIEUT. H. FOSTER R.N.

A Scale of Four Nautical Miles

Latitude	70° 40' S.A.	by the
Long.ᵈᵉ	23. 43. 40 E	observations
Dip of the Mag.ᵗ Needle	77° 42. 0 N	of
Variation	29. 37. 23 E	Captain Parry
High water	2.ʰ 4.ᵐ P.M.	and
Ves.ᵗ Moon		Lieut. Foster
Rise of Tide	7 feet 1 inch	H.M.S. Hecla
		A.D. 1827

Note The Coasts of the adjacent Islands not examined

offing, we had no prospect of making any progress till the morning of the 29th, when we weighed at six, A M   I cannot omit this opportunity of expressing my acknowledgments to all the gentlemen at Hammerfest, whom I have before mentioned, for the ready assistance they afforded us on all occasions, and also to Mr. Capellan, Sheriff of the District of West Finmark, who accompanied Mr Woodfall from Bosecop, where he resides, and where he behaved with extreme attention to Lieutenant Crozier and his boat's crew.

After the detailed and interesting account already given of Hammerfest, and of the inhabitants of this part of Lapland, by Captain de Capell Brooke *, it would be useless, as well as presumptuous in me, to attempt any thing further in this way. I shall, therefore, only add a few hydrographical remarks, which may be useful to ships bound to this port, and such as I should myself have been very glad to possess, when entering it on this occasion.   Some local information of this nature is the more necessary, since the fishermen will not come out to any distance to pilot a ship to the anchorage.

The little harbour of Hammerfest is by no means easy for a stranger to find, in the present imperfect state of our charts of the coast of Lapland, on account of the number of deep inlets, or "fiords,' by which the shores are indented, and the sameness in the appearance of most of the land in its

* A Winter in Lapland and Sweden, &c

neighbourhood. This latter also differs materially at different seasons, according to the quantity of snow which is lying upon it. The southern entrance, by Hasvig, which is situated towards the south-western extremity of Soroe, is not to be so much recommended as that to the northward, on account of the greater distance which a ship has to go between the high lands, where the wind varies in every turning, and sometimes blows in heavy squalls down the inlets, making it a tedious business to get in or out, even with a tolerably favourable breeze. Perhaps the best direction for approaching the northern entrance, is to get into the latitude of 70° 55′, which will lead a ship close to the north-eastern extreme of Soroe, at a short distance off which lies a remarkable craggy rock or islet, which was, at this season, almost entirely clear of snow. After passing to the eastward of it, it becomes somewhat of this shape,

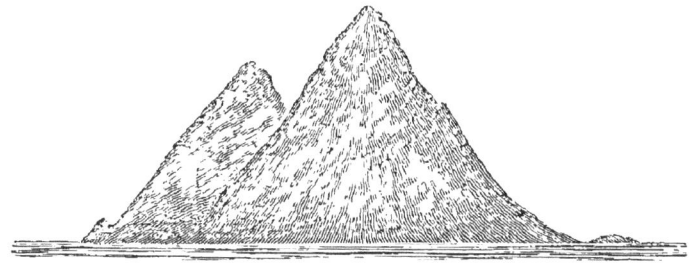

and there will then be in sight another small but high rocky island to the S.E., having a smoothly rounded appearance at the top in almost every point of view, and which bears from the outer point of Milk Island, near Hammerfest, N. 8° E. (true). To the southward of this will also be seen another small and *low* rocky island, which, as well as the round topped island, was now free from snow. A ship must leave these both to the eastward, keeping between them and Soroe, when a S.S.E course by compass will lead towards Milk Island, and the two small but high islands called the Great and Little Helm will then come in sight, which being kept in one, afford a good leading mark for the port of Hammerfest, as shown in the accompanying survey made by Lieutenant Foster, in the Gripei, in 1823. The bower anchor may be dropped in eighteen to twenty fathoms, on a muddy bottom, rather on the Fugleness side, and a stream laid out to the S.S.E ; it is also recommended to make a hawser fast to a ring on the shore upon that side. There is said to be no danger from sunken rocks in any part of this navigation; a remark which is considered equally applicable to the whole of the coast of Lapland, to the northward of 68°.

The latitude of Fugleness, by our observations, is 70° 40′ 8″ N.; the longitude by chronometers 23° 45′ 40″ E.; the dip of the magnetic needle 77° 12′ N.; and the variation 10° 14′ 12″ westerly. It was high water on the day of new moon at 2 40, p.m, the rise of tide being seven feet one inch. There is a tide and half tide, the stream running about three hours longer than the time of high or low water

C

1827.
April.

by the shore ; and, considering the depth of water, we found it stronger than might have been expected.

Lieutenant Crozier's observations make the latitude of the town of Bosecop 69° 57' 37": and the variation of the needle there was 9° 54' 30" westerly. It was high water at 9·30, P.M., on the 21st of April, the rise of tide being three feet and a half.

In sailing out, along the island of Soroe, near the north-eastern point of it, where the dip of the gneiss (of which all these islands appear composed) is very distinctly exhibited, we observed it to incline to the S.W., at a measured angle of 27°. We found the wind at north on the outside, which, continuing for several days, led us to the W.N.W., and occasioned us to notice a remarkable belt of comparatively warm water, as shown in the following table.

DAYS.	Between the parallels of	Between the meridians of	Temperature of	
			Sea water.	Air.
April 29th and 30th	70 55 and 71 9 N	23 0 and 22 10 E	36 to 37	25 to 31
30th and May 1st	71 9 — 71 40	22 10 — 18 40	38 — 39	26 — 32
May 1st to 3d . . .	71 40 — 72 38	18 40 — 14 10	39 — 40	23½ — 26
3d and 4th . . .	72 38 — 73 29	14 10 — 8 20	38 — 32 gradually	24 — 23

During the whole of the time we remained in water of this higher temperature, the wind, though in general light, and the weather fine, was constantly coming in puffs of greater or less force, and then relapsing again almost into a

calm; a circumstance so unusual in an open sea, that it appeared to us, at the time, to have some connexion with the
temperature of the water compared with that of the air, as
in the Gulf-stream. The horizon seemed broken into little
detached lumps, and the dip of the sea, as measured by Dr.
Wollaston's dip-sector, indicated a depression very considerably greater than that given in the Tables. In one instance
the excess amounted to 2′ 3″, the temperature of the air
being $23\frac{1}{2}°$, and that of the water 40°.

On the 5th of May, being in latitude 73° 30′, and longi- Saturday,
5th.
tude 7° 28′ E., we met with the first straggling mass of
ice, after which, in sailing about 110 miles in a N.N.W.
direction, there was always a number of loose masses in sight;
but it did not occur in continuous "streams," till the morning of the 7th, in latitude 74° 55′, a few miles to the east- Monday,
7th.
ward of the meridian of Greenwich. Early on the morning
of the 9th, while running, with all the studding-sails set, Wednesday,
9th.
through "sailing ice," we were taken aback with a sudden
and violent squall of wind from the northward. Soon after,
it fell calm, and a light air from the eastward having succeeded for a short time, we were a second time taken aback
with a fresh gale from the northward. At half past nine we
saw two whale ships, which joined us in the course of the
day. They proved to be the Alpheus, and the Active, of
Peterhead. By the former I wrote to the Secretary of the
Admiralty, acquainting him with the Hecla's arrival in the

C 2

1827.
May
Thursday,
10th.

latitude of 77°. On the following day several other whalers were in sight, and Mr. Bennett, the master of the Venerable, of Hull, whom we had before met in Baffin's Bay, in 1818, came on board. From him I learned that several of the ships had been in the ice since the middle of April, some of them having been so far to the westward as the island of Jan Mayen, and that they were now endeavouring to push to the northward. They considered the ice to offer more obstacles to the attainment of this object than it had done for many years past*. None of the ships had yet taken a single whale, which, indeed, they never expect to do to the southward of about 78°.

In the afternoon, after waiting for some time for the ice to open, we again entered it, in company with all the

Friday,
11th

whalers, and by the following morning had succeeded in pushing about fifty miles farther to the northward, though not without some heavy blows in "boring" through the ice. The weather had been almost constantly thick with snow since our leaving Hammerfest; but, on its clearing up this morning, we saw the land about Black Point, the southern extreme of Prince Charles's Island or Foreland,

* I find it to be the universal opinion among the most experienced of our Whalers, that there is much less ice met with, of late years, in getting to the northward, in these latitudes, than formerly was the case Mr Scoresby, to whose very valuable local information, contained in his "Account of the Arctic Regions," I have been greatly indebted on this occasion, mentions the circumstance as a generally-received fact.

bearing N E b.E., distance about nine leagues. We were
here stopped by close ice, the weather becoming again very
thick with snow, and a fresh gale blowing from the E.S.E.
The whalers, twelve in number, and two of these Dutch,
hove to an hour or two before us, being now about their
fishing-latitude.

1827
May.

On the 12th we had strong gales to the southward, with
thick snowy weather; and the thermometer, which had
generally been from 16° to 20° since our entering the ice,
had now risen to 31° We saw a black whale, and one of
the ships sent her boats in pursuit of it; this was only the
third we had seen. The dovekies, (*Colymbus Grylle,*) and
eider-ducks, were very numerous. In the afternoon there
was a slight swell perceptible, which led us to believe we
were not far from open water inshore, and on the weather
clearing up on the following morning, this conjecture proved
correct, nearly the whole space between us and Prince
Charles's Foreland, not less than six or seven leagues in
breadth, being quite clear, except of " young ice ;" and this,
though covering the greater part of the sea, was now so soft
and broken up, as scarcely to impede a ship's progress
Being still favoured by a southerly wind, we proceeded without impediment, the same, or even a greater, breadth of open
water continuing along the land At five, A.M., on the
14th, we passed Magdalena Bay, and by ten o'clock had
arrived off Hakluyt's Headland, round which we hauled

Saturday,
12th.

Sunday,
13th.

Monday,
14th

to the south-eastward, to look for anchorage in Smeren-burg Harbour In this, however, we were disappointed, the whole place being occupied by one unbroken floe of ice, still firmly attached to the land on each side. Here we made fast, though not without considerable difficulty, the wind, which was now freshening from the southward, blow-ing in such violent and irregular gusts off the high land, that the ship was scarcely manageable. Walruses, dovekies, and eider-ducks were very numerous here, especially the former; and four rein-deer came down upon the ice near the ship.

We now prepared a quantity of provisions and other stores to land at Hakluyt's Headland, as a supply for my party on our return from the northward ; so that, in case of the ship being obliged to go more to the southward, or of our not being able at once to reach her, we should here be furnished with a few days' resources of every kind. Our intentions were, however, frustrated for the present ; for we had scarcely secured our hawsers, when a hard gale came on from the southward, threatening every moment to snap them in two, and drive us from our anchorage. We held on for several hours, till, at 9 P M., some swell having set in upon the margin of the ice, it began to break off and drift away. Every possible exertion was instantly made to shift our stream-cable farther in upon the floe, but it broke away so quickly as to baffle every endeavour, and at 10 the

1827.
May.

ship went adrift, the wind blowing still harder than before.
Having hauled in the hawsers, and got the boats on board,
we set the close-reefed topsails, to endeavour to hang to
windward; but the wind blew in such tremendous gusts
off the high land as almost to lay the ship on her beam-
ends, so that we were obliged to reduce our canvass to the
main-topsail and storm-sails, and let her drive to leeward *.
After wearing several times between the island called Vogel
Sang and a narrow stream of ice that lay to the westward and
kept off a considerable sea which was rolling on the outside
of it, we had driven as far as the northern extreme of the
island; and at 1, A M, the main body of packed ice was
seen, only a mile or two under our lee.   The situation of
the ship now appeared a very precarious one, the wind still
blowing with unabated violence. and with every appearance
of a continuance of stormy weather.   Under these circumstances, it was the general opinion of the officers. as well as
my own, that it was advisable to take advantage of the comparatively smooth water within the stream of ice before-
mentioned, and to run the ship into the pack, rather than
incur the risk of having to do the same thing in a heavy sea.
This plan succeeded remarkably well; a tolerably smooth and
open part of the margin being selected, the ship was forced

---

* It was probably some such gale as this which has given to Hakluyt's Headland, in an old Dutch chart, the appellation of "Duyvel's
Hoek.'

into it at three, A.M.; when, after encountering a few severe blows from the heavy washed pieces which always occur near the sea-edge, she was gradually carried onwards under all sail, and at four, A.M., we had got into a perfectly smooth and secure situation, half a mile within the margin of the " pack*."

The wind subsided in the course of the day, and clear and cloudless weather succeeded. We were glad to take advantage of our quiet situation to give the officers and men the rest which they much needed. The wind continuing from the southward, the ice soon drifted as far north as it could go, and we then drove rapidly with it to the eastward, past Cloven Cliff, and along the northern coast of Spitzbergen. At noon our observed latitude was 80° 04' 13", and longitude by chronometers 12° 35' E, the depth of water being twenty-five fathoms, on a hard bottom The temperature of the air rose to 41° in the shade, and to 48° in the sun, which was the more remarkable from the low temperature which followed this for several days afterwards. On
the 16th the wind was light from the northward, and the thermometer falling to 17° in the course of the day, and to 14° at midnight, the pack was cemented together by the

---

* It is remarkable that the position of the Hecla, and the circumstances under which she was placed on this occasion, were almost the same as those in which His Majesty's Ship the Dorothea received very serious damage in the expedition of 1818, and but for the smooth place which we fortunately found, we should probably have incurred similar injury

frost. The ship still drove with the ice to the eastward, and
inshore withal, and we were now off the remarkable part of
the land called Red Beach, which was at this season as white
as an entire covering of snow could make it. A young bear
was killed close to the ship, and some ivory gulls and eider-
ducks were flying about, the latter in considerable flocks

It was impossible not to consider ourselves highly fortunate in having thus early, and with no great difficulty, succeeded in reaching the highest latitude to which it was our
object to take the ship. But, from what we had already
seen at Smerenburg, it was also impossible not to feel
much anxiety as to the prospect of getting her into any
secure harbour, before the proper time of my departure to
the northward should arrive. However, we could only wait
patiently for the result of a few more days, and, in the mean
time, every body was busily employed in completing the
arrangements for our departure, so that, if an opportunity
did offer of securing the ship, we might have nothing else
to attend to. Our deer were in good order, having been
thriving well ever since they came on board; they make
excellent sailors, and do not seem to mind bad weather,
always lying down quite comfortably whenever there is
any sea.

On the 18th, being only six or seven miles from the Red
Beach, and the ice appearing close between us and the shore,
I sent Lieutenant Ross with a party to endeavour to land,

D

1827
May.
Friday, 18th,
continued
being desirous to know what this remarkable looking place was composed of. Lieutenant Ross was not, however, enabled to land, there being a considerable lane of water inshore, too broad for the party to ferry over on pieces of ice. In order to try what our chances were, at the present low temperature, of procuring water upon the ice without expense of fuel, we laid a black-painted canvass cloth, and also a piece of black felt, upon the surface of the snow; the temperature of the atmosphere being from 18° to 23°. These substances had, in a couple of hours, sunk half an inch into the snow, but no water could be collected. I was desirous also of ascertaining whether any part of the real sea ice was so entirely fresh, when melted, as to be drank without injury or inconvenience. For this purpose we cut a block of ice from a large hummock, about ten feet high above the sea, and having broken, pounded, and melted it, without any previous washing, we found it, both by the hydrometer and by the chemical test (nitrate of silver) *more* free from salt than any which we had in our tanks, and which was procured from Hammerfest I considered this satisfactory, because, in the autumn, the pools of water met with upon the ice, generally become very brackish, in consequence of the sea-water being drawn up into them by capillary action as the ice becomes more " rotten" and porous ; and we might, therefore, have to depend chiefly on melted ice for our daily supply.

Saturday,
19th
On the 19th, the wind freshened up strong from the

W N.W., which is here rather upon the land, and the ice settled together and inshore, occasioning the ship such violent pressure as few others could have withstood, and much endangering the rudder, which we had not been able to unship In about half an hour, however, it remained quiet, leaving the ship so closely pressed in every part, that the lead for sounding could not any where be dropped until we had dug a hole for the purpose. The thermometer fell to 12°, with thick snowy weather. No change took place till the 21st, when, on the weather clearing up, we found that Monday.
21st the open water we had left to the westward was now wholly closed up, and that there was none whatever in sight It was now also so close inshore, that on the 22d, Lieutenant Tuesday,
22d Ross, with a party of officers and men, succeeded in landing without difficulty. They found a small floe of level ice close to the beach, which appeared very lately formed. Walking up to a little conspicuous eminence near the eastern end of the beach, they found it to be composed of clay-slate, tinged of a brownish red colour. The few uncovered parts of the beach were strewed with smooth schistose fragments of the same mineral, and in some parts a quantity of thin slates of it lay closely disposed together in a vertical position. On the little hillock were two graves, bearing the dates of 1741 and 1762 on some of the stones which marked them, and a considerable quantity of fir drift wood lay upon the beach.

D 2

In the evening of the 22d, a light air at length sprung up from the eastward, and on the following morning had, in a slight degree, increased, opening a few holes of water here and there, and giving us great hopes of our being released from our present confinement. To help the ice a little in opening, we set all the sails, which certainly produced some effect in the course of the day; but the wind was so very light,
that though it still continued on the 24th, nothing like an opening was afforded for us to get out. Indeed, the ship was still closely squeezed up by the ice all round her, though she moved a little to the westward now and then *with* it.

The air of wind again dying away, and some of the holes again closing, I now clearly saw that there was, for the present, no reasonable prospect of our getting towards any harbour, and I could not but feel confident that, even if we did get to the entrance of any, some time must be occupied in securing the ship It may be well imagined how anxious I had now become to delay no longer in setting out upon the main object of the expedition I felt that a few days at the commencement of the season, short as it is in these regions, might be of great importance as to the result of our enterprise, while the ship seemed to be so far secure from any immediate danger, as to justify my leaving her, with a reduced crew, in her present situation. It appeared to me that the present case was one which their Lordships could not foresee, nor provide against in my Instructions, and that I was, therefore, called upon to use my own judgment and discretion, now that it had arisen, and to pursue such a plan as might best contribute to the success of our enterprise in its principal object. The nature of the ice was, beyond all comparison, the most unfavourable for our purpose that I ever remember to have seen It consisted only of loose pieces, scarcely any of them fifteen or twenty yards square, and when any so large did occur, their margins were surrounded by the smaller ones thrown up by the recent pressure into ten thousand various shapes, and presenting high and sharp angular masses at every other step. The men compared it to a stone-mason's yard, which, except that the stones were of ten times the usual dimensions, it indeed very much resembled. The only inducement to set out over such a road, was the certainty that floes and fields lay beyond it, and the hope that they were not *far* beyond it. In this respect, indeed, I considered our present easterly position as a probable advantage, since the ice was much less likely to have been disturbed to any great extent northwards in this meridian than to the westward, clear of the land, where every southerly breeze was sure to be making havock among it. Another very important advantage in setting off on this meridian appeared to me to be, that, the land of Spitzbergen lying immediately over against the ice, the

1827
May

Sunday,
27th

latter could never drift so much or so fast to the southward, as it might further to the westward.

Upon these grounds it was that I was anxious to make an attempt, at least, as soon as our arrangements could be completed; and the officers being of the same opinion with myself, we hoisted out the boats early in the morning of the 27th, and having put the things into one of them, endeavoured, by way of experiment, to get her to a little distance from the ship. Such, however, were the irregularities of the ice that, even with the assistance of an additional party of men, it was obvious that we could not have gained a single mile in a day, and what was still more important, not without almost certain and serious injury to the boats by their striking against the angular masses. Under these circumstances, it was but too evident to every one that it would have been highly imprudent to persist in setting out, since, if the ice after all should clear away, even in a week, so as to allow us to get a few miles nearer the main body, time would be ultimately saved by our delay, to say nothing of the wear and tear, and expense of our provisions I was, therefore, very reluctantly compelled to yield to this necessity, and to order the things to be got on board again. In the mean time I despatched Lieutenant Ross, with a couple of men, to make a rapid journey over the ice to the northward, in order to gain some information respecting the nature and state of

it in that direction. Lieutenant Ross returned at night,
having travelled about ten miles, in the course of which he
passed over one good floe, from two to three miles wide, and
the rest was of the same kind as near the ship   Upon the
whole, his report did not offer us much encouragement to
set off from our present station.

On the following morning I sent Lieutenant Crozier, with
a small party, to the E.N E., with the same object ; but he
had not travelled above four miles, and therefore not beyond
the limit of our view from the ship, when the ice beginning
to open, I was obliged to recall him.   The ice, however,
soon settled back again into its former place, as it had done
several times before, moving about two hundred yards one
way or other, according to the winds, and perhaps the tide.

Immediately that we had, on the 27th, proved experi-
mentally the extreme difficulty of transporting our boats
and stores over the ice which now surrounded us, I made
up my mind to the very great probability there seemed to
be of the necessity of adopting such alterations in our original
plans as would accommodate them to these untoward circumstances at the outset. The boats forming the main
impediment, not so much on account of their absolute weight,
as from the difficulty of managing so large a body upon a
road of this nature, I made preparations for the possible
contingency of our having to take only one, continuing the
same number of men in our whole party.   All that I saw

reason to apprehend from having only a single boat on our outward journey, was some occasional delay in ferrying over spaces of water in two trips instead of one , but we considered that this would be much more than compensated by the increased rate at which we should go whenever we were upon ice, as we expected to be nine days out of ten   The principal disadvantage, therefore, consisted in our not all being able to sleep in the boat, and this we proposed to obviate in the following manner.

We constructed, out of the Lapland snow-shoes, fourteen sledges, each sledge consisting of two pair, well fastened together.   Upon these we proposed dragging almost all the weight, so as to keep the boat nearly without any cargo in her, as we found by experiment that a man could drag about three hundred pounds on one of the sledges, with more facility than he could drag the boat when his proportion did not exceed one hundred pounds.   Upon these sledges we proposed lodging half our party alternately each night, placing them under the lee of the boat, and then stretching over them, as a sloped roof, a second awning which we fitted for the purpose   Upon this plan we likewise could afford to make our boat considerably stronger, adding some stout iron knees to the supports of her runners, and increasing our store of materials for repairing her.   The weight reduced by this arrangement, would have been above two thousand pounds, without taking away any article conducive to our comfort, except

the boat and her geer.   I proposed to the officers and men,
who had been selected to accompany me, this change in our
equipment, and I need scarcely say that they all clearly saw
the probable necessity of it, and cheerfully acquiesced in its
adoption, if requisite.

On the 29th, I sent Lieutenants Foster and Crozier with
the greater part of the ship's company, and with a third or
spare travelling-boat, to endeavour to land her on Red Beach,
together with a quantity of stores, including provisions, as a
deposit for us on our return from the northward, should it
so happen, as was not improbable, that we should return
to the eastward.   It is impossible to describe the labour
attending this attempt.   Suffice it to say that, after working
for fourteen hours, they returned on board at midnight, having accomplished about four miles out of the six.   The next
day they returned to the boat, and after several hours' exertion
landed her on the beach with the stores.   What added to
the fatigue of this service, was the necessity of taking a
small boat to cross pools of water on their return, so that
they had to drag this boat both ways, besides that which
they went to convey.   Having, however, had an opportunity
of trying what could be done upon a regular and level floe
which lay close to the beach, every body was of opinion, as
I had always been, that we could easily travel twenty miles
a day on ice of that kind.

Every one was now occupied in completing our arrange-

E

ments on the new plan of taking only one boat, stowing all our provisions on the sledges, and adopting every possible expedient to save weight and labour. Another week was fast passing without any improvement in the prospect of our getting the ship free, so as either to carry us farther north, or to put her into harbour. It may here be remarked that our only chance of this latter seemed at the time to depend on our getting to the westward, since there were no known places of shelter on the northern side of Spitzbergen; beside which it would be much more difficult to get hence in the autumn. Now it so happened, whether from any local cause or not I cannot say, that during the sixteen days we had already been beset, there had not been wind enough from the eastward to fill a skysail; added to which we found a decided easterly set, which carried the ship a little now and then in that direction.

It will not, then, be wondered at if this apparent hope-lessness of getting the ship free for the present again suggested the necessity of my own setting out; and I had once more, after an anxious consultation with my officers, resolved on making a second attempt, when the ice near us, which had opened at regular hours with the tide for three or four days past, began to set us much more rapidly than usual to the eastward, and towards a low point which runs off from Red Beach, near its eastern end, causing us to shoal the

water, in a few hours, from fifty-two to twenty fathoms, and

on the following morning to fourteen and a half. By send-
ing a lead-line over the ice a few hundred yards beyond us,
we found ten fathoms water. However unfavourable the
aspect of our affairs seemed before, this new change could
not fail to alter it for the worse. The situation of the ship
now, indeed, required my whole attention; for though the
ice occasionally opened and shut within twenty or twenty-
five yards of us on the inshore side, the ship herself was
still very firmly imbedded by the turned-up masses which
had pressed upon her on the 19th, and which, on the other
side, as well as ahead and astern, were of considerable extent.
Thus she formed, as it were, part of a floe, which went
drifting about in the manner above-described. This was of
little importance while she was in sixty fathoms of water, as
she was for the first fourteen days of our besetment, and at
a distance of five or six miles from the land; but now that
she had shoaled the water so considerably, and approached
the low point within two or three miles, it became a matter
of importance to try whether any labour we could bestow
upon it would liberate the ship from her present imbedded
state, so as to be at least ready to take advantage of slack
water, should any occur, to keep her off the shore. All
hands were, therefore, set to work with handspikes, capstan
bars, and axes, it being necessary to detach every separate
mass, however small, before the larger ones could be moved.
The harassing and laborious nature of this operation is such

1827.
June

E 2

as nothing but experience can possibly give an idea of, especially when, as in this case, we had only a small pool of clear
water near the margin, in which the detached pieces could
be floated out. However we continued at work, with only
the necessary intermissions for rest and meals, during this
Sunday, 3rd. and the two following days, and on the evening of the third,
had accomplished all that the closeness of the ice would
permit; but the ship was still by no means free, numberless
masses of ice being doubled under her, even below her
keel, and which could not be moved without more space
for working.

While thus employed, we had once more deepened the water,
the ice continuing to set more or less rapidly to the eastward,
except for a few hours on the 2nd, when a fresh breeze springing up from the S.E. carried us, *with* the ice, and by the
help of all our sails, about one mile to the N.W., but the
moment the wind fell (which it did just as it had opened a
few holes of water to the westward) we began again to move
over the ground in the opposite direction. At midnight,
Monday, 4th. on the 3rd, the ice slackened about us very quickly, and the
ship was immediately found to be setting more rapidly than
ever to the eastward. In three-quarters of an hour the
water shoaled from fifty-two to twenty-five fathoms, and
in ten minutes after we had nine and three-quarters, the
ship driving at the rate of two miles an hour past a low
point which runs off from under the high land of Grey

Hook.   There being now a little open water at the margin of the floe in which we had been imbedded, we succeeded in freeing the ship, and then laid out hawsers in each direction, in readiness for moving her, should she drive into still shoaler water.   Happily, however, this was not the case, the ice soon after closing us in towards the entrance of Weyde Bay, and the water gradually deepening to thirty-seven, and then to sixty-seven fathoms.

Painful as was this protracted delay in setting out upon the principal object of the expedition, the absolute necessity of it will scarcely, I think, be doubted by any person conversant in such matters   So long as the ship continued undisturbed by the ice, nearly stationary, and in deep water, for several days together, I had, in my anxiety to lose not a moment's time, ventured to flatter myself with the hope that, in a case of such unlooked-for emergency, when every moment of our short and uncertain season was of importance, I might be justified in quitting my ship at sea; and in this opinion the zeal of my officers, both those who were to accompany me, and those who were to remain on board, induced them unanimously to concur.   But the case was now materially altered; for it had become plain to every seaman in the ship—first, that the safety of the Hecla, if thus left with less than half her working hands, could not be reckoned upon for an hour—and, secondly, that no human foresight could enable us to conjecture, should we

set out while she was thus situated, when or where we
should find her on our return. In fact. it appeared to us
at this time, as indeed it was, a very providential circumstance, that the impracticable nature of the ice for travelling
had offered no encouragement to persevere in my original
intention of setting out a week before this time. While,
therefore, it occasioned me inexpressible regret to be thus
detained, I could not entertain a doubt that I was performing an imperative duty in remaining on board; for, to have
done otherwise, under such circumstances, would have been
to abandon the ship to her fate, on the one hand; and,
on the other, to expose my own party to almost certain
destruction. So that all I could do was to wait for some
favourable turn which would enable me to get the ship into
security, and then to proceed to the northward, in full confidence of finding her on my return.

I have before stated, that our hopes of finding a harbour
had hitherto rested on our getting the ship to the westward.
Such, however, was the decided tendency of the ice to drift in
the contrary direction, that it now appeared next to impossible that we could effect that object in any reasonable time.
Indeed, we had for a week past wholly lost sight of the
open water about Cloven Cliff; but as we continued to drive
to the eastward, we observed a constant darkness, and very
frequently a dense fog-bank, in the horizon, from about a
N.E.b.E. to a N.N.E. bearing, which we considered an

indication of open water in that direction. To this quarter,
therefore, we now more particularly turned our attention;
and on the 4th we were almost certain that we could, from
the mast-head, discover the water, extending two or three
points to the northward from Verlegen Hook. This circumstance excited new hopes; for could we only have had
room to move about in, we did not doubt our being soon
able to discover some place of shelter for the ship.

For the two following days we continued closely beset, but
still driving to the eastward across the mouth of Weyde Bay,
which is here six or seven miles in breadth, and appeared to
be very deep, the land in the centre receding to a distance
of full eight leagues. In the afternoon of the 6th, we had
driven within five miles of a point of land, beyond which,
to the eastward, it seemed to recede considerably; and this
appearing to answer tolerably to the situation of Muscle or
Mussell Bay, as laid down in most of the charts, I was very
anxious to discover whether we could here find shelter for
the ship. A lane of water leading towards the land at no
great distance from us, I hauled a boat over the ice, and
then rowed on shore, accompanied by Lieutenant Foster
and some of the other officers, taking with me another small
store of provisions, to be deposited here, as a future resource
for my party, should we approach this part of the coast.

Landing at half past six, P.M., and leaving Mr. Bird to
bury the provisions, Lieutenant Foster and myself walked

without delay to the eastward, and on ascending the point,
found that there was, as we had supposed, an indentation
in the coast on the other side. We now began to conceive the most flattering hopes of discovering something
like a harbour for the ship, and pushed on with all possible
haste to examine the place further; but, after three hours'
walking, were much mortified, on arriving at its head,
to find that it was nothing but an open bay, entirely
exposed to the inroads of all the northern ice, and therefore quite unfit for the ship. We returned to the boat
greatly disappointed, and reached the Hecla at 1. 30, A.M.,
on the 7th.

This bay, which is very small, but appears the only one
which answers to Muscle or Mussell Bay, lies ten miles to
the S.W. of Verlegen Hook, and is about two miles in
depth, having a beach composed of small rounded stones, and
covered with great quantities of drift-wood, which, indeed,
is the case with every part of this coast on which we landed.
Some of the trees, with their roots attached to them, were
not less than eighteen inches in diameter; and the smaller
ones were very abundant, the whole being of the pine tribe.
The rocks are composed of mica-slate, which Mr. Beverly
remarked to dip to the eastward, generally at an angle of
about 70°, and sometimes to lie still nearer a perpendicular
direction. The land to the eastward of this part of the
coast, as Phipps has justly remarked, assumes a very dif-

ferent aspect from that to the westward; the latter being the most rugged and acuminated that I ever saw, and this becoming of a more smooth and rounded outline. We were a good deal surprized, on landing, to find that large streams of water were rushing down the sides of all the hills, and that there were large ponds of it in every direction; a circumstance the less expected by us, since we had certainly never seen it half so abundant in any of our winter stations at this season; not even at Winter Island, which lies in latitude $66°\frac{1}{4}$, or nearly 14° to the southward of this. The water was running copiously, even at a height of three or four hundred feet above the sea, almost at midnight, and the *Saxifraga Oppositifolia* was quite out in flower at a similar height. We saw several rein-deer, and killed a small one. It was high water at 10 40, P M, the tide having risen two feet ten inches in about four hours. There was here an extensive floe of land-ice, filling the upper part of the bay, as shown by the broken line in the chart; but it was so thin and watery, that we could have cut through it, at least half a mile, in two days, had the place been such as to require it. This operation I had always anticipated as likely to be requisite, wherever the ship should be placed. The variation of the magnetic needle, as observed upon the ice near this spot, was 18° 10′ 30″, westerly.

From the hills we could plainly distinguish a considerable space of open water to the eastward of Verlegen Hook, as

F

we had supposed to be the case when on board; and I could not help feeling great confidence that, could we now have been enabled to place the Hecla in security, we might have got the boats into this water, which appeared to lead directly to the northward, and thus have reached the main ice without much difficulty. As it was, we were obliged to submit to the necessity of still awaiting some favourable change; and those only, who have been in similar situations, can conceive how painful such a necessity was.

I never remember to have experienced in these regions such a continuance of beautiful weather as we now had, during more than three weeks that we had been on the northern coast of Spitzbergen Day after day we had a clear and cloudless sky, scarcely any wind, and, with the exception of a few days previously to the 23d of May, a warm temperature in the shade, and quite a scorching sun. On the 3d of June we had a shower of rain, and on the 6th it rained pretty hard, for two or three hours. After the 1st of June we could procure abundance of excellent water upon the ice, and by the end of the first week the floe pieces were looking blue with it in some parts, and the snow had everywhere become too soft to bear a man's weight.

On the 7th, the ship, still closely beset, had drifted much more to the eastward, being within a mile of the spot where the provisions had been deposited the preceding evening. There was now no other ice between us and the land, except

the floe to which we had been so long attached; and round
this we were occasionally obliged to warp, whenever a little
slackening of the ice permitted, in order to prevent our getting too near the rocks. In this situation of suspense and
anxiety we still remained until the evening of the 8th,
when a breeze, at length, springing up from the southward,
began to open out the ice from the point near which we
lay. As soon as the channel was three or four hundred
yards wide, we warped into the clear water and, making
sail, rounded the point in safety, having no soundings with
twenty fathoms, at one-third of a mile from a small rocky
islet lying off it. In the mean time the wind had been
driving the ice so fast off the land as to form for us a clear
communication with the open water before seen to the eastward; and thus were we at length liberated from our confinement, after a close and tedious " besetment" of twenty-
four days.

This escape appeared to give us all fresh animation, and
we now entertained the most confident hopes of being able
shortly to effect the object we had so long had at heart,
that of securing the Hecla in some harbour previously to our
departure in the boats; an object which the events of the
last few days had shown to be indispensably necessary, before
I could venture to set out. With this view we stretched
along the low point of Verlegen Hook, round which we
found some swell coming in from Waygatz Strait, the wind

blowing strong from the southward, with heavy rain, during
the night. We, therefore, lay to under this land till the
wind had moderated, and the weather cleared; and early in
the morning of the 9th, made sail to the N.N.E., towards
the Seven Islands, finding a clear sea in that direction.

On the low shore near Verlegen Hook, we saw a house,
which appeared in a ruinous state, and which we supposed
to have belonged to some Russian settlers. Near this
Hook, too, we found, for the first time on the north coast
of Spitzbergen, heavy grounded ice, such as we had formerly
been accustomed to find upon all shelving shores. This
circumstance appeared to us worthy of remark, as seeming
to afford a proof that the heavy or field ice seldom, if ever,
comes actually home upon these shores; for otherwise it
would leave many traces of that kind. We were pleased to
see that, except these grounded masses, there was, along this
shore, no other ice attached to the land.

At noon, being in latitude 80° 16′ 40″ by observation, and
the high land of Verlegen Hook bearing south (true) distant from four to five leagues, we had no bottom with ninety
fathoms of line. A haze clearing off about this time, we
saw the land to the eastward, and hauled up for it, towards
Brandywine Bay, with the intention of examining that part
of the coast for a harbour. The " packed" ice was at this
time four or five miles to the westward of us, and the blink
was very strongly marked, and of a yellowish colour, over

the whole of the northern and western horizons At two,
P.M, after standing about six miles to the eastward, we
struck soundings in seventeen, and immediately afterwards
in fifteen fathoms. As no land could be seen within many
leagues of us, we tacked till a boat could be got a-head to
sound, and then kept to the E.N.E, having from fourteen
to ten fathoms for several miles in that direction. The
weather had now become hazy, and the wind light ; but we
could perceive, to the south-eastward, a quantity of heavy ice,
apparently aground, at four or five miles' distance; this we
supposed to be lying around the " Low Island" of Phipps,
which conjecture subsequently proved correct. The weather
becoming more thick, with rain, sleet, and snow, we were
obliged to put the ship's head to the N W., and lie to ; and
in drifting to the northward soon dropped off into deep
water, the hand-leads not reaching the bottom.

The weather continued so thick that, impatient as we were
to stand in towards the eastern land, we could not venture
to do so till eleven A.M, on the 10th, when we made sail
towards Brandywine Bay, the wind being now from the
W.S.W., or nearly dead upon that shore. The weather
clearing up at 1·15, P M, we saw the eastern land, and soon
after discovered the grounded ice off Low Island ; Walden's Island was also plainly in sight to the N.E. The Bay
seemed deeply indented, and very likely to afford nooks such

as we wanted; and where so large a space of open water, and consequently some sea, had been exerting its influence for a considerable time, we flattered ourselves with the most sanguine hopes of now having access to the shores, sufficiently near, at least, for sawing into some place of shelter. How, then, shall I express our surprize and mortification in finding that the whole of the coast, from the islands northwards to Black Point, and apparently also as far as Walden's Island, was rendered inaccessible by one continuous and heavy floe, everywhere attached to the shores, and to the numberless grounded masses about the island, this immense barrier being in some places six or seven miles in width, and not less than twelve feet in thickness near the margin!

In standing in towards this floe, from the north-westward, we had no bottom with thirty-five fathoms of line; but, after sailing *out* on the opposite tack about a mile, we suddenly struck soundings in ten, and before the ship's head came round, had decreased to seven fathoms. Lowering a boat, I immediately went away to sound, and found that some heavy masses of ice, near us, and lying close off the margin of the floe, were aground in six fathoms, our distance from the north-eastern part of the island being about four or five miles. Nearer to the island the water deepened again to thirteen and fifteen fathoms; so that this appears to be a bank lying by itself at that distance; and upon

which there is, perhaps, less water than I found, as the floe
prevented my sounding more to the eastward about the shoalest part.

The prospect from our masthead at this time was certainly enough to cast a damp over every sanguine expectation I had formed, of being *soon* enabled to place the Hecla in security; and more willingly than ever would I, at this period, have persuaded myself, if possible, that I should be justified in quitting her at sea. Such, however, was the nature of this navigation, as regarded the combined difficulties arising from ice and a large extent of shoal and unsurveyed ground, that, even with our full complement of officers and men on board, all our strength and exertions might scarcely have sufficed, in a single gale of wind, to keep the ship tolerably secure, and much less could I have ensured placing her ultimately in any proper situation for picking up an absent party; for, if once again beset, she must, of course, be at the mercy of the ice. The conclusion was, therefore, irresistibly forced upon my mind, that thus to have left the ship would have been to expose her to imminent and certain peril, rendering it impossible to conjecture where we should find her on our return, and therefore rashly to have placed all parties in a situation from which nothing but disaster could reasonably be expected to ensue

The wind having now freshened up from the S.W bW.,

which might be expected to bring the drift ice from the
" pack " in upon the land, we stood to the N.W. to gain an
offing, and, after sailing eighteen miles, came to a quantity
of ice which was streaming off from the margin.   When we
tacked, at 11 P.M., our estimated latitude, by our run from
Low Island, was 80° 36´; and there was at this time so
much clear water to the northward and N.N.E. of us, that
we might probably have run, without any obstruction, to
80°⅔, had there been any object in our doing so.   I now
determined to take advantage of the westerly wind, and of
the lee afforded by the ice, to stand back to the southward
towards Waygatz Strait, where a dark purple sky seemed to
indicate clear water, and where, on this account, as well as
from the clearness of the shores about Verlegen Hook, we
hoped there might be access to the land near some harbour.
In keeping in that direction, in the course of the night, we
found that the ice was drifting very fast to the eastward,
and on the morning of the 11th, it was not without some
difficulty that we got to windward of the shoal ground off
the west end of Low Island ; so near had the ice now approached it, though, forty-eight hours before, none was to
be seen from the ship's deck, in a much more westerly position than this.   When we had proceeded a little farther to
the southward, we found that the same effect had been
produced in a much more surprising degree under all the

lands about the entrance of Waygatz Strait, and towards Verlegen Hook, where it was now not possible to approach the shores in any one place in sight from our masthead.

My intentions being thus again baffled, and there being every probability that, if the westerly wind lasted, it would soon leave us no space in which to keep under way, we now pushed back again to the northward, preferring to be beset in a high latitude, if we were to be beset at all. However, in the course of the 12th, the wind shifted to the north- ward; of which circumstance I gladly took advantage to endeavour to get a sight of the main ice, and at the same time to examine about Walden Island, though with little hopes of finding a harbour on so small a spot of land. This island was regarded by us at this time with no common interest, since it now appeared probable that it would form one of the stations to which provisions and information would be carried, as an assistance to our party on their return from the northward.

After beating through much ice, which was all of the drift or broken kind, and had all found its way hither in the last two days, we got into an open space of water inshore, and about six miles to the northward of Low Island, and on the morning of the 13th stretched in to- wards Walden Island, around which we found, as we had feared, a considerable quantity of fixed ice It was certainly much less here than elsewhere; but the inner, or eastern

G

side of the island was entirely enveloped by it   In fact, the very circumstance which tended to clear the northern and western sides of any land hereabouts, and to retain the ice on the northern and eastern, (namely, the exposure of the former, and the sheltered situation of the latter, relatively to the open water,) tended also to delay the accomplishment of our wishes; for it was against the sea and the pressure of ice from the south and west alone that it was very important at present to secure the ship, and from any such shelter we were still unavoidably shut out.

Having from twenty-six to twenty-four fathoms at the distance of four miles from Walden Island, I was preparing two boats, with the intention of going to sound about its northern point, which was the most clear of ice, and not without a faint hope of finding something like shelter there; but I was prevented by a thick fog coming on.   Indeed, ever since we had got into open water, we had scarcely once seen the blue sky, and for ten hours out of every twelve we had experienced fog, sleet, or snow.   Continuing, therefore, to beat to the northward, we passed occasionally a good deal of loose drift-ice, but with every appearance of much clear water in that direction; and the weather clearing about midnight, we observed in latitude 80° 43′ 32″.   The Seven Islands were in sight to the eastward, and the " Little Table Island " of Phipps's bore E.N.E. (true), distant about nine or ten miles.   It is a mere craggy rock, rising perhaps from three to four hundred feet above the level of the sea, and with a small low islet lying off its northern end. This island, being the northernmost known land in the world, naturally excited much of our curiosity; and bleak and barren and rugged as it is, one could not help gazing at it with intense interest

The wind freshened from the northward on the 14th, and as this was likely to clear the margin of the main ice, we still continued to beat up towards it under all sail, in the confident hope of soon meeting it, or at least of forming some idea, from appearances, where we might expect to do so in the boats. As we advanced to the northward, we fell in with more and more drift-ice; but at noon, when in latitude, by observation, 80° 49' 6", or one mile to the northward of Phipps's furthest, nothing like the heavy or main ice could be seen. In the evening the drift-ice still increased, and we passed one or two floes, but not of a heavy kind. At midnight we had reached the latitude of 81° 5' 32". Our longitude, by chronometers, at this time was 19° 34' East, Little Table Island bearing S. 26° E (true), distant six or seven leagues, and Walden Island S. 4° E *   The depth

* I have been thus particular in noticing the Hecla's position, because our observations would appear to be, with one exception, the most northern on record at that time. The Commissioners of Longitude, in their memorial to the King in Council, in the year 1821, consider that the " progress of discovery has not arrived northwards, according to any well-authenticated accounts, so far as eighty-one degrees of north latitude " Mr Scoresby subsequently states his having observed in lat 81° 12 42".

of water was ninety-seven fathoms, on a bottom of greenish
mud; and the temperature, at ninety-five fathoms, by Six's
thermometer, was 29°8, that at the surface being 31°, and
of the air 28'. All that could here be seen to the northward was loose drift-ice. To the north-east it was particularly open, and I have no doubt that we might have gone
many miles further in that direction, had it not been a much
more important object to keep the ship free, than to push
her to the northward. We were, however, much disappointed in seeing no indication of the main ice from this
station; unless, indeed, the yellow blink which overspread
the northern horizon, but which we had seen quite as bright
when forty miles further south, could so be considered
There was, in fact, scarcely a loose mass to be seen, that
could have ever belonged to a very heavy floe, such as the
main ice is considered to be; so that, although we were now
twenty-five miles to the northward of the station in which
Phipps remarked that " the ice appeared flat and unbroken,"
as seen from a considerable height on shore, all that we
could discover was quite of a contrary description. Thus
we were still at a loss to know the position of the main ice
at this time; while the nature and quantity of that through
which we had been sailing for so many miles were extremely
unfavourable to the progress of boats over it, whenever it
should become " packed "

We now stood back again to the southward, in order

again to examine the coast wherever we could approach it, but found, on the 15th, that none of the land was at all accessible, the wind having got round to the W.N.W and loaded all the shores with drift-ice. Our attention was, indeed, pretty well occupied in keeping the ship at liberty; which, however, she probably would not have been for twenty-four hours longer, had the westerly breeze continued; for the ice came driving back very quickly from that quarter, and would have very soon beset us. Fortunately, however, on the evening of the 15th, it shifted to the eastward, and a fresh breeze blowing from that quarter sent it away once more to the westward in a few hours, leaving us a clear space of water inshore. I now determined to examine, if possible, every part of the coast, while this easterly wind kept it clear of drift-ice, and wherever the shore could be approached, either by water, or by walking over the ice, to search for a sheltered place for the ship, that we might at least know of such a place, and then take the first opportunity of getting into it.

Walden Island being the first part clear of the loose ice, we stretched in for it on the 16th, and, when within two miles, observed that about half that space was occupied by land ice, even on its north-western side, which was the only accessible one, the rest being wholly enclosed by it. However, being desirous of obtaining a better view than our crow's-nest commanded, and also of depositing here a small

1827.
June
Friday, 15th.

Saturday,
16th

supply of provisions, I left the ship at 1 P.M., accompanied
by Lieutenant Foster in a second boat, and, landing upon
the ice, walked over about three-quarters of a mile of high
and rugged hummocks to the shore Ascending two or
three hundred feet, we had a clear and extensive view of
the Seven Islands, and of some land far beyond them to the
eastward; and here the whole sea was covered with one
unbroken land-floe attached to all the shores, extending
from the island where we stood, and which formed an abut-
ment for it, each way along the land as far as the eye could
reach.   After this discouraging prospect, which wholly
destroyed every hope of finding a harbour among the Seven
Islands, we returned to the place where the men had deposited the provisions, and after making the necessary observations for the survey, returned immediately on board.

This island, which in some parts is about five hundred
feet above the sea, and precipitous towards the middle,
consists of coarse-grained granite, most of which is black and
white: in the rest the felspar is of a bright flesh-colour,
giving the rock a red hue, and the mica is very abundant and
shining in both kinds.   In one place, it seemed to dip to the
north-east, at an angle of 30°; but it was not very distinctly
marked.   A few plants, mosses, and lichens were found.
Of the last-mentioned, the tripe-de-roche (*Gyrophora Pro-
boscidea*), the rein-deer moss (*Cenomyce Rangiferina*), and
the black woolly-looking *Cornicularia divergens*, were most

abundant. A few eider ducks and dovekies were the only
animals seen; but there were traces of rein-deer having
been upon the island. The latitude of the north-west end
is 80° 35′ 38″; the longitude, by chronometer, 19° 51′ 16″ E.,
and the variation of the magnetic needle 17° 42′ westerly;
the latter phenomenon still exhibiting a regular decrease as
we advanced to the eastward. The soundings appeared
deep around the island; we had thirty-three fathoms at the
margin of the land-ice.

Observing from the island that the sea was perfectly clear
to the northward, we now stood for Little Table Island,
with some slight hope that the rock off its northern end
might afford shelter for the ship; at all events, being the
most exposed, on account of its situation, it was the most
likely to be free from ice. A thick fog prevented our getting near it till the morning of the 17th, when, having
approached it within a mile and a half, I sent Lieutenant
Ross on shore to the little islet, which was quite clear of ice,
and where he deposited another small store of provisions,
but found nothing like shelter for the ship. The islet consists
of gneiss, having garnets imbedded in some specimens; Mr
Beverly could not discover in what direction it dipped. This
small rock, with specimens of which (as being the northernmost known land in the world) the boat returned loaded,
is about one hundred feet above the sea, and the Table
Island about four or five hundred, both occupying an extent

of perhaps one-third of a square mile. Lieutenant Ross
described the rocks as covered with abundance of very large
tripe-de-roche, some rein-deer moss, and other lichens; and
there was abundance of good water in pools   A few brent-
geese, eider-ducks, and a *Lestris Parasiticus,* were all the
animals seen   We place this island, by a meridian altitude
observed on board this day, in latitude 80° 48′; but the
observation was an indifferent one, and with the sea horizon,
which is never to be trusted. We had no bottom with
thirty-five fathoms, at one mile distance, on the north and
west sides, and Lieutenant Ross found twelve fathoms
alongside the rocks.   This was the only island round which
a ship might, at this time, have sailed; all the others in
sight being entirely enclosed by a barrier of fixed ice.

Having no further business here, and the easterly wind
still continuing, I thought the best thing we could do,
would be to run again to the southward of Low Island, and
try once more to approach the shores about the entrance
of the Waygatz Strait.   We, therefore, bore up under all
sail to the south-west.

It would be vain to deny that I had lately begun to
entertain the most serious apprehensions, as related to the
accomplishment of our principal object.   The 17th of June
had now arrived, and all that we saw afforded the most
discouraging prospect as to our getting the Hecla into harbour; while every day's experience showed how utterly rash

a measure it would be to think of quitting her in her present
situation, which, even with all her officers and men, was
one of extreme precariousness and uncertainty. Although
I was in the habit of daily and almost hourly communication
with my officers, yet I thought it my duty once more to
require from them officially their opinions upon this subject,
which I found to agree entirely with my own. Indeed,
there could not, under present circumstances, be two opinions upon the subject.

Standing to the S.W. after passing Walden Island, we
came, as usual, pretty suddenly into sixteen fathoms, when
at the distance of six or seven miles from the north side of
Low Island. In running for the grounded hummocks off
the west extremity, which is itself so low as to be scarcely
discernible when any ice lies near it, we soon had from
twelve to ten; but in keeping *out*, in order to deepen the
water, we suddenly fell into seven, and, for more than an
hour's quick run, did not get a cast above ten. There
being at this time a considerable swell, and too much ice
still adhering to the island to enable us to seek a shelter
there, I did not choose to risk getting the ship on the
ground, and therefore hauled to the southward, towards
Verlegen Hook, to prosecute our search for a harbour once
more in that quarter. On the evening of the 18th, while
standing in for the high land to the eastward of Verlegen Hook,
which, with due attention to the lead, may be approached

H

with safety, we perceived from the crow's-nest what appeared a low point, possibly affording some shelter for the ship, and which seemed to answer to an indentation of the coast laid down in an old Dutch chart *, and there called *Treurenburg Bay*.

On the following morning I proceeded to examine the place, accompanied by Lieutenant Ross in a second boat, and, to our great joy, found it a considerable bay, with one part affording excellent land-locked anchorage, and, what was equally fortunate, sufficiently clear of ice to allow the ship to enter. Having sounded the entrance, and deter-termined on the anchorage, we returned to the ship to bring her in; and I cannot describe the satisfaction which the information of our success communicated to every individual on board. The main object of our enterprise now appeared almost within our grasp, and every body seemed anxious to make up, by renewed exertions, for the time we had una-voidably lost. The ship was towed and warped in with the

greatest alacrity, and at 1. 40, A M., on the 20th, we dropped the anchor in Hecla Cove, in thirteen fathoms, on a bottom of very tenacious blue clay, and made some hawsers fast to the land-ice which still filled all the upper part of the bay. After resting a few hours, we sawed a canal, a quarter of a mile in length, through which the ship was removed into a

* Nieuwe afteckening van Het Eyland Spits-Bergen, opgegeven deor de Commandeurs Giles en Outger Rep, en in't Light gebragt en uytgegeven door Gerard Van Keulen, &c. &c

better situation, a bower-cable taken on shore and secured
to the rocks, and an anchor with the chain-cable laid out
the other way.   On the morning of the 21st, we hauled the
launch up on the beach, it being my intention to direct such
resources of every kind to be landed, as would render our
party wholly independent of the ship, either for returning
to England or for wintering, in case of the ship being driven
to sea by the ice ; a contingency against which, in these
regions, no precaution can altogether provide.   I directed
Lieutenant Foster, upon whom the charge of the Hecla
was now to devolve, to land without delay the necessary
stores, keeping the ship sea-worthy by taking in an equal
weight of ballast ; and, as soon as he should be satisfied of
her security from ice, to proceed on the survey of the eastern
coast ; but should he see reason to doubt her safety, with a
still further diminution of her crew, to relinquish the survey, and attend exclusively to the ship.   I also gave directions that notices should be sent, in the course of the
summer, to the various stations where our depôts of provisions were established, acquainting me with the situation
and state of the ship, and giving me any other information
which might be necessary for my guidance on our return
from the northward.   These and other arrangements being
completed, I left the ship at five, P.M., with our two boats,
which we named the Enterprise and Endeavour, Mr. Beverly
being attached to my own, and Lieutenant Ross, accompa-

H 2

nied by Mr. Bird, in the other.   Besides these, I took Lieutenant Crozier in one of the ship's cutters, for the purpose
of carrying some of our weight as far as Walden Island, and
also a third store of provisions to be deposited on Low
Island, as an intermediate station between Walden Island
and the ship.   As it was still necessary not to delay our
return beyond the end of August, the time originally
intended, I took with me only seventy-one days' provisions;
which, including the boats and every other article, made up
a weight of 260 lbs. per man; and as it appeared highly
improbable, from what we had seen of the very rugged
nature of the ice we should first have to encounter, that
either the rein-deer, the snow-shoes, or the wheels would
prove of any service for some time to come, I gave up the
idea of taking them.   We, however, constructed out of the
snow-shoes four excellent sledges, for dragging a part of our
baggage over the ice; and these proved of invaluable service
to us, while the rest of the things just mentioned would
only have been an incumbrance

Having received the usual salutation of three cheers from
those we left behind, we paddled through a quantity of
loose ice at the entrance of the bay, and then steered, in a
perfectly open sea, and with calm and beautiful weather, for
the western part of Low Island, which we reached at half
past two on the morning of the 22nd.   The low beach on
which we landed was principally composed of rounded frag-

ments of limestone, intermixed with some of clay-slate ; and
several small rounded pieces of pumice-stone were also
found.   The drift-wood lined the beach in great quantities,
the whole being of the pine tribe, as usual, and a Greenland
whaler's harpoon was found lying among it.

Having deposited the provisions, we set off at four, A M.,
paddling watch and watch, to give the people a little rest.
It was still quite calm ; but there being much ice about the
island, and a thick fog coming on, we were several hours
groping our way clear of it.   The walruses were here very
numerous, lying in herds upon the ice, and plunging into the
water to follow us as we passed.   The sound they utter is
something between bellowing and very loud snorting, which,
together with their grim, bearded countenances and long
tusks, makes them appear, as indeed they are, rather formidable enemies to contend with   Under our present circumstances, we were very well satisfied not to molest them, for
they would soon have destroyed our boats, if one had been
wounded ; but I believe they are never the first to make
the attack.   We landed upon the ice still attached to Walden Island, at 3. 30, A M., on the 23rd.   Our flat-bottomed
boats rowed heavily with their loads, but proved perfectly
safe and very comfortable.   The men being much fatigued,
we rested here some hours, and, after making our final
arrangements with Lieutenant Crozier, parted with him at
three in the afternoon, and set off for Little Table Island.

Finding there was likely to be so much open water in this neighbourhood in the autumn, I sent directions to Lieutenant Foster to have a spare boat deposited at Walden Island, in time for our return, in case of any accident happening to ours.

The land-ice. which still adhered to the Seven Islands, was very little more broken off than when the Hecla had been here a week before, and we rowed along its margin a part of the way to Little Table Island, where we arrived at ten, p.m. We here examined and re-secured the provisions left on shore, having found our depôt at Walden Island disturbed by the bears. The prospect to the northward at this time was very favourable, there being only a small quantity of loose ice in sight; and the weather still continuing calm and clear, with the sea as smooth as a mirror, we set off, without delay, at half past ten, taking our final leave of the Spitzbergen shores, as we hoped, for at least two months Steering due north, we made good progress, our latitude by the sun's meridian altitude at midnight being 80° 51' 13". A beautifully coloured rainbow appeared for some time, without any appearance of rain falling. We observed that a considerable current was setting us to the eastward just after leaving the land, so that we had made a N.N E. course, distance about ten miles, when we met with some ice, which soon becoming too close for further progress, we landed upon a high hummock to obtain a better view.

1827
June

We here perceived that the ice was close to the northward, but to the westward discovered some open water, which we reached after two or three hours paddling, and found it a wide expanse, in which we sailed to the northward without obstruction, a fresh breeze having sprung up from the S.W. The weather soon after became very thick, with continued snow, requiring great care in looking out for the ice, which made its appearance after two hours run, and gradually became closer, till at length we were stopped by it at noon, and obliged to haul the boats upon a small floe-piece, our latitude by observation being 81° 12′ 51″.

Our plan of travelling being nearly the same throughout this excursion, after we first entered upon the ice, I may at once give some account of our usual mode of proceeding. It was my intention to travel wholly at night, and to rest by day, there being, of course, constant daylight in these regions during the summer season. The advantages of this plan, which was occasionally deranged by circumstances, consisted first, in our avoiding the intense and oppressive glare from the snow during the time of the sun's greatest altitude, so as to prevent, in some degree, the painful inflammation in the eyes, called " snow-blindness," which is common in all snowy countries. We also thus enjoyed greater warmth during the hours of rest, and had a better chance of drying our clothes ; besides which, no small advantage was derived from the snow being harder at night

foɪ travelling.   The only disadvantage of this plan was, that
the fogs were somewhat more frequent and more thick by
night than by day, though even in this respect there was
less diffeɪence than might have been supposed, the tem-
peɪatuɪe during the twenty-four hours undergoing but little
variation   This travelling by night and sleeping by day so
completely inveɪted the natuɪal order of things, that it was
difficult to persuade ourselves of the reality.   Even the
officeɪs and myself, who were all furnished with pocket
chronometers, could not always bear in mind at what part
of the twenty-four hours we had arrived ; and there weɪe
several of the men who declaɪed, and I believe truly, that they
never knew night fɪom day duɪing the whole excursion *.

When we rose in the evening, we commenced ouɪ day by
pɪayers, after which we took off our fur sleeping-dɪesses,
and put on those for travelling ; the former being made of
camblet, lɪned with racoon-skɪn, and the latteɪ of strong blue
box-cloth.   We made a point of always putting on the same
stockings and boots foɪ tɪavelling in, whether they had dried
duɪing the day or not ; and I believe it was only in five or

* Had we succeeded in reachɪng the higher latitudes, where the change of
the sun's altitude during the twenty-four hours is still less peɪceptible, it would
have been essentially necessary to possess the certaɪn means of knowɪng this , sɪnce
an eɪror of twelve hours of tɪme would have caɪɪied us, when we intended to
return, on a merɪdɪan opposɪte to, or 180° from, the rɪght one.   To obvɪate the
possɪbɪlɪty of this, we had some chronometers constɪucted by Messrs Paɪkɪnson
and Fɪodsham, of whɪch the houɪ-hand made only one revolution in the day,
the twenty-four houɪs beɪng marked round the dial-plate.

1827
June

six instances, at the most, that they were not either still wet
or hard-frozen. This, indeed, was of no consequence, beyond
the discomfort of first putting them on in this state, as they
were sure to be thoroughly wet in a quarter of an hour after
commencing our journey; while, on the other hand, it was
of vital importance to keep dry things for sleeping in. Being
"rigged" for travelling, we breakfasted upon warm cocoa
and biscuit, and after stowing the things in the boats and on
the sledges, so as to secure them, as much as possible, from
wet, we set off on our day's journey, and usually travelled
from five to five and a half hours, then stopped an hour to
dine, and again travelled four, five, or even six hours, according to circumstances. After this we halted for the night,
as we called it, though it was usually early in the morning,
selecting the largest surface of ice we happened to be near,
for hauling the boats on, in order to avoid the danger of its
breaking up by coming in contact with other masses, and
also to prevent drift as much as possible. The boats were
placed close alongside each other, with their sterns to the
wind, the snow or wet cleared out of them, and the sails,
supported by the bamboo masts and three paddles, placed
over them as awnings, an entrance being left at the bow.
Every man then immediately put on dry stockings and fur
boots, after which we set about the necessary repairs of
boats, sledges, or clothes; and, after serving the provisions
for the succeeding day, we went to supper. Most of the

I

officers and men then smoked their pipes, which served to
dry the boats and awnings very much, and usually raised the
temperature of our lodgings 10° or 15°. This part of the
twenty-four hours was often a time, and the only one, of real
enjoyment to us; the men told their stories and " fought all
their battles o'er again," and the labours of the day, unsuccessful as they too often were, were forgotten. A regular
watch was set during our resting-time, to look out for bears
or for the ice breaking up round us, as well as to attend to
the drying of the clothes, each man alternately taking this
duty for one hour. We then concluded our day with
prayers, and having put on our fur-dresses, lay down to
sleep with a degree of comfort, which perhaps few persons
would imagine possible under such circumstances; our chief
inconvenience being, that we were somewhat pinched for
room, and therefore obliged to stow rather closer than was
quite agreeable. The temperature, while we slept, was
usually from 36° to 45°, according to the state of the external
atmosphere; but on one or two occasions, in calm and warm
weather, it rose as high as 60° to 66°, obliging us to throw
off a part of our fur-dress. After we had slept seven hours,
the man appointed to boil the cocoa roused us, when it was
ready, by the sound of a bugle, when we commenced our
day in the manner before described.

Our allowance of provisions for each man per day was as
follows :—

Biscuit . . . . . . 10 ounces.

Pemmican . . . . 9 ,,

Sweetened Cocoa Powder 1 ,, to make one pint.

Rum . . . . . . 1 gill.

Tobacco . . . . . 3 ounces per week.

Our fuel consisted entirely of spirits of wine, of which two pints formed our daily allowance, the cocoa being cooked in an iron boiler over a shallow iron lamp, with seven wicks; a simple apparatus, which answered our purpose remarkably well. We usually found one pint of the spirits of wine sufficient for preparing our breakfast, that is, for heating twenty-eight pints of water, though it always commenced from the temperature of 32°. If the weather was calm and fair, this quantity of fuel brought it to the boiling point in about an hour and a quarter; but more generally the wicks began to go out before it had reached 200°. This, however, made a very comfortable meal to persons situated as we were. Such, with very little variation, was our regular routine during the whole of this excursion.

We set off on our first journey over the ice at ten, P.M., on the 24th, Table Island bearing S.S W., and a fresh breeze blowing from W.S.W., with thick fog, which afterwards changed to rain. The bags of pemmican were placed upon the sledges, and the bread in the boats, with the intention of securing the latter from wet , but this plan we were very soon obliged to relinquish. We now commenced upon very

I 2

slow and laborious travelling, the pieces of ice being of small extent and very rugged, obliging us to make three journies, and sometimes four, with the boats and baggage, and to launch several times across narrow pools of water. This, however, was nothing more than we had expected to encounter at the margin of the ice, and for some distance within it; and every individual exerted himself to the very utmost, with the hope of the sooner reaching the main or field ice. We stopped to dine at five, A.M., on the 25th, having made, by our log, (which we kept very carefully, marking the courses by compass, and estimating the distances,) about two miles and a half of northing; and again setting forward, proceeded till eleven, A M., when we halted to rest, our latitude by observation at noon being 81° 15' 13".

Setting out again at half past nine in the evening, we found our way to lie over nothing but small loose rugged masses of ice, separated by little pools of water, obliging us constantly to launch and haul up the boats, each of which operations required them to be unloaded, and occupied nearly a quarter of an hour. It came on to rain very hard on the morning of the 26th; and finding we were making very little progress, (having advanced not more than half a mile in four hours,) and that our clothes would be soon wet through, we halted at half past one, and took shelter under the awnings. The weather improving at six o'clock, we again moved forward, and travelled till a quarter past eleven, when we hauled the boats upon the only tolerably large floe-piece in sight. The rain had very much increased the quantity of water lying upon the ice, of which nearly half the surface was now covered with numberless little ponds of various shapes and extent. It is a remarkable fact that we had already experienced, in the course of this summer, more rain than during the whole of seven previous summers *taken together*, though passed in latitudes from 7° to 15° lower than this. A great deal of the ice over which we passed to-day presented a very curious appearance and structure, being composed, on its upper surface, of numberless irregular needle-like crystals, placed vertically, and nearly close together , their length varying, in different pieces of ice, from five to ten inches, and their breadth in the middle about half an inch, but pointed at both ends. The upper surface of ice having this structure sometimes looks like greenish velvet; a vertical section of it, which frequently occurs at the margin of floes, resembles, while it remains compact, the most beautiful satin-spar, and asbestos, when falling to pieces. At this early part of the season, this kind of ice afforded pretty firm footing, but as the summer advanced, the needles became more loose and moveable, rendering it extremely fatiguing to walk over them, besides cutting our boots and feet, on which account the men called them " penknives." It appeared probable to us that this peculiarity might be produced by the heavy drops of rain piercing

their way downwards through the ice, and thus separating
the latter into needles of the form above described, rather
than to any regular crystallization when in the act of freezing;
which supposition seemed the more reasonable, as the needles
are always placed in a vertical position, and never occur
except from the upper surface downwards.

We pursued our journey at half past nine, P M., with the
wind at N.E , and thick weather, the ice being so much in
motion as to make it very dangerous to cross with loaded
boats, the masses being all very small. Indeed, when we
came to the margin of the floe-piece on which we had slept,
we saw no road by which we could safely proceed, and therefore preferred remaining where we were, to the risk of
driving back to the southward on one of the smaller masses.
On this account we halted at midnight, having waded three-
quarters of a mile through water from two to five inches
deep upon the ice. The thermometer was at 33°. In the
course of this short journey, we saw several rotges and dovekies, and a few kittiwakes, ivory gulls, and mallemuckes.

The weather continued so thick that we could only see
a few yards around us; but the wind backing to the southward, and beginning to open out the loose ice at the edge
of the floe, we proceeded at half past ten, P.M., and after
crossing several small pieces, came to the first tolerably heavy
ice we had yet seen, but all broken up into masses of small
extent. At seven, A M., on the 28th, we came to a floe

covered with high and rugged hummocks, which opposed a formidable obstacle to our progress, occurring in two or three successive tiers, so that we had no sooner crossed one than another presented itself. Over one of these we hauled the boats with extreme difficulty, by a " standing pull," and the weather being then so thick that we could see no pass across the next tier, we were obliged to stop at nine, A.M. While performing this laborious work, which required the boats to be got up and down places almost perpendicular, James Parker, my coxswain, received a severe contusion in his back, by the boat falling upon him from a hummock, and the boats were constantly subject to very heavy blows, but sustained no damage *. The weather continued very foggy during the day, but a small lane of water opening out at no great distance from the margin of the floe, we launched the boats, at eight in the evening, among loose drift-ice, and after some time landed on a small floe to the eastward, the only one in sight, with the hope of its leading to the north-ward. It proved so rugged that we were obliged to make three, and sometimes four journies with the boats and pro-

---

* I may here mention that notwithstanding the heavy blows which the boats were constantly receiving, all our nautical and astronomical instruments were taken back to the ship without injury. This circumstance makes it, perhaps, worth while to explain that they were lashed upon a wooden platform in the after locker of each boat, sufficiently small to be clear of the boat's sides, and playing on strong springs of whalebone, which entirely obviated the effects of the severe concussions to which they would otherwise have been subject

visions, and this by a very circuitous route; so that the road by which we made a mile of northing was full a mile and a half in length, and over this we had to travel at least five, and sometimes seven times. Thus, when we halted to dine, at two, A M, after six hours' severe toil, and much risk to the men and boats, we had only accomplished about a mile and a quarter in a N.N.E. direction. After dining we proceeded again till half past six, and then halted, very much fatigued with our day's work, and having made two miles and a half of northing. One of the carpenter's mates was a good deal hurt by a loaded sledge running against him, which laid him up for a day or two We were here in latitude, by account, 81° 23', and in longitude, by the chronometers, 21° 32' 34″ E., in which situation the variation of the magnetic needle was observed to be 15° 31', westerly. We now enjoyed the first sunshine since our entering the ice, and a great enjoyment it was, after so much thick and wet weather. We rose at half past four, P.M., in the hopes of pursuing our journey, but after hauling the boats to the edge of the floe, found such a quantity of loose rugged ice to the northward of us, that there was no possibility, for the present, of getting across or through it. Soon afterwards the whole of it became in motion, and driving down upon the floe, obliged us to retreat from the margin, and wait for some favourable change. We here tried for soundings, but found no bottom with two hundred fathoms of line. The

weather was beautifully clear, and the wind moderate
from the S.W. From this situation we saw the eastern-
most of the Seven Islands, bearing S. b W.; but Little
Table Island, though more to the northward, yet being
less high, was not in sight. Observing a small opening
at 10.30, P.M., we launched the boats, and hauled them
across several pieces of ice, some of them being very light
and much decayed. Our latitude, by the sun's meridian
altitude at midnight, was 81° 23'; so that we had made
only eight miles of northing since our last observation at
noon on the 25th.

The 30th commenced with snowy and inclement weather,
which soon rendered the atmosphere so thick, that we could
no longer see our way, obliging us to halt till two, P.M., when
we crossed several small pools with great labour and loss of
time. We had generally very light ice this day, with some
heavy rugged pieces intermixed; and when hauling across
these we had sometimes to cut with axes a passage for the
boats among the hummocks. We also dragged them through
a great many pools of fresh water, to avoid the necessity of
going round them. The wind freshening up from the
S S.W., we afterwards found the ice gradually more and
more open, so that, in the course of the day, we made by
rowing, though by a very winding channel, five miles of
northing, but were again stopped by the ice soon after
midnight, and obliged to haul up on the first mass that we

K

could gain, the ice having so much motion that we narrowly
escaped being "nipped" We had passed, during this day's
journey, a great deal of light ice, but, for the first time,
one heavy floe, from two to three miles in length, under
the lee of which we found the most open water. A number
of rotges and ivory-gulls were seen about the "holes" of
water, and now and then a very small seal. We set out
again at 11 30, A.M., the wind still fresh from the S.W., and
some snow falling; but it was more than an hour before we
could get away from the small piece of ice on which we
slept, the masses beyond being so broken up, and so much
in motion, that we could not at first venture to launch the
boats. Our latitude, observed at noon, was 81° 30′ 41″.
After crossing several pieces, we at length got into a good
"lead" of water, four or five miles in length; two or three
of which, as on the preceding day, occurred under the lee
of a floe, being the second we had yet seen that deserved
that name. We then passed over four or five small floes,
and across the pools of water that lay betwixt them. The
ice was now less broken up, and sometimes tolerably level;
but from six to eighteen inches of soft snow lay upon it in
every part, making the travelling very fatiguing, and obliging us to make at least two, and sometimes three journies
with our loads. We now found it absolutely necessary to
lighten the boats as much as possible, by putting the bread-
bags on the sledges, on account of the "runners" of the

boats sinking so much deeper into the snow; but our bread ran a great risk of being wetted by this plan

As soon as we landed on a floe-piece, Lieutenant Ross and myself generally went on ahead, while the boats were unloading and hauling up, in order to select the easiest road for them. The sledges then followed in our track, Messrs. Beverly and Bird accompanying them; by which the snow was much trodden down, and the road thus improved for the boats. As soon as we arrived at the other end of the floe, or came to any difficult place, we mounted one of the highest hummocks of ice near at hand, (many of which were from fifteen to five-and-twenty feet above the sea) in order to obtain a better view around us; and nothing could well exceed the dreariness which such a view presented The eye wearied itself in vain to find an object but ice and sky to rest upon, and even the latter was often hidden from our view by the dense and dismal fogs which so generally prevailed. For want of variety, the most trifling circumstance engaged a more than ordinary share of our attention; a passing gull, or a mass of ice of unusual form, became objects which our situation and circumstances magnified into ridiculous importance; and we have since often smiled to remember the eager interest with which we regarded many insignificant occurrences. It may well be imagined, then, how cheering it was to turn from this scene of inanimate desolation, to our two little boats in the distance, to see the moving figures

K 2

of our men winding with their sledges among the hummocks, and to hear once more the sound of human voices
breaking the stillness of this icy wilderness.   In some cases
Lieutenant Ross and myself took separate routes to try the
ground, which kept us almost continually floundering among
deep snow and water. The sledges having then been brought
up as far as we had explored, we all went back for the boats;
each boat's crew, when the road was tolerable, dragging their
own, and the officers labouring equally hard with the men.
It was thus we proceeded for nine miles out of every ten
that we travelled over ice; for it was very rarely indeed
that we met with a surface sufficiently level and hard to
drag all our loads at one journey, and in a great many
instances, during the first fortnight, we had to make three
journies with the boats and baggage , that is, to traverse the
same road five times over.

　　We halted at eleven, P.M, on the 1st, having traversed
from ten to eleven miles, and made good, by our account,
seven and a half in a N.b W. direction. We again set for-
Monday,2nd. ward at ten, A.M, on the 2nd, the weather being calm, and
the sun oppressively warm, though with a thick fog.   The
temperature in the shade was 35° at noon, and only 47° in
the sun ; but this, together with the glare from the snow,
produced so painful a sensation in most of our eyes, as to
make it necessary to halt at one, P.M., to avoid being blinded.
We therefore took advantage of this warm weather to let

the men wash themselves, and mend and dry their clothes,
and then set out again at half past three. The snow was,
however, so soft as to take us up to our knees at almost
every other step, and frequently still deeper ; so that we
were sometimes five minutes together in moving a single
empty boat, with all our united strength. It being impossible to proceed under these circumstances, I determined,
by degrees, to fall into our night-travelling again, from which
we had of.late insensibly deviated. We therefore halted
at half past five, the weather being now very clear and
warm, and many of the people's eyes beginning to fail. We
did not set out again till after midnight, with the intention
of giving the snow time to harden after so warm a day ; but
we found it still so soft as to make the travelling very
fatiguing. Our way lay at first across a number of small
loose pieces, most of which were from five to twenty yards
apart, or just sufficiently separated to give us all the labour
of launching and hauling up the boats, without the advantage of making any progress by water ; while we crossed, in
other instances, from mass to mass, by laying the boats over,
as bridges, by which the men and the baggage passed. By
these means, we at length reached a floe about a mile in
length, in a northern direction . but it would be difficult to
convey an adequate idea of the labour required to traverse
it. The average depth of snow upon the level parts was
about five inches. under which lay water four or five inches

deep; but the moment we approached a hummock, the depth to which we sank increased to three feet or more, rendering it difficult at times to obtain sufficient footing for one leg, to enable us to extricate the other. The pools of fresh water had now also become very large, some of them being a quarter of a mile in length, and their depth above our knees. Through these we were prevented taking the sledges, for fear of wetting all our provisions; but we preferred transporting the boats across them, notwithstanding the severe cold of the snow-water, the bottom being harder for the " runners " to slide upon. On this kind of road we were, in one instance, above two hours in proceeding a distance of one hundred yards.

We halted at half past six, A.M., to dine, and to empty our boots and wring our stockings, which, to *our* feelings, was almost like putting on dry ones; and again set out in an hour, getting at length into a " lane " of water one mile and a quarter long, in a N.N.E direction. We halted for the night at half an hour before midnight, the people being almost exhausted with a laborious day's work, and our distance made good to the northward not exceeding two miles and a quarter. We allowed ourselves this night a hot supper, consisting of a pint of soup per man, made of an ounce of pemmican each, and eight or ten birds which we had killed in the course of the last week; and this was a luxury which persons thus situated could perhaps alone duly appreciate. We had·seen. in the course of the day, a few 10tges, a dovekie, a loom, a mallemucke, and two or three very small seals.

We rose and breakfasted at nine, P.M.; but the weather had gradually become so inclement and thick, with snow, sleet, and a fresh breeze from the eastward, that we could neither have seen our way, nor have avoided getting wet through, had we moved. We, therefore, remained under cover; and it was as well that we did so, for the snow soon after changed to heavy rain, and the wind increased to a fresh gale, which unavoidably detained us till 7. 30, P.M., on the 4th, when we found, on setting out, that there was nothing but loose drift-ice for us to haul over; nor from the highest hummock could we discover a single floe, much less a field, towards which to direct our course On two or three small floe-pieces which we did cross, none of which were a quarter of a mile in extent, we found the hummocks occurring, ridge after ridge, with only fifty or sixty yards of level ice between them. The rain had produced even a greater effect than the sun, in softening the snow. Lieutenant Ross and myself, in performing our pioneering duty, were frequently so beset in it, that sometimes, after trying in vain to extricate our legs, we were obliged to sit quietly down for a short time to rest ourselves, and then make another attempt, and the men, in dragging the sledges, were often under the necessity of crawling upon all-fours, to make any progress at all. Nor would any kind of snow-shoes have been of the least service, but rather an incumbrance to us, for the surface was so irregular, that they would have thrown us down at every other step. We had hitherto made use of the Lapland shoes, or *kamoogas*, for walking in, which are excellent for dry snow; but there being now so much water upon the ice, we substituted the Esquimaux boots, which had been made in Greenland expressly for our use *, and which are far superior to any others for this kind

Thursday, 5th

of travelling. Just before halting, at six, A.M., on the 5th, the ice at the margin of the floe broke, while the men were handing the provisions out of the boats ; and we narrowly escaped the loss of a bag of cocoa, which fell overboard, but fortunately rested on a " tongue." The bag being made of Mackintosh's waterproof canvas, the cocoa did not suffer the slightest injury †. We had seen, in the course of our last journey, a few rotges, a loom, an ivory-gull, a malle-mucke, and a tern (*Sterna Arctica*). We here observed the dip of the magnetic needle to be 82° 4′.7, and the variation 13° 16′ westerly; the latitude being 81° 45′ 15″, and

---

* For these we are greatly indebted to the kindness of Lieutenant Holboll, of the Danish Navy, through whose means we obtained them from Greenland

† Of this invaluable manufacture, which consists, I believe, in applying a solution of elastic gum, or caoutchouc, between two parts of canvas, it is impossible to speak too highly. I know of no material which, with an equal weight, is equally durable and water-tight. In the latter quality, indeed, it is altogether perfect, so long as the material lasts.

the longitude, by chronometers, 24° 23′ East, by which we found that we had been drifted considerably to the eastward. In this situation we tried for soundings with four hundred fathoms of line, without reaching the bottom, the temperature at that depth, by Six's thermometer, was 30°, that at the surface, at the time, being $32\frac{1}{2}$°, and of the air 34°.

We rose at five, P.M., the weather being clear and fine, with a moderate breeze from the south, no land was in sight from the highest hummocks, nor could we perceive any thing but broken loose ice in any direction. We hauled across several pieces which were scarcely fit to bear the weight of the boats, and in such places used the precaution of dividing our baggage, so that, in case of the ice breaking or turning over, we should not lose all at once. The farther we proceeded, the more the ice was broken; indeed, it was much more so here than we had found it since first entering the "pack." The labour required to drag the boats over the hummocks, and from one mass to another, was so great that we were obliged to have recourse to what seamen call a "bowline-haul" for many minutes together; which so exhausted the men, that it was necessary for them every now and then to sit down and take breath. After stopping at midnight to dine, and to obtain the meridian altitude, we passed over a floe full of hummocks, a mile and a half in length; but any kind of floe was relief to us after the constant difficulty we had experienced in passing over loose ice. Many of the hummocks were smooth regular cones,

L

much resembling in shape the aromatic pastiles sold by chemists: this roundness and regularity of form indicate age, all the more recent ones being sharp and angular　We had now for several days ceased to observe any ice covered with mud or soil, called by the sailors "dirty ice," which was frequently met with during the first week after our leaving the open water.　We often, however, noticed parts of the ice, which at a distance appeared of an iron-rust colour; but on coming near it, and taking up some in the hand, we could detect nothing with a magnifying glass.

Friday, 6th.
After several hours of very beautiful weather, a thick fog came on early on the morning of the 6th, and at five, A.M., we halted, having got to the end of the floe, and only made good two miles and a half to the northward.　The men were greatly fatigued by this day's exertions, and we served an extra ounce of bread and one of pemmican for their supper; an addition to the original allowance which we were frequently obliged to make, after this time, to prevent our going to bed hungry.　The fog continued very thick all day; but being unwilling to stop on this account, we set out again at half past six in the evening, and passed over several small flat pieces with no great difficulty, but with much loss of time in launching and hauling up the boats.　The fog

Saturday, 7th.
still continued very thick, and the ice of the same broken kind as before; till, towards the end of our day's journey, we landed on the only really level floe we had yet met with. It was, however, only three quarters of a mile in length,

but being almost clear of snow, afforded such good travelling, that although much fatigued at the time, we hauled the boats, and all the baggage, across it at one journey, at the rate of about two miles an hour, and halted at the northern margin at five A.M., on the 7th. The prospect beyond was still very unfavourable, and at eight in the evening, when we again launched the boats, there was not a piece of large or level ice to be seen in a northern direction. After an hour, we arrived at a very difficult pass, which required all our strength, as well as care, to accomplish   We had first to launch the boats into the water over a high and rugged margin, and then to haul them across a number of irregular and ill-connected masses, sometimes making bridges of them for the conveyance of ourselves and our provisions, and once having to cut a passage through a ridge of hummocks which lay across our path. We were thus more than two hours in proceeding a distance not exceeding one hundred and fifty yards. Notwithstanding these discouraging difficulties, the men laboured with great cheerfulness and good-will, being animated with the hope of soon reaching the more continuous body which had been considered as composing the " main ice" to the northward of Spitzbergen, and which Captain Lutwidge, about the same meridian, and more than a degree to the southward of this, describes as " one continued plain of smooth, unbroken ice, bounded only by the horizon.*"

* Phipps's Voyage towards the North Pole, p. 60.

L 2

1827
July.

Sunday, 8th

Monday, 9th.

Tuesday,
10th

We halted at six A.M., on the 8th, in time to avoid a great deal of rain which fell during the day, and again proceeded on our journey at eight in the evening, the wind being fresh from the E.S.E., with thick wet weather. We now met with detached ice of a still lighter kind than before, the only floe in sight being much to the eastward of our course. This we reached, after considerable labour, in the hope of its leading to the northward, which it did for about one mile, and we then came to the same kind of loose ice as before. We observed in one place a little mud in some small holes in the ice, being the first we had seen for a week. On the morning of the 9th, we enjoyed the indescribable comfort of two or three hours' clear dry weather, but had scarcely hung up our wet clothes, after halting at five, A M., when it again came on to rain ; but as every thing was as wet as it could be, we left them out to take their chance. We again allowed ourselves the luxury of a hot supper, having shot eight or nine birds since our last. The rain continued most of the day, but we set out at half past seven, P.M., crossing loose ice, as usual, and much of the surface consisting of the detached vertical needles before described. After an hour, the rain became so heavy, that we halted to save our shirts, which were the only dry clothes belonging to us. Soon after midnight, the rain being succeeded by one of the thickest fogs I ever saw, we again proceeded, groping our way almost yard by yard from one small piece of ice to another, and were very fortunate in hitting upon some with level surfaces, and also a few tolerable-sized holes of water. At half past two we reached a floe, which appeared at first a level and large one; but on landing we were much mortified to find it so covered with immense ponds, or rather small lakes of fresh water, that to accomplish two miles in a north direction, we were under the necessity of walking from three to four, the water being too deep for wading, and from two hundred yards to one-third of a mile in length. Towards the northern margin we came among large hummocks, having very deep snow about them, so that this floe, which had appeared so promising, proved very laborious travelling, obliging us, in some parts, to make three journeys with our loads; that is, to traverse the same road five times over We halted at six, A.M., having made only one mile and three quarters in a N.N.W. direction, the wind still blowing fresh from the eastward, with a thick fog. We were in latitude 82° 3′ 19″, and longitude by chronometers 23° 17′ E., and we found the variation of the magnetic needle to be 13° 41′, westerly. We moved again at seven, P.M., with the weather nearly as foggy as before, our road lying across a very hummocky floe, on which we had considerable difficulty in getting the boats, the ice being extremely unfavourable both for launching and hauling them up. We afterwards passed over two or three other small floes, and crossed a lane of water a mile

long in an east and west direction, but not more than two
hundred yards wide from north to south. After stopping
an hour at midnight to dine, we were again annoyed by a
heavy fall of rain, a phenomenon almost as new to us in
these regions, until this summer, as it was harassing and un-
healthy. Being anxious, however, to take advantage of a
lane of water that seemed to lead northerly, we launched the
boats, and by the time that we had crossed it, which gave
us only half a mile of northing, the rain had become much
harder, and our outer clothes, bread-bags, and boats, were
thoroughly wet. To keep our shirts dry (which was the
more necessary as we had only one spare one between every
two individuals) we got under the shelter of our awnings,
and, the rain abating in half an hour, again proceeded, giving
the men a small quantity of rum and a mouthful of biscuit,
by way of refreshing them a little in this uncomfortable condition. After this we had better travelling on the ice, and
also crossed one or two larger holes of water than we had
met with for a long time, and halted, for our night's rest, at
half past seven, A.M., after nearly twelve hours hard, but not
altogether unsuccessful labour, having traversed about twelve
miles, and made good, by our account, seven and a half, in a
N.W.b.N. direction. We had gradually met with fewer
birds as we advanced to the northward; to-day we saw only
one kittiwake, and a boatswain, (*lestris parasiticus.*) The
floes now around us were heavier than any that we had

before passed; perhaps about the same as those usually met
with in Baffin's Bay. The rain ceased soon after we had
halted, but was succeeded by a thick wet fog, which obliged
us, when we continued our journey, to put on our travelling
clothes in the same dripping state as when we took them
off The wind continued fresh from the south-eastward, and
at nine, P.M , the weather suddenly cleared up, and gave us
once more the inconceivably cheering, I had almost said the
blessed sight of a blue sky, with hard well-defined white
clouds floating across it. There was not, however, much
dryness in the atmosphere, the dew point, by Daniell's
hygrometer, being 35° at nine, P.M., when the temperature
of the atmosphere was the same. We considered ourselves
fortunate in having any floes to cross, though only one or
two exceeded a quarter of a mile in length, and all very
rugged and much covered with ponds of water; but this
was better than the more frequent and hazardous launching
among small pieces. Halting at midnight to dine, we
obtained the sun's altitude, which placed us in latitude
82° 11′ 51″. On continuing our journey, after dinner, we
still had small floe-pieces to pass over, several of which gave
us much labour, and occupied considerable time, being just
too widely separated to make bridges of the boats, so that
launching them was unavoidable. We halted at six, A M,
after making, by our day's exertions, only three miles and a
half of northing, and then obtained the dip of the magnetic

needle 82° 16'.3, and the variation 15° 6' westerly, our
latitude at this time being 82° 14' 28", and our longitude
by chronometers 22° 4' E.   Some observations for the magnetic intensity were also obtained at this place. This proved
a remarkably clear and fine day, with a moderate breeze from
the S.E.   The thermometer was from 35° to 36° in the
shade during most of the day, and this, with a clear sky
overhead, was now absolute luxury to us.   Setting out again
at seven, P M , we crossed a small lane of water to another
floe, but this was so intersected by ponds, and by streams
running into the sea, that we had to make a very circuitous
route, some of the ponds being half a mile in length.   If anything could have compensated for the delay these occasioned
us, it would have been the beautiful blue colour peculiar to
these super-glacial lakes, which is certainly one of the most
pleasing tints in nature.   Notwithstanding the immense quantity of water still upon the ice, and which always afforded us
a pure and abundant supply of this indispensable article, we
now observed a mark round the banks of all the ponds, shew-
ing that the water was less deep in them, by several inches,
than it had been somewhat earlier in the summer, and,
indeed, from about this time, some small diminution in its
quantity began to be perceptible to ourselves.   We also
encountered to-day a more than usual proportion of the
" penknife" ice, the needles of which were fourteen inches
long, and so loose as to occasion great labour in walking and

dragging the boats over it   A parhelion, slightly tinged
with the prismatic colours, appeared on the western side of
the sun, and remained for two or three hours.   At ten, P M,
we exchanged a troublesome floe for still more troublesome
loose ice, which kept us constantly launching and hauling
up the boats, with extreme risk to them as well as to the
provisions, and most harassing labour to the officers and
men.   Still our work went on cheerfully, our hope resting
on at length meeting with something like continuous and
level ice.   We halted for our resting-time at six, A.M., on the
13th, having gained only two miles and a half of northing,
over a road of about four, and this accomplished by ten hours
of fatiguing exertion.   We saw, in the course of this journey,
besides an ivory-gull and a mallemucke, one of the very
beautiful gulls first discovered by Lieutenant Ross at Arlag-
nuk, in our voyage of 1823, and named, in compliment to
him, *Larus Rossii**.   We were here in latitude, by the
noon observation, 82° 17′ 10″, and could find no bottom with
four hundred fathoms of line.   The temperature of some
water brought up from that depth in a copper bottle contrived for the purpose, was 31° on coming to the surface,
and its specific gravity, when weighed at the temperature
of 41°, 1 0283.   The temperature of the surface-water at the
time was $32°\frac{1}{2}$, and its specific gravity only 1·0004, owing to

* Narrative of the Second Voyage, p 449; and Dr. Richardson's Zoological
Appendix, p 359.

the intermixture of fresh water from the ice. A thermometer, having its bulb placed upon the surface of the ice, stood at 33°, the air being 36°, and the temperature of the streams and pools of fresh water was 32°½. We launched the boats at seven in the evening, the wind being moderate from the E S.E with fine clear weather, and were still mortified in finding that no improvement took place in the road over which we had to travel ; for the ice now before us was, if possible, more broken up and more difficult to pass over than ever. Much of it was also so thin as to be extremely dangerous for the provisions, and it was often a nervous thing to see our whole means of existence lying on a decayed sheet, having holes quite through it in many parts, and which the smallest motion among the surrounding masses might have instantly broken into pieces. There was however no choice, except between this road, and the more rugged though safer hummocks, which cost ten times the labour to pass over. Mounting one of the highest of these at nine P.M., we could discover nothing to the northward but the same broken and irregular surface ; and we now began to doubt whether we should at all meet with the solid fields of unbroken ice which every account had led us to expect in a much lower latitude than this. The weather was to-night remarkably clear, with the most regular and beautiful mackarel sky I ever saw, and no land, nor any indication of it, was visible from a height of thirty to forty feet above the level of the sea, to which eleration many of the hummocks rose. A very strong yellow ice-blink overspread the whole northern horizon. We stopped to dine at half an hour past midnight, after more than five hours' unceasing labour, in the course of which time we had only accomplished a mile and a half due north, though we had traversed from three to four, and walked at least ten, having made three journeys a great part of the way We had launched and hauled up the boats four times, and dragged them over twenty-five separate pieces of ice. After dinner we continued the same kind of travelling, which was, beyond all description, harassing to the officers and men. In crossing from mass to mass, several of which were separated about half the length of our sledges, the officers were stationed at the most difficult places to see that no precaution was omitted, which could ensure the safety of the provisions. Only one individual was allowed to jump over at a time, or to stand near either margin, for fear of the weight being too great for it ; and when three or four men had separately crossed, the sledge was cautiously drawn up to the edge, and the word being given, the men suddenly ran away with the ropes, so as to allow no time for its falling in, if the ice should break. In one or two instances this day, we were obliged to have recourse to the still more hazardous expedient of ferrying all our provisions across a narrow pool of water upon a small piece of ice, the situation being such that our boats could not be thus made use of. Wherever

M 2

the boats could possibly be hauled across with the provisions in them, we prefered this as a safer mode of proceeding; but this very precaution had nearly cost us dear to-day, for while we were thus dragging one of them along, the ice on which she rested began to sink and then turned over on one side, almost upsetting the boat with the provisions in her. However, a number of the men jumped upon the ice, with great activity, in order to restore its balance by their weight, and having cautiously unloaded and hauled her back, we got her over in another place.   Having at length succeeded in reaching a small floe, we halted at half past six, A M, much wearied by nearly eleven hours' exertion, by which we had only advanced three miles and a half in a N.N.W. direction. The wind again freshened up strong from the S.E.b.E., with a thick fog, which shortly after changed to rain.   We saw only a single mallemucke and a bear in our last journey ; the latter was wounded, but easily escaped our pursuit, and this to our no small disappointment, for we began to find our allowance of provisions too little to satisfy us, and would gladly have added to it by a supply of this kind.   We rose at six P.M., and prepared to set out, but it rained so hard and so incessantly that it would have been impossible to move without a complete drenching   I had never before seen any rain in the Polar regions to be compared to this, which continued, without intermission, for twenty-one hours, sometimes falling with great violence, and in large drops,

especially about two A.M., on the 15th. It held up a little
at five, and at six we set out, but the rain soon recommenced, though less heavily than before. In proceeding over the floe on which we had slept, we found it alternately level and " hummocky," the former affording sufficiently good travelling to allow us to carry all our baggage at one journey with great ease, one boat's crew occasionally assisting the other for a few yards together; but the hummocks cost us immense labour, nothing but a " bowline haul" being sufficient, with all our hands, to get the boats across or between them. At eight the rain again became heavier, and we got under shelter of our awnings for a quarter of an hour, to keep our shirts, and other flannel clothes, dry, these being the only things we now had on, which were not thoroughly wet. At nine we did the same, but before ten were obliged to halt altogether, the rain coming down in torrents, and the men being much exhausted by continued wet and cold, though the thermometer was at 36°, which was somewhat above our usual temperature. The wind shifted to the W.S.W. in the afternoon, and the rain was succeeded by a thick fog, after it had been falling for thirty hours out of the last thirty-one. At half past seven P.M., we again pursued our journey, and after much laborious travelling, were fortunate, considering the fog, in hitting upon a floe which proved the longest we had yet crossed, being three miles from south to north, though alternately rugged and flat. From this we launched

into a lane of water half a mile long from east to west, but which only gave us a hundred and fifty yards of northing. We had then several other smaller pools to cross, and on one occasion were obliged to cut a place for hauling up the boats, the margin consisting of a tier of high and continuous hummocks. In hauling one of the boats over a " tongue" of ice, where she only floated in part, her bottom-boards were raised by the pressure against the ice below, but so strong and elastic was their construction that she did not suffer the slightest external injury. We frequently, during fogs, saw a broad white fog-bow opposite the sun ; but one which appeared to-night was strongly tinged with the prismatic colours.

The floe on which we stopped to dine at one, A.M., on the 16th, was not more than four feet thick, and its extent half a mile square ; and on this we had the rare advantage of carrying all our loads at one journey. At half past six the fog cleared away, and gave us beautiful weather for drying our clothes, and once more the cheerful sight of the blue sky. We halted at half past seven, after being twelve hours on the road, having made a N.b W. course, distance only six miles and a quarter, though we had traversed nine miles. The thermometer was unusually high in the shade, having risen to $37°\frac{3}{4}$; in the sun it stood at $47°$; a blackened bulb raised it to $51°\frac{1}{2}$; and the same thermometer, held against the black painted side of the boat, rose to $58\frac{1}{2}°$. This was during a calm; but almost the smallest breath of wind immediately reduced them all below 40° We saw, during this last journey, a mallemucke and a second Ross gull; and a couple of small flies (to us an event of ridiculous importance) were found upon the ice. We here observed the variation of the magnetic needle to be 17° 28′ westerly, being in latitude, by observation, 82° 26′ 44″ (or two miles to the southward of our reckoning), and in longitude by chronometers 20° 32′ 13″ East.

We again pursued our way at seven in the evening, having the unusual comfort of putting on dry stockings, and the no less rare luxury of delightfully pleasant weather, the wind being moderate from the S.S.E. It was so warm in the sun, though the temperature in the shade was only 35°, that the tar was running out of the seams of the boats; and a blackened bulb held against the paint-work raised the thermometer to 72°. We were to-day also unusually fortunate in meeting with some open water, one lane of which gave us, though by a very crooked course, a mile and a half of northing, besides other smaller ones. The sea-water, in one of the largest of these lanes, was at the temperature of 34°, being almost the only instance I remember of such an occurrence in a sea thus loaded with ice, and at so short a distance from it. We now no longer saw any birds in the "holes" of water, as we had done farther south. From a hummock forty feet above the level of the sea, and with a

very clear and transparent atmosphere, nothing but ice,
with a few small patches of water, could be discerned in any
direction. The floes were larger to-day, and the ice, upon
the whole, of heavier dimensions than any we had yet met
with. The general thickness of the floes, however, did not
exceed nine or ten feet, which is not more than the usual
thickness of those in Baffin's Bay and Hudson's Strait;
while it is a great deal less than the ordinary dimensions of
the ice about Melville Peninsula, and not half the thickness
of that towards the western extremity of Melville Island,
though these places lie from eight to twenty degrees south
of our present latitude. We found the snow this night
very soft, in consequence of the warmth of the weather and
the late heavy rains; making the travelling extremely laborious. In fact, the upper surface of the heavier floes is *all*
snow; so that every warm day, even to the very close of the
summer, softens it to the depth of several inches. We also
met to-night with a great deal more of the "penknife" ice,
the margins of some of the floes exhibiting a section of it
having the needles above eighteen inches in length, and all
quite loose and easily detached by the hand. I may also
here mention another peculiar kind of ice, consisting of
oblong slabs, which appear to have been imbedded by heavy
pressure in the surface of the floe, and have at length, by
alternate thawing and freezing, become a part of it. These
slabs, still retaining their angular shape, and assuming a

smoothly polished and handsome surface, appear not unlike the lumps of feldspar in porphyry, on which account we called it " porphyritic " ice. For one or two nights past we had observed the clouds near and opposite to the sun to be tinged with a little red towards midnight, the sun having probably been too high before this period

The 17th of July being one of the days on which the Royal Society of Edinburgh have proposed to institute a series of simultaneous meteorological observations, we commenced an hourly register of every phenomenon which came under our notice, and which our instruments and other circumstances would permit, and continued most of them throughout the day. We this morning crossed a floe three miles in length, which was equal in extent to any we had seen : the thickness of this, as measured in a large hole near the middle of it, was only from five to six feet. We halted at seven, A.M., after a long and fatiguing journey, our distance made good in a north direction being six miles and a half. Being more fatigued than usual, and the last week having produced us no birds for supper, we allowed ourselves a mess of hot cocoa, which seemed quite a cordial to us. Our latitude, observed at noon, was 82° 32' 10", being more than a mile to the southward of the reckoning, though the wind had been constantly from that quarter during the twenty-four hours. We had seen, in our last journey, only one ivory-gull, one mallemucke, and another Ross gull.

N

The 17th proved one of the warmest and most pleasant days to the feelings that we had during the whole time we were upon the ice; the thermometer in the shade being from 36° to 40° for several hours, and in the sun from 42° to 51°. It produced, however, as usual, the serious disadvantage of rendering the snow very soft, and increasing the fatigue of travelling. Besides this, on setting out at eight, P.M., we found our road to be over some of the most broken ice we had ever yet encountered, obliging us to make bridge after bridge with the boats almost every thirty or forty yards, for three hours together, in which time we scarcely made half a mile of northing. The small floe-piece which we at length reached was a very rugged one, and the sun was so bright as to render the glare of the snow painfully oppressive to the eyes. The latitude, observed at midnight, was 82° 32′ 15″, or nearly the same as at noon, though we had certainly walked one mile to the northward.

After midnight the road became, if possible, worse, and the prospect to the northward more discouraging than before; nothing but loose and very small pieces of ice being in sight, over which the boats were dragged almost entirely by a "standing-pull." When we halted to dine, at two A.M on the 18th, we were not sorry to see a fog coming on, our eyes having begun to fail for some time. Setting out again in an hour, we found no improvement in the travelling; but being the more anxious to get past this harassing

kind of road, we continued our work till half past eight, when we reached a small floe-piece, the only one in sight, and there halted for the night. Thus, after more than eleven hours' actual labour, requiring, for the most part, our whole strength to be exerted, we had travelled over a space not exceeding four miles, of which only two were made good in a N.N.W. direction. The men were so exhausted with their day's work, that it was absolutely necessary to give them something hot for supper, and we again served a little cocoa for that purpose. They were also put into good spirits by our having killed a small seal, which, the following night, gave us an excellent supper. The meat of these young animals is tender, and free from oiliness; but it certainly has a smell and a look which would not have been agreeable to any but very hungry people like ourselves. We also considered it a great prize, on account of its blubber, which gave us fuel sufficient for cooking six hot messes for our whole party, though the animal only weighed thirty pounds in the whole. These animals, of which we usually saw two or three in almost every day's journey, are, when very small, best procured by shooting them in the head with small shot; but, if quite killed at once, they are apt to sink immediately and be lost. The temperature of this seal was 98°, immediately after death.

The fog dispersing before noon, we had another clear and fine day, but, as usual, paid dear for this comfort by the

N 2

increased softness of the snow and the oppressive glare
reflected from it.   Setting out at half past seven in the
evening, we found the sun more distressing to the eyes than
we had ever yet had it, bidding defiance to our crape veils
and wire-gauze eye-shades *; but a more effectual screen
was afforded by the sun becoming clouded about nine, P M.
Our way still lay over small loose masses, to which we were
now so accustomed as scarcely to expect any other; for it
was evident enough that we were not improving in this
respect as we advanced northwards.   At half past nine we
came to a very difficult crossing among the loose ice, which,
however, we were encouraged to attempt by seeing a floe of
some magnitude beyond it.   We had to convey the sledges
and provisions one way, and to haul the boats over by
another.   One of the masses over which the boats came,
began to roll about while one of them was upon it, ·giving
us reason to apprehend its upsetting, which must have been
attended with some very serious consequence; fortunately,
however, it retained its equilibrium long enough to allow
us to get the boat past it in safety, not without several of
the men falling overboard in consequence of the long jumps
we had to make, and the edges breaking with their weight.
Towards midnight we had some smart showers of rain,
Thursday, with dry clear intervals between them, just as on an April
19th.

* We found the best preservative against this glare to be a pair of spectacles,
having the glass of a bluish-green colour, and with side-screens to them.

day in England. This kind of weather, which continued
for several hours, harassed the men very much, as it was
too warm for working with their jackets on, and they wetted
their shirt-sleeves when they took them off. I think the
blue sky between the clouds this night was as transparent,
and almost of as deep a blue as I ever saw it. We had
nearly incurred a second disaster in launching one of the
boats from an awkward-shaped mass, which brought her
gunwale close to the water, and there kept her for a quarter
of an hour in a very dangerous situation, without our being
able to move her one way or the other, while the loose ice
was in motion about us at the time. At length, however,
we contrived to reach the floe, after consuming the best part
of the day's journey in effecting it; and when we halted to
rest at half past seven a.m, twelve hours' labour had not
been repaid by more than three miles and a half gained, on
a N.N.E. course.

It is remarkable that we had hitherto been so much favoured by the wind, that only a single northerly one, and
that very moderate, and of short duration, appears upon
our journals up to this day, when a breeze sprung up from
that quarter, accompanied by a thick fog. Though this
wind appeared to be the means of opening several lanes
of water, of which we gladly took advantage when we set
out at eight p m, yet we were aware that any such effect
could only be produced by the ice drifting to the southward,

and would, therefore, have willingly dispensed with this apparent facility in proceeding. We found the temperature of the sea-water, in a large lane, to be 34°, and once as high as $34°\frac{1}{2}$, which, as before remarked, is very unusual in the middle of a large body of ice. We hauled over one very heavy floe, about half a mile in length, of which the thickness was from fifteen to twenty feet, with huge hummocks at the margin, indicating a tremendous pressure at some time or
other. On the morning of the 20th, we came to a good deal of ice, which formed a striking contrast with the other, being composed of flat bay-floes, not three feet thick, which would have afforded us good travelling, had they not recently been broken into small pieces, obliging us to launch frequently from one to another. These floes had been the product of the last winter only, having probably been formed in some of the interstices left between the larger bodies; and, from what we saw of them, there could be little doubt of their being all dissolved before the next autumnal frost. We halted at seven A.M., having, by our reckoning, accomplished six miles and a half in a N.N.W. direction, the distance traversed being ten miles and a half. It may, therefore, be imagined how great was our mortification in finding that our latitude, by observation at noon, was only 82° 36′ 52″, being less than *five* miles to the northward of our place at noon on the 17th, since which time we had certainly travelled *twelve* in that direction.

Under these discouraging circumstances, which we carefully avoided making known to the men, we pursued our
journey at eight P.M , the wind blowing from the N W.b.N ,
with overcast but clear weather. A little small snow fell
during the night, composed of very minute irregular needles.
We were, as usual, much annoyed by the numerous loose
pieces over which we had to pass, but a large proportion of
these being composed of flat bay-ice, we made tolerable progress. At eleven P.M , we could see nothing before us but
this thin ice, much of which was not fit to bear the weight
of our boats and provisions, and more caution than ever was
requisite in selecting the route by which we were to pass
At five A M., on the 21st, having gone ahead, as usual, upon
a bay-floe, to search for the best road, I heard a more than
ordinary noise and bustle among the people who were bringing up the boats behind. On returning to them, I found
that we had narrowly, and most providentally, escaped a
serious calamity ; the floe having broken under the weight of
the boats and sledges, and the latter having nearly been
lost through the ice. Some of the men went completely
through, and one of them was only held up by his drag-
belt being attached to a sledge which happened to be on
firmer ice. Fortunately the bread had, by way of security,
been kept in the boats, or this additional weight would
undoubtedly have sunk the sledges, and probably some of
the men with them. As it was, we happily escaped, though

we hardly knew how, with a good deal of wetting ; and cautiously approaching the boats, drew them to a stronger part
of the ice, after which we continued our journey till half
past six A.M., when we halted to rest, having travelled about
seven miles N.N.W. We here found the dip of the magnetic needle to be 82° 21'.8, and the variation 19° 5' westerly,
our longitude by chronometers being 19° 52' East, and the
latitude 82° 39' 10", being only two miles and a quarter to
the northward of the preceding day's observation, or four
miles and a half to the southward of our reckoning

Our sportsmen had the good fortune to kill another seal
to-day, rather larger than the first, which again proved a
most welcome addition to our provisions and fuel. Indeed,
after this supply of the latter, we were enabled to allow
ourselves every night a pint of warm water for supper, each
man making his own soup from such a portion of his bread
and pemmican as he could save from dinner. Setting out
again at seven in the evening, we were not sorry to find the
weather quite calm, which sailors account " half a fair wind ;"
for it was now evident that nothing but a southerly breeze
could enable us to make any tolerable progress, or to regain
what we had lately lost. The weather was warm and pleasant, though the thermometer was only 35°. At half past
eight we observed a fog-bank rising to the southward, and
another equally fast to the north. While we were anxiously
watching to see which would prevail, that from the south

1827.
July

first came over us, with a light air from that quarter; this, however, was of short duration, the weather again becoming calm and perfectly clear in an hour afterwards. We observed this night, and only on three or four other occasions, the most brilliant prismatic colours imaginable reflected from the snow crystals on the ice, the tints being principally the red, orange, green, and violet. This phenomenon, which occurred when the sun was low, (and, I suppose, only with crystals of a peculiar form,) is always seen, of course, between the sun and the observer, and the reflecting surfaces cover a space which assumes this kind of semi-elliptical form, *a* being next the eye. It becomes more distant and less distinct as the sun rises, and is then altogether lost. This beautiful natural appearance may possibly be familiar to many persons, but as it was new to us, I have described it just as it occurred.

Our travelling to-night was the very best we had during this excursion, for though we had to launch and haul up the boats frequently, an operation which, under the most favourable circumstances, necessarily occupies much time, yet the floes being large and tolerably level, and some good lanes of water occurring, we made, according to the most moderate calculation, between ten and eleven miles in a N.N E. direction, and traversed a distance of about seventeen. We halted at a quarter past eight, A M, after more than twelve hours' actual travelling, by which the people were extremely

Sunday,
22nd.

O

fatigued; but while our work seemed to be repaid by anything like progress, the men laboured with great cheerfulness
to the utmost of their strength. A solitary rotge, two small
seals, and a fish twelve inches long, (of which we had before
noticed one or two,) were the only living creatures seen
to-day, notwithstanding the unusual extent of the open water.
The ice over which we had travelled was by far the largest
and heaviest we met with during our whole journey :
this, indeed, was the only occasion on which we saw anything
answering, in the slightest degree, to the descriptions given
of the main ice   The largest floe was from two and a half to
three miles square, and in some places the thickness of the
ice was from 15 to 20 feet.   Still these were not " fields ";
for in no one instance had we any difficulty in seeing the
margin of them in more directions than one, by mounting a
tolerably high hummock; and from a much less elevation
than that of a ship's masthead, the whole extent and form
of such floes would have been very easily discernible. However, it was a satisfaction to observe that the ice had certainly improved ; and we now ventured to hope that, for the
short time that we could still pursue our outward journey,
our progress would be more commensurate with our exertions than it had hitherto proved.   In proportion, then, to
the hopes we had begun to entertain, was our disappointment in finding, at noon, that we were in latitude 82° 43′ 5″,
or not quite four miles to the northward of yesterday's

observation, instead of the ten or eleven which we had travelled! However, we determined to continue to the last
our utmost exertions, though we could never once encourage
the men by assuring them of our making good progress, and,
setting out at seven in the evening, soon found that our
hope of having permanently reached better ice was not to
be realized; for the floe on which we slept was so full of
hummocks, that it occupied us just six hours to cross it, the
distance in a straight line not exceeding two miles and a half.
At midnight on the 22d, we had a good observation in latitude
82° 43' 32", being, as usual, the mean of two observers. After
this, our road once more consisted of small rugged masses,
and little pools of water, requiring many launches In
addition to these impediments, the wind, which had been from
the W.N.W. at our setting out, again shifted to north, and
freshened up considerably. We halted at seven, A M, after
a laborious day's work, and, I must confess, a disheartening
one to those who knew to how little effect we were struggling; which, however, the men did not, though they often
laughingly remarked that " we were a long time getting to
this 83°!" Being anxious to make up, in some measure, for
the drift which the present northerly wind was, in all probability, occasioning, we rose earlier than usual, and set off
at half past four in the evening. At half past five, P M, we
witnessed a very beautiful natural phenomenon. A broad
white fog-bow first appeared opposite the sun, as was very

O 2

commonly the case; presently it became strongly tinged
with the prismatic colours, and soon afterwards no less than
five other complete arches were formed within the main
bow, the interior ones being gradually narrower than those
without, but the whole of them beautifully coloured. The
larger bow, and the one next within it, had the red on the
outer or upper part of the circle, the others on the inner
side.   Lieutenant Ross measured the altitude of the outer
arch, which was 20° 45′ in the centre, its extent at the
horizon 72°½, the altitude of the sun, which was bright at
the time, being 20° 40′.   The fog was quite wet, while the
smaller bows were visible, which was only for about twenty
minutes; though the large one remained, as usual, for hours
together.   We were now once more annoyed by a quantity
of broken ice, so thin as to require increased caution in
trusting our loads upon it; indeed, we passed, during this
night, some of the lightest ice we had yet seen. Several of
us began to feel, in our eyes, the bad effects of having set
out somewhat earlier in the day than usual.   My own were
so painful with having strained them in looking out for the
road, that I was unable any longer to see my way, and was
therefore obliged, for a time, to give up the pioneering duty
to Lieutenant Ross

We halted at a quarter past three on the morning of the
24th, having made four miles and a half N.N.E., over a road
of about seven and a half, most of which we traversed, as

usual, three times.   The only notice of animal life occurring
in our journals in the course of this day's travelling, consists
in our having "*heard* a rotge"!   The wind continued fresh
from the northward, with small snow, of which about two
inches fell in twenty-four hours.   We moved again at four,
P M, over a difficult road composed of small and rugged ice.
Lieutenant Ross, in exerting himself to drag his boat along,
received a severe squeeze between her gunwale and a hummock of ice, which gave Mr. Beverly reason to apprehend
at first, from the numbness and sickness which ensued, that
his spine might be affected; but happily no such bad con-
sequences followed this accident.   So small was the ice now
around us, that we were obliged to halt for the night at
two, A.M., on the 25th, being upon the only piece in sight,
in any direction, on which we could venture to trust the
boats while we rested.   Such was the ice in the latitude of
$82°\frac{3}{4}$!   We had travelled, during this journey, two miles
and three-quarters N $\frac{1}{2}$E., and saw but one mallemucke and
one Ross gull in the course of it.

The wind had now got round to the W.N.W., with raw
foggy weather, and continued to blow fresh all day.   Snow
came on soon after our halting, and about two inches had
fallen when we moved again at half past four P.M.   We
continued our journey, in this inclement weather, for three
hours, hauling from piece to piece, and not making more
than three quarters of a mile progress, till our clothes and

bread-bags had become very wet, and the snow fell so thick that we could no longer see our way. It was, therefore, necessary to halt, which we did at half past seven, putting the awnings over the boats, changing our wet clothes, and giving the men employment for the mere sake of occupying their minds. We were housed just in good time; for the wind soon after freshened to a gale at W.N.W., with sleet and rain, and a most inclement night succeeded. The
weather improving towards noon on the 26th, we obtained the meridian altitude of the sun, by which we found ourselves in latitude 82° 40′ 23″; so that, since our last observation (at midnight on the 22d), we had lost by drift no less than thirteen miles and a half; for we were now more than three miles to the *southward* of that observation, though we had certainly travelled between ten and eleven due north in this interval! Again, we were but one mile to the north of our place at noon on the 21st, though we had estimated our distance made good at twenty-three miles. Thus it appeared that, for the last five days, we had been struggling against a southerly drift exceeding four miles per day.

It had, for some time past, been too evident that the nature of the ice with which we had to contend was such, and its drift to the southward, especially with a northerly wind, so great, as to put beyond our reach any thing but a very moderate share of success in travelling to the north-

ward. Still, however, we had been anxious to reach the
highest latitude which our means would allow, and, with
this view, although our whole object had long become
unattainable, had pushed on to the northward for thirty-five
days, or until half our resources were expended, and the
middle of our season arrived.   For the last few days, the
eighty-third parallel was the limit to which we had ventured
to extend our hopes; but even this expectation had become
considerably weakened since the setting in of the last
northerly wind, which continued to drive us to the southward, during the necessary hours of rest, nearly as much as
we could gain by eleven or twelve hours of daily labour.
Had our success been at all proportionate to our exertions,
it was my full intention to have proceeded a few days beyond
the middle of the period for which we were provided,
trusting to the resources we expected to find at Table Island.
But this was so far from being the case, that I could not
but consider it as incurring useless fatigue to the officers
and men, and unnecessary wear and tear for the boats, to
persevere any longer in the attempt.   I determined, therefore, on giving the people one entire day's rest, which they
very much needed, and time to wash and mend their clothes,
while the officers were occupied in making all the observations which might be interesting in this latitude; and then
to set out on our return on the following day.   Having
communicated my intentions to the people, who were all

much disappointed in finding how little their labours had effected, we set about our respective occupations, and were much favoured by a remarkably fine day.

The dip of the magnetic needle was here 82° 21'.6, and the variation 18° 10' westerly, our latitude being 82° 40' 23", and our longitude 19° 25' East of Greenwich. The highest latitude we reached was probably at seven, A M, on the 23rd, when, after the midnight observation, we travelled, by our account, something more than a mile and a half, which would carry us a little beyond 82° 45'. Some observations for the magnetic intensity were obtained at this station. We here found no bottom with five hundred fathoms of line; the specific gravity of some water brought up from that depth was 1·0340, being at the temperature of 37° when weighed. A Six's thermometer attached to the lead failed to indicate the temperature below, owing to the mercury rising past the index. The sea-water from the surface was, as usual near the ice in the summer time, so nearly fresh as to require only three grains to be added to the hydrometer; and at six fathoms below the surface it was 1·0225, at temperature 37°. At the extreme point of our journey, our distance from the Hecla was only 172 miles in a S. 8° W. direction. To accomplish this distance we had traversed, by our reckoning, two hundred and ninety-two miles, of which about one hundred were performed by water, previously to our entering the ice. As we travelled by far

the greater part of our distance on the ice three, and not
unfrequently five times over, we may safely multiply the length of the road by two and a half; so that our whole distance, on a very moderate calculation, amounted to five hundred and eighty geographical, or six hundred and sixty-eight statute miles, being nearly sufficient to have reached the Pole in a direct line.   Up to this period we had been particularly fortunate in the preservation of our health; neither sickness nor casualties having occurred among us, with the exception of the trifling accidents already mentioned, a few bowel complaints which were soon removed by care, and some rather troublesome cases of chilblains arising from our constant exposure to wet and cold

Our day of rest proved one of the warmest and most
pleasant to the feelings we had yet had upon the ice, though the thermometer was only from 31° to 36° in the shade, and 37° in the sun, with occasional fog; but to persons living constantly in the open air, calm and tolerably dry weather affords absolute enjoyment, especially by contrast with what we had lately experienced.   Our ensigns and pendants were displayed during the day, and sincerely as we regretted not having been able to hoist the British flag in the highest latitude to which we had aspired, we shall perhaps be excused in having felt some little pride in being the bearers of it to a parallel considerably beyond that mentioned in any other well-authenticated record.

P

During some intervals of very clear weather, we could perceive nothing like land in any direction from our present situation, and a strong yellow ice-blink always overspread the northern horizon. At three A.M., on the 27th, we observed a phenomenon resembling that mentioned on the 23rd, but much less perfect and distinct, three smaller fog-bows at times appearing within a large one, the legs of the arches being distinctly coloured as before. The sun's altitude at this time was $12°\frac{1}{2}$, that of the centre of the outer arch 28°, and its extent at the horizon $77°\frac{1}{2}$. At 4. 30, P.M., we set out on our return to the southward, and I can safely say that, dreary and cheerless as were the scenes we were about to leave, we never turned homewards with so little satisfaction as on this occasion. To afford a chance of determining the general set of the current from this latitude, we left upon a hummock of ice a paper, sewn up in a water-proof canvas bag, and then inclosed in a water-tight tin cannister, giving an account of the place where it was deposited, and requesting any person who should find it, to send it to the Secretary of the Admiralty. The wind sprung up from the S.E., and, as usual with any *change* of wind, opened a few holes among the ice, which assisted us a little; but, notwithstanding this, so unfavourable was the ice for travelling, that, when we halted at three A.M., on the 28th, we had only made three miles and a quarter of southing. The wind then gradually shifted to the N.E and freshened up, with

heavy snow, which continued to fall during the whole day.
Nothing worthy of particular notice occurred on this and
the following day, on each of which we travelled eleven
hours, finding the water somewhat more open and the floes
less rugged than usual.   Two of these were from two to
three miles in length, and in one instance the surface was
sufficiently level to allow us to drag the boats for three
quarters of a mile, with the sledges *in tow*.   Towards the
end of our journey on the morning of the 30th, we came to
an extensive collection of light bay-ice, such as we had
passed on our outward journey, only that it was now broken
into much smaller pieces.   It was probably, indeed, the
same ice, as we saw our old tracks on some of the larger
floes   Our latitude, observed at noon, was 82° 20' 37", or
twelve miles and a half to the southward of the preceding
day's observation, though we had travelled only seven by
our account; so that the drift of the ice had assisted us in
gaining five miles and a half in that interval.

   Setting out to continue our journey at five P.M., we could
discover nothing from a high hummock but the kind of
bay-ice before noticed, except the floe on which we had
slept.   We were therefore obliged to go along the margin
of this floe, a long way out of our road to the south-eastward,
to avoid the danger as well as labour of crossing it, and at
length discovered some more secure ice beyond it, though
still in small detached pieces.   We saw to-day a great many

P 2

small seals, and wounded several, but could not get them, though we tried as hard as hungry people could do. The wind had now backed to the north, and still blew fresh; towards midnight it veered to the N.W., with small snow. The travelling was very laborious, but we were obliged to go on, till we could get to a secure floe for resting upon,
which we could not effect till half past four on the 31st, when, in eleven hours and a half, we had not made more than two miles and a quarter of southing. However, we had the satisfaction, which was denied us on our outward journey, of feeling confident that we should keep all that we gained, and probably make a good deal more; which, indeed, proved to be the case, for at noon we found our latitude by observation to be 82° 14′ 25″, or four miles to the southward of the reckoning. The variation of the magnetic needle observed here was 22° 23′ 16″ westerly, the longitude being 17° 18′ 19″ E, showing an increase in that phenomenon in going westward, in this as well as in lower latitudes.

Our next day's journey, which we commenced at 6.30, P M, was one of the most laborious we had yet experienced, the ice being composed of loose rugged pieces, very dangerous as well as difficult to pass over with the provisions, and requiring a " bowline-haul " with the boats during a great
part of the journey. We halted at five, A.M, on the 1st of August, the officers and men being quite knocked up, and having made by our account only two miles of southing,

over a road not less than five in length. Heavy rain prevented our setting out again till eight in the evening, when the weather cleared up, the wind now blowing fresh from the W.S.W. We had, as usual, a great quantity of loose ice to pass through, or over, before we could get to anything like a floe. As we came along, we had seen some recent bear-tracks, and soon after discovered Bruin himself. Halting the boats, and concealing the people behind them, we drew him almost within gun-shot; but after making a great many traverses behind some hummocks, and even mounting one of them to examine us more narrowly, he set off and escaped—I must say, to our grievous disappointment; for we had already, by anticipation, consigned a tolerable portion of his flesh to our cooking kettle, over a fire of his own blubber.

In the course of this day's journey we met with a quantity of snow, tinged, to the depth of several inches, with some red colouring matter, of which a portion was preserved in a bottle for future examination. This circumstance recalled to our recollection our having frequently before, in the course of this journey, remarked that the loaded sledges, in passing over hard snow, left upon it a light rose-coloured tint, which at the time we attributed to the colouring matter being pressed out of the birch of which they were made. To-day, however, we observed that the runners of the boats, and even our own footsteps, exhibited the same appearance,

and on watching it more narrowly afterwards, we found the
same effect to be produced, in a greater or less degree, by
heavy pressure, on almost all the ice over which we passed,
though a magnifying-glass could detect nothing to give it
this tinge. The colour of the red snow which we bottled,
and which only occurred in two or three spots, appeared
somewhat different from this, being rather of a salmon than
a rose colour, but both were so striking as to be the subject
of constant remark. Halting at seven, A.M., after making
only three miles and a half of southing, we observed the
variation of the magnetic needle to be 20° 46' 54" westerly,
being in latitude 82° 6', and longitude 17° 45' 33" East. A
fog, which prevailed during most of the day, cleared away
soon after our setting out, at eight in the evening, and we
enjoyed, during the night, some of the most beautiful weather that we experienced during our whole excursion, the
wind being light from the S.W. The temperature of the
air at midnight did not exceed 31°½ in the sun, and yet on
the north side of the hummocks the water was dropping
from the ice The _small_ ponds of fresh water on the ice
were frozen, but there was little or no young ice, even in
the smallest pools, upon the sea. We saw some seals, and
five or six birds, among the rest two Ross gulls, during this
journey. Halting at seven, A.M., on the third, after launching and hauling up the boats a great number of times, we had
not only the comfort of drying all our wet clothes, but were

1827.
August.

even able to wash many of our woollen things, which dried in a few hours The latitude observed at noon was 82° 1′ 48″, or twelve miles and half to the southward of our place on the 31st, which was about three more than our log gave, though there had been southing in the wind during the whole interval.

We proceeded on our journey southward at eight, P.M, and were again favoured with a clear and beautiful night, though the travelling was as slow and laborious as ever, there being scarcely a tolerable floe lying in our road Almost the only one over which we passed was so intersected by deep ponds and water-courses, that, although it was in other respects level, we were obliged to walk nearly two miles to gain one of southing The water was again dropping from the sunny side of the hummocks about midnight, the thermometer in the shade being 29°½, and in the sun 36°. The temperature of the sea-water was 32°¼. The sun now became so much lower at night, that we were seldom annoyed by the glare from the snow. It was also a very comfortable change to those who had to look out for the road, to have the sun behind us, instead of facing it, as on our outward journey We stopped to rest at a quarter past six, A.M., after accomplishing three miles in a south direction, over a troublesome road of nearly twice that length. It was almost calm, and to *our* feelings oppressively warm during the day, the thermometer within the boats rising as high as 66°,

Saturday,
4th

which put our fur dresses nearly "out of commission,"
though the mercury exposed to the sun outside did not rise
above 39°. Pursuing our journey at eight, P.M., we paid, as
usual, for this comfort, by the extreme softness of the snow.
The upper crust would sometimes support a man's weight
for a short time, and then suddenly let him down two or
three feet, so that we could never make sure of our footing
for two steps together. We saw patches of the red snow in
two or three different places, and always near the margin of
a floe. The weather continued beautifully clear, with a
light air from the eastward. The thermometer at midnight
was $29°\frac{1}{2}$ in the shade, and 32° in the sun. No young ice
appeared upon the sea, nor upon the larger ponds upon the
ice, but the small ones were quite frozen over. For several

hours after midnight we remarked to the southward, for the
first time since we had entered the ice, a great deal of that
appearance which is called by our Greenland sailors the
" tree-ing" of ice. It consists in the ice being apparently
raised in the horizon by refraction ; sometimes so considerably, as it was in the present instance, as to resemble a perpendicular wall of some height above the general level   It
is usually considered an indication of open water in that
quarter, though I believe it is by no means an infallible one.
However, on this occasion we were willing to flatter ourselves
that the popular notion might be the right one, as indeed it
subsequently proved to be, though we scarcely dared to hope

1827
August.

that we could as yet be very near the open water to the southward. The temperature of the sea in a large hole of water was $33°\frac{1}{2}$, which is unusually high in a sea thus incumbered with ice. The floes were larger to-day than any we had seen for some time; and one over which we passed was considered to be from two to three miles in length, though not in the direction of our course. We halted on another at seven, A.M., and observed at noon in latitude 81° 54' 47", which agreed very well with our reckoning, notwithstanding the southing in the winds for some days past. The temperature of the air in the shade at noon was 35°, and in the sun as high as 42°. We moved again at eight, P.M., travelling over floes of tolerable size, but so covered with hummocks, water, and snow, that our progress was but slow. Several of the men were also suffering much at this time from chilblains, which, from the constant wet and cold, as well as the irritation in walking, became serious sores, keeping them quite lame. With many of our people, also, the epidermis, or scarf-skin, peeled off in large flakes, not merely in the face and hands, which were exposed to the action of the sun and the weather, but in every other part of the body; this, however, was attended with no pain, nor with much inconvenience.

One variety in our monotonous mode of travelling was afforded this day by our rowing across a lake of fresh water in the boats, in order to avoid passing some heavy hum-

Q

mocks. It was a quarter of a mile long, and varied in depth from two to four feet, which, together with an island that happened to be in the middle of it, the rugged ice by which it was bounded, and the beautiful blue of the water, gave it a singular and picturesque appearance. We halted at a

quarter past six, A.M , on the 6th, after making three miles of southing. A thick wet fog prevailed during the day, and the breeze freshened from the S.E.b.E. We again proceeded

at eight P.M., and travelling till half past six on the following morning, had accomplished only three miles of southing over a difficult road of five in length. Some small rain fell during the night, but we were fortunate in getting housed before it came down more heavily, which it did the whole day. A fat she-bear crossed over a lane of water to visit us, and approaching the boats within twenty yards was killed by Lieutenant Ross. The scene which followed was laughable, even to us who participated in it. Before the animal had done biting the snow, one of the men was alongside of him with an open knife, and being asked what he was about to do, replied that he was going to cut out his heart and liver to put into the pot, which happened to be then boiling for our supper. In short, before the bear had been dead an hour, all hands of us were employed, to our great satisfaction, in discussing the merits, not only of the said heart and liver, but a pound per man of the flesh ; besides which, some or other of the men were constantly frying steaks, during the whole day, over a large fire made of the blubber. The consequence of all this, and other similar indulgences, necessarily was, that some of them complained, for several days after, of the pains usually arising from indigestion; though they all, amusingly enough, attributed this effect to the quality, and not the quantity of meat they had eaten. The fact, however, is, that the flesh of the bear is just as wholesome, though not quite as palatable, as any other; and had they eaten moderately of it, as the officers did, they would have suffered no inconvenience whatever. However, notwithstanding these excesses at first, we were really thankful for this additional supply of meat, for we had observed, for some time past, that the men were evidently not so strong as before, and would be the better for more sustenance. A second bear being attracted by the smell of our fire, was wounded, but luckily (for us') escaped. We had also more birds about us than usual, and a narwhal, the only one we had seen since leaving the ship, was blowing in a small hole of water near us

The rain continued so hard, at our usual time of setting out, that I was obliged to delay doing so till six P.M., on the 8th, when it ceased a little, after falling hard for twenty-four hours, and less violently for twelve more. When we first launched the boats, our prospect of making progress seemed no better than usual, but we found one small hole of water leading into another in so extraordinary a manner that,

Q 2

though the space in which we were rowing seemed to be always coming to an end, we continued to creep through narrow
passages, and when we halted to dine at half an hour before
midnight. had only hauled the boats up once, and had
made, though by a winding channel, four or five miles of
southing. This was so unusual a circumstance, that we could
not help entertaining some hope of our being at no great
distance from the open sea, which seemed the more probable
from our having seen seven or eight narwhals, and not less
than two hundred rotges, a flock of these little birds occurring in every hole of water.   The wind was from the southward, with a thick fog, and the clear water increased so much,
as we proceeded, that at six, A.M., on the 9th, instead of
hauling up the boats as usual, we served an extra supper,
and then pursued our way.   However, at nine o'clock, the
wind having freshened from the southward, and there being
only one floe in sight, with immense spaces of open water
between the streams of loose ice, I thought it better to halt
upon the floe, than to incur the probable risk of being driven
back, should we be obliged to rest on any of the smaller
pieces.   It was fortunate that we adopted this plan ; for, the
wind still increasing from the southward, the loose ice continued to drive past us to the northward, during the whole
of this and the following day, at the rate of a mile and a half
an hour, and we were, therefore, very glad to retain our
present quarters.   The weather being wet, with fog, we

occupied the men in making additional sails out of our empty bread-bags, and in filling the empty vessels with water, since it now appeared more than probable that we were close to the open sea. At noon, on the 10th, we observed in latitude 81° 40′ 13″, which was only four miles to the northward of our reckoning from the last observation, although there had been almost constantly southing in the wind ever since, and it had been blowing strong from that quarter for the last thirty hours. This circumstance afforded a last and striking proof of the general tendency of the ice to drift southward, about the meridians on which we had been travelling. Another bear came towards the boats in the course of the day, and was killed. We were now so abundantly supplied with meat, that the men would again have eaten immoderately, had we not interposed the necessary authority to prevent them. As it was, our encampment became so like an Eskimaux establishment, that we were obliged to shift our place upon the floe, in the course of the day, for the sake of cleanliness and comfort.

The wind falling towards midnight, we launched the boats at half past one, A.M., on the 11th, paddling alternately in large spaces of clear water, and among streams of loose "sailing-ice." We soon afterwards observed such indications of an open sea as could not be mistaken, much of the ice being "washed" as by a heavy sea, with small rounded fragments thrown on the surface, and a good deal of "dirty ice" occurring   We also met with several pieces of drift-wood and birch-bark, the first since we had entered the ice; and the sea was crowded with shrimps and other sea-insects, principally the *Clio Borealis* and *Argonauta Arctica*, on which numerous birds were feeding.   After passing through a good deal of loose ice, it became gradually more and more open, till at length, at a quarter before seven, A.M., we heard the first sound of the swell under the hollow margins of the ice, and in a quarter of an hour had reached the open sea, which was dashing with heavy surges against the outer masses.   We hauled the boats upon one of these, to eat our last meal upon the ice, and to complete the necessary supply of water for our little voyage to Table Island, from which we were now distant fifty miles, our latitude being 81° 34', and longitude 18°¼ E.   A light air springing up from the N.W., we again launched the boats, and at eight, A M, finally quitted the ice, after having taken up our abode upon it for forty-eight days.

The wind dying away, our progress wholly depended on the paddles, which made it very laborious for the men.   At two, P.M., we came to some loose ice a mile or two wide, but so open as scarcely to oblige us to alter our course.   At three the temperature of the sea had increased to 36°, the air being the same; and at nine, P.M., both had risen to 38°, not a piece of ice being in sight in any direction.   The weather continued quite calm, and the atmosphere very

pleasant to our feelings. We saw a great many seals sport-
ing about, as well as large flocks of rotges, the latter feeding
on the *Argonauta Arctica*, which now swarmed in myriads.
We also passed a great many pieces of drift-wood, and laid
in a stock, as fuel, lest we should find none at Table Island.

We had some fog during the night, so that we steered
entirely by compass, according to our last observations by
the chronometers, which proved so correct, that at five, A.M.,
on the 12th, on the clearing up of the haze, we made the
island right ahead. At ten, A M., when within three miles
of it, the temperature of the air was as high as 41°, and the
sea still continued at 38°. At eleven, A.M., we reached the
island, or rather the rock to the northward of it, where our
provisions had been deposited; and I cannot describe the
comfort we experienced in once more feeling a dry and
solid footing. We found that the bears had devoured all
the bread (one hundred pounds), which occasioned a remark
among the men, with reference to the quantity of these
animals' flesh that we had eaten, that " Bruin was only
square with us." We also found that Lieutenant Crozier
had been here since we left the island, bringing some materials for repairing our boats, as well as various little luxuries
to which we had lately been strangers, and depositing in
a copper cylinder a letter from Lieutenant Foster, giving
me a detailed account of the proceedings of the ship up to
the 23rd of July. By this I learned that the Hecla had

been forced on shore on the 7th of July, by the breaking-
up of the ice at the head of the bay, which came down upon
her in one solid mass; but by the unwearied and zealous
exertions of the officers and men, she had again been hove
off without incurring the slightest damage, and placed in
perfect security. Finding the ship thus liable to be disturbed by ice, Lieutenant Foster had prudently relinquished
the idea of leaving her for any length of time, so as to make
an extended survey of the eastern coast, confining himself to
the neighbouring parts of Waygatz Strait, which were more
within his reach. Among the supplies with which the anxious care of our friends on board had now furnished us, some
lemon-juice and sugar were not the least acceptable; two
or three of the men having for some days past suffered from
œdematous swellings of the legs, and evinced other symptoms apparently scorbutic, and which soon improved after
administering this valuable specific.

Having got our stores into the boats, we rowed round
Table Island, to look for a place on which to rest, the men
being much fatigued; but so rugged and inhospitable is
this northern rock, that not a single spot could we find where
the boats could possibly be hauled up, or lie afloat in security. I therefore determined to take advantage of the
freshening of the N.E wind, and to bear up for Walden
Island, which we accordingly did at two, p m. To the islet
which lies off Little Table Island, and which is interesting

1827
August.

as being the northernmost known land upon the globe, I have applied the name of Lieutenant Ross in the chart; for I believe no individual can have exerted himself more strenuously to rob it of this distinction. We had scarcely made sail when the weather became extremely inclement, with a fresh gale and very thick snow, which obscured Walden Island from our view. Steering by compass, however, we made a good land-fall, the boats behaving well in a sea; and at seven, P.M., landed in the smoothest place we could find under the lee of the island. Everything belonging to us was now completely drenched by the spray and snow; we had been fifty-six hours without rest, and forty-eight at work in the boats, so that, by the time they were unloaded, we had barely strength left to haul them up on the rock. We noticed, on this occasion, that the men had that wildness in their looks which usually accompanies excessive fatigue; and though just as willing as ever to obey orders, they seemed at times not to comprehend them. However, by dint of great exertion, we managed to get the boats above the surf; after which, a hot supper, a blazing fire of drift-wood, and a few hours' quiet rest quite restored us.

The next morning I despatched Lieutenant Ross, with a party of hands, to the N.E. part of the island, to launch the spare boat which, according to my directions, Lieutenant Foster had sent for our use, and to bring round the stores

Monday.
13th.

R

deposited there, in readiness for our setting off for Low
Island. They found everything quite undisturbed; but,
by the time they reached us, the wind had backed to the
westward, and the weather become very wet, so that I
determined to remain here till it improved.

The south-eastern, or lowest part of Walden Island, which
we had not before visited, is composed of coarse-grained red
and grey granite. Mr. Beverly remarked, that "on the
face of the rock may be observed veins of a finer grey granite, from twelve to twenty inches wide, bordered by a
ribbon of whitish felspar, about three inches wide on each
side, and dipping at an angle of 10° to the south-eastward."
Heaps of large rounded masses of granite, in regular horizontal beds, are lying at the height of thirty to forty feet
above the present level of the sea, but giving the idea
of their having once been washed by it. A great number
of female eider-ducks, with their flocks of young, were
swimming about the island; and the *tripe de roche* and *coch-
learia* were here more luxuriant than we had ever seen
them. Drift-wood was, as usual, in great abundance in
every spot where it could effect a landing We here observed the dip of the magnetic needle to be 81° 24'.19
North; and, in taking angles for the survey, discovered a
very dangerous rock, with the sea breaking upon it, at the
distance of a mile and a half from the island, which I have
distinguished as the "Hecla Rock" upon the chart. No

ice was here in sight, to the utmost limit of a very extensive view.

At ten, A.M., on the 14th, the weather being fine, we launched our three boats, and left Walden Island; but the wind backing more to the westward, we could only fetch into a bay on the opposite or southern shore, where we hauled the boats up on very rugged rocks, under cliffs about six hundred feet high, and of the same granite formation as Walden Island. We found the eastern land of this bay to be an island separated by a narrow strait; and this, and another to the westward of it, having no names in the chart, I have distinguished them by those of our fellow-travellers, Messrs. Beverly and Bird. The wind shifted to the eastward in the night, and at eight, A.M., on the 15th, we set out for Low Island, where we arrived at four, P.M., landing upon the west point, which is composed of a schistose quartz rock, dipping at an angle of 70° to the S.E., with a fine smooth beach of small pebbles of quartz and clay-slate, strewed in every part with immense quantities of drift-wood. Beds of clay-slate occur further inland, of a blue, red, and yellow colour, and dipping in various directions. Off this point, and at the distance of one mile, we observed several small rocky islets which had before escaped notice, being then covered with ice. In fact, the whole neighbourhood of this island should be approached very cautiously in a ship, the soundings being irregular and

uncertain. We here saw a bear, a great many tern and
eider-ducks with their young, and several deer, two of which
were killed. By the time we had prepared for setting out,
the wind had freshened almost to a gale, with every appearance of dirty weather, which induced me to remain here
for the night. Messrs. Ross and Beverly took a long walk
about the island, and found it much intersected by ponds
and lagoons, with very little vegetation in any part. In
the mean time I observed the dip of the magnetic needle,
which was 81° 22′ 9; and at nine, A M., on the following
morning, set off for the Hecla; but as we approached the
point which I have distinguished by the name of " Shoal
Point" on the chart, the wind shifted to the southward, and
raised a sea which obliged us to bear up for the south point
of Low Island, where we landed at one, P.M., on a long
narrow beach, almost entirely composed of clay-slate, with
a lagoon within it. Near this point is a hill about one
hundred and fifty feet above the sea, which is the highest
and only conspicuous part of the island. The rocks which
compose the hill are of reddish schistose quartz, approaching in some places to sandstone, the strata being disposed
in a direction quite vertical. We saw nothing here resembling the hexagonal stones mentioned by Dr. Irving, in
Phipps's Voyage *, as occurring about the northern part of

---

* Voyage towards the North Pole, p. 58.

the island   Having a commanding view from this eminence, we obtained angles for the survey, and afterwards
found that Lieutenant Crozier had observed the latitude
not far from our present landing-place to be 80° 15′ 25″.
Within, or to the eastward of the island, is a considerable
bay, in which some heavy masses of ice were lying aground,
reminding us more than any that we had seen about Spitzbergen of the smaller bergs in Baffin's Bay, though of
much less dimensions   There appears to be a great deal
of shoal water in this neighbourhood, and many detached
rocks appear above water.   No drift-ice was in sight in any
direction.

The wind dying away on the morning of the 17th, we
once more set out for the ship at nine, A.M.; but having
a second time nearly reached Shoal Point, were again met
by a strong breeze as we opened Waygatz Strait, and were
therefore obliged to land upon the low shore to the southward of Low Island.   It was, however, some time before
we discovered a spot on which any fresh water could be
obtained; for we found this coast to consist almost entirely
of narrow strips of beach, within which are very extensive
lagoons, and most of the water near them is brackish
The formation here was different from any we had yet met
with about Spitzbergen; the rocks consisting chiefly of
a black marble with white and red veins intersecting it,
and the flat parts of the land covered with small detached

fragments of decomposed limestone. In some places, also, there are beds of clay-slate of considerable extent. A narrow line of marble rock here and there projects into the sea, like jetties thrown out by art, and having fine beaches between them. We found one piece of bituminous wood-coal, which burned with a clear, bright flame, and emitted a pleasant odour. On this and all the land hereabouts, where lagoons occur, enormous quantities of drift-wood line the inner beach, which is now quite inaccessible to the sea, and this wood is always more decayed than that which lies on the outer or present sea-beach; by which it appears that the latter has been thrown up, to the exclusion of the sea, long since the inner wood was landed. A great many small rounded pieces of pumice-stone are also found on this part of the coast, and these generally occur rather above the inner line of drift-wood, as if they had reached the highest limit to which the sea has ever extended.

On the 18th the wind increased to a strong breeze from the S.W., with rain and sleet, which afterwards changed to snow in some of the largest flakes I ever saw, completely changing the whole aspect of the land from summer to
winter in a few hours. On the following morning we prepared to move at an early hour, but the wind backed more to the westward, and soon after increased to a gale, raising so much surf on the beach as to oblige us to haul the boats higher up. The rain, which fell heavily, keeping us pri-

soners under our awnings, dissolved nearly all the snow on the low lands. As the wind now blew so much upon the shore, I was in momentary expectation of seeing some ice come in, but we were agreeably surprised to find that none appeared This circumstance appeared to us the more remarkable from the extraordinary rapidity with which, in the month of June, the very lightest air from the westward brought the drift-ice in upon the land, rendering these shores quite inaccessible in the course of a few hours.

On the 20th, tired as we were of this tedious confinement, and anxious to reach the ship, the wind and sea were still too high to allow us to move, and it was not till

half past seven, A.M, on the 21st, that we could venture to launch the boats. Having now, by means of the drift-wood, converted our paddles into oars, and being occasionally favoured by a light breeze, with a perfectly open sea, we made tolerable progress, and at half past four, P M., when within three or four miles of Hecla Cove, had the gratification of seeing a boat under sail, coming out to meet us. Mr. Weir soon joined us in one of the cutters; and, after hearing good accounts of the safety of the ship, and of the welfare of all on board, together with a variety of details, to us of no small interest, we arrived on board at seven, P.M., after an absence of sixty-one days, being received with that warm and cordial welcome, which can alone be felt, and not described.

The distance traversed during this excursion was five hundred and sixty-nine geographical miles; but allowing for the number of times we had to return for our baggage during the greater part of the journeys over the ice, we estimated our actual travelling at nine hundred and seventy-eight geographical, or eleven hundred and twenty-seven statute miles. Considering our constant exposure to wet, cold, and fatigue, our stockings having generally been drenched in snow-water for twelve hours out of every four-and-twenty, I had great reason to be thankful for the excellent health in which, upon the whole, we reached the ship. There is no doubt that we had all become, in a certain degree, gradually weaker for some time past; but only three men of our party now required medical care, two of them with badly swelled legs and general debility, and the other from a bruise; but even these three returned to their duty in a short time.

I cannot conclude the account of our proceedings without endeavouring to do justice to the cheerful alacrity and un-wearied zeal displayed by my companions, both officers and men, in the course of this excursion; and if steady perse-verance and active exertion on their parts could have accom-plished our object, success would undoubtedly have crowned our labours. I must also mention, to the credit of the officers of Woolwich dock-yard, who took so much pains in the con-struction of our boats, that, notwithstanding the constant and severe trial to which their strength had been put—and a more severe trial could not well be devised—not a timber was sprung, a plank split, or the smallest injury sustained by them; they were, indeed, as tight and as fit for service when we reached the ship as when they were first received on board, and in every respect answered the intended purpose admirably.

An abstract of our meteorological observations during this excursion, is given in the Appendix, together with those kept on board the Hecla. In this there is nothing so remarkable as the extraordinary quantity of rain, of which it may safely be said that *twenty times* as much fell in the course of this one summer, as during any preceding one we had passed in the polar regions, even in latitudes from 8° to 16° lower.

ON my arrival on board, I learned from Lieutenant Crozier that Lieutenant Foster, finding that no further disturbance from ice was to be apprehended, and after making an accurate plan of the bay and its neighbourhood, had proceeded on the survey of Waygatz Strait, and proposed returning by the 26th, the day to which I had limited his absence. I found the ship quite ready for sea, with the exception of getting on board the launch, with the stores deposited by

S

my direction on the beach.   Lieutenant Foster's report
informed me that, after the ship had been hauled off the
ground *, they had again suffered considerable disturbance
for several days, in consequence of some heavy masses of ice
driving into the bay, which dragged the anchors, and again
threatened them with a similar accident.   However, after
the middle of July no ice had entered the bay, and, what is
still more remarkable, not a piece had been seen in the
offing for some weeks past, even after hard northerly and
westerly gales.   I must here not omit to do justice to the
zealous and unwearied exertions which had been made by
Lieutenant Foster, and every officer and man left on board,
as well to preserve the Hecla from injury, under circumstances of considerable danger, as to get on board all the
stores and ballast after they had been landed for the purpose
of heaving her off; in the course of which service, the conduct of every individual was highly meritorious.   It was also
a source of great satisfaction to find everybody on board in
good health, with the exception of Mr. Crawford, the Greenland Master, who had for some time past been in a declining

* I cannot here omit to mention the invaluable advantage derived, on this
occasion, from one of our cutters (a twenty-five feet boat) having been fitted on
Mr. Cow's ingenious principle for weighing anchors in the centre, instead of the
extremity of the boat   By this beautiful contrivance, six men could weigh the
Hecla's bower-anchor, of thirty cwt., with ease, and transport it any distance
with safety.   Indeed, but for this facility, added to that afforded by Phillips's
Capstan, the Hecla's reduced crew would probably have been unable to haul her
off the ground at all on this occasion.

state, and now evinced dropsical symptoms, indicating a gradual and rapid decay.

No opportunity had been lost of making such observations as, in this latitude, may be considered interesting to science, and in collecting specimens of natural history; in all which pursuits the officers were constantly employed, during every moment that could be spared from the necessary duties of the ship. Among other magnetic observations, an interesting series of hourly experiments had been made on the diurnal changes of variation and intensity, and continued for several days without intermission, by Lieutenants Foster and Crozier. By these it appears that there is a diurnal oscillation of the magnetic needle, usually amounting to about a degree and a half, and in some instances to $2°\frac{3}{4}$; the maximum westerly variation occurring at about five, P.M, and the minimum about $4^h\ 22^m$, A.M. The experiments on the change of intensity were not less satisfactory and conclusive; exhibiting an increased action about $10^h\ 20^m$, A M, and a minimum intensity about midnight. There was also observed a remarkable coincidence between these two phenomena, the largest amount of diurnal variation and the greatest changes of intensity usually occurring on the same days.

On the 22d, as soon as our people had enjoyed a good Wednesday, 22nd night's rest, we commenced bringing the stores on board from the beach, throwing out such a quantity of the stone ballast as was necessary for trimming the ship; after which

S 2

the cables and hawsers were cast off from the shore, and the ship hauled off to single anchor. Lieutenant Foster returned on board on the 24th, having surveyed the greater part of the shores of the Strait, as far to the southward as 79° 33'. This Strait was found to vary in breadth from four to eleven miles; and Lieutenant Foster recognised distinctly almost every feature of the lands delineated in the old Dutch chart before alluded to, though the position of these is, in general, very erroneously laid down, both in latitude and longitude. Still, however, there is enough to shew that they have been delineated from a sketch actually made upon the spot. The land within the Strait, especially that which he saw to the southward of 79°½, Lieutenant Foster considered to be much higher than any of the northern shores of Spitzbergen, being in some parts probably not less than three thousand feet.

He found in some places a good deal of alluvial soil, such as occurs at the base of the hills in almost every part of this coast on which we have landed. Some islands near the middle of the Strait, to which I have ventured to affix the name of Lieutenant Foster, are composed of hornblende; but at a short distance to the westward of these, a limestone formation occurred, with numerous fossils imbedded in the rock, upon a prominent headland forming the eastern point of entrance to Bear or Loom Bay, and which Lieutenant Foster distinguished by the name of Cape Fanshawe   A striking feature of the land on the western coast of the

Strait consists in the numerous ice-bergs with which the cliffs are in many parts lined. One of these, marked in the chart, is not less than nine miles in length, and one hundred and fifty feet high , immense masses of ice were constantly falling from them at this season, with a sound resembling that of thunder. Several of these ice-bergs are faithfully laid down in the Dutch Chart.

Lieutenant Foster saw some sea-horses, narwhals, and white whales, in the course of this excursion, but no black whales; nor did we, in the whole course of the voyage, see any of these, except on the ground already frequented by our whalers, on the western coast of Spitzbergen. It is remarkable, however, that the " crown-bones,' and other parts of the skeleton of whales, are found in most parts where we landed on this coast. The shores of the Strait, like all the rest in Spitzbergen, are lined with immense quantities of drift-wood, wherever the nature of the coast will allow it to land.

That part of Treurenburg Bay, to which I have affixed the name of Hecla Cove, is the only good anchorage it contains, the water being either too deep or too shoal in most other parts. The Hecla's anchorage is perfectly land-locked and secure, except from the incursions of ice, which, in these regions, occasionally finds its way into every corner; but even in this respect, there was nothing to apprehend after the middle of July   The holding-ground is excellent, consisting of a tenacious blue clay, in which the anchors were quite imbedded. The latitude of the flag-staff marked in the Plan, on which a copper-plate was fixed, giving an account of the Hecla's visit, is 79° 55′ 20″, and its longitude by our chronometers 16° 48′ 45″ east. The dip of the magnetic needle by that employed by Lieutenant Foster is 80° 45′.91, and by mine 81° 4′.58. The mean variation is 18° 46′ 12″ westerly. The time of high water at full and change is 2ʰ 26ᵐ, the highest rise at spring tides being four feet two inches, and the smallest at the neaps seventeen inches ; both of these occurring at the fourth tide after the full moon, and the last quarter, respectively.

The animals met with here, during the Hecla's stay, were principally rein-deer, bears, foxes, kittiwakes, glaucous and ivory gulls, tern, eider-ducks, and a few grouse. Looms and rotges were numerous in the offing. Seventy rein-deer were killed, chiefly very small, and, until the middle of August, not in good condition They were usually met with in herds of from six or eight to twenty, and were most abundant on the west and north sides of the bay. Three bears were killed, one of which was somewhat above the ordinary dimensions, measuring eight feet four inches from the snout to the insertion of the tail. The vegetation was tolerably abundant, especially on the western side of the bay, where the soil is good ; a considerable collection of plants, as well as minerals, was made by Mr. Halse, and of birds by Mr. M'Cormick.

The following remarks by Mr. Beverly, made during our

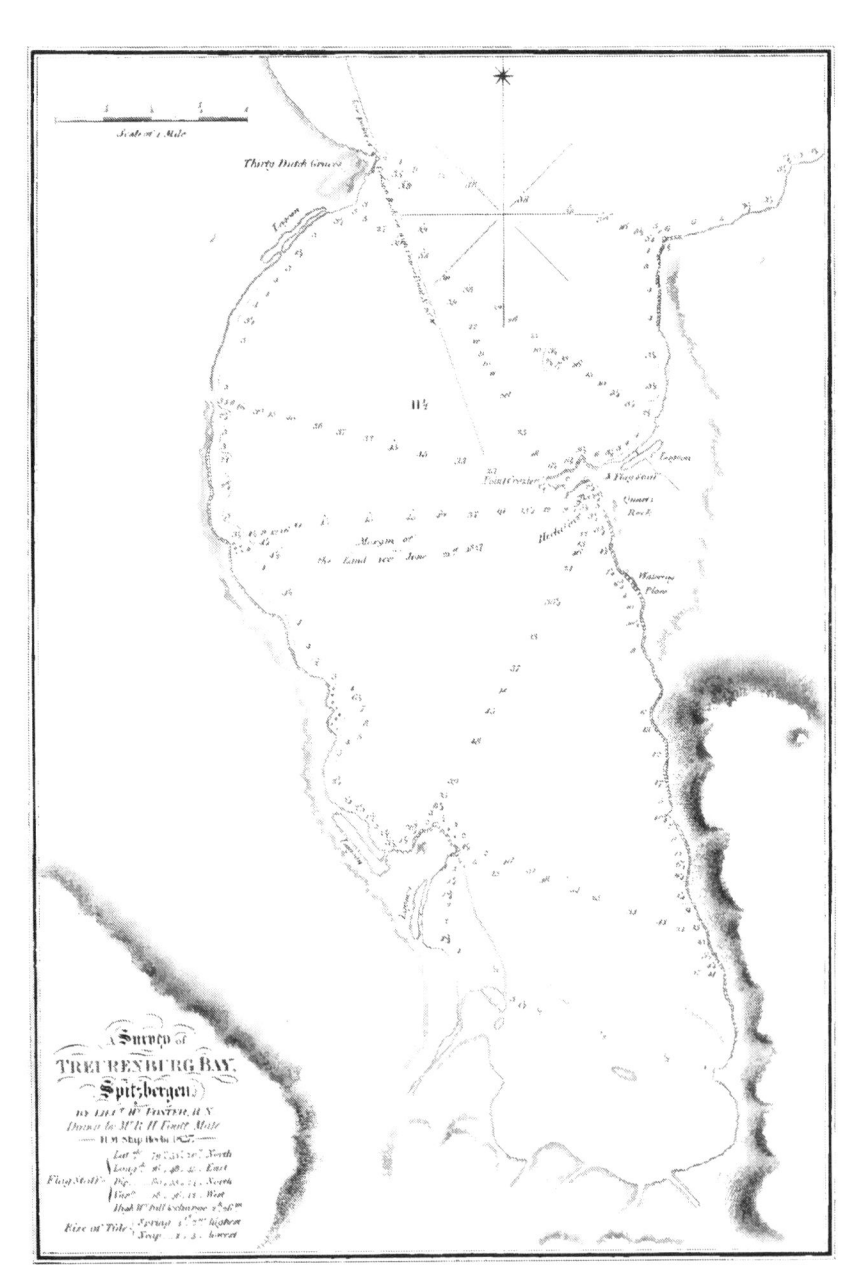

Thirty Dutch Graves

11½

Point Crozier

Flagstaff

Quaer's Rock

Hecla Cove

Walrous Point

Margin of
the Land ice June 20th 1827

A Survey of

TREURENBURG BAY,

Spitzbergen,

BY LIEUT W. FINLEY, R.N.
Drawn by Mr. R. H. Gault, Mate
H.M. Ship Hecla 1827.

short stay in Hecla Cove, after returning from the north, may be interesting to geologists. " The land on the east side of this bay, near the Cove, is a flat, from two to three miles in extent, and is composed, in some parts, of a fine deep alluvial soil, probably formed by the decomposition of the rocks which compose the hills to the southward.   On this plain there are beds of schistose quartz, nearly approaching to sand-stone, and chiefly of a pale red colour.   Beds of clay-slate also occur, in some places of greenish gray, and in others of a brick-red colour.   Next the sea is a fine bold beach, composed of rounded pieces of the above rock, with limestone intermixed.   At about a quarter of a mile from the base of the high land, immense masses of a very coarse-grained rock lie scattered about, and appear to have been precipitated from the upper stratum of the mountain.   They are composed of ferruginous sand and hornblende, in such a state of decomposition as to crumble to powder under the blow of the hammer

" The range of mountains beyond this plain lies in an E.b S , and afterwards in a more southerly, direction, forming the west shore of Waygatz Strait ; and, as far as I was able to ascertain, is composed of the same rock, which, being soft, gives their summit a smooth and rounded form.   The debris extends about five hundred yards on the plain, and consists of loose fragments, rendering the ascent to the perpendicular face of the rock very difficult   That part of the hill which faces the harbour is composed of quartz rock, in some places schistose, in others massive, with a waxy fracture. This terminates abruptly about a mile and a half to the eastward, where the clay-slate formation commences, being of a deep lead colour, a firm texture, and less talcose than that on the plain. The inclination of this stratum, as well as that of the quartz rock, is to the south-east, at an angle of about sixty degrees

" The formation of the rocks on the opposite or western side of the bay, appeared, as far as I had an opportunity of examining them, to be much the same. At the foot of the hills there is a broad belt of flat alluvial ground, much of which consists of a fine deep soil, thickly covered with mosses and other vegetation ; upon this flat ground are lying large boulders of mica-slate."

The height of the hill nearest to Hecla Cove, as measured barometrically by Lieutenant Foster, is about two thousand feet; but the barometer having subsequently been found defective, this measure can only be considered an approximation. The hills on the south side of the bay are considerably higher than this.

The neighbourhood of this bay, like most of the northern shores of Spitzbergen, appears to have been much visited by the Dutch at a very early period ; of which circumstance records are furnished on almost every spot where we landed, by the numerous graves which are met with. There are thirty of these on a point of land on the north side of the bay *. The bodies are usually deposited in an oblong wooden coffin, which, on account of the difficulty of digging the ground, is not buried, but merely covered by large stones; and a board is generally placed near the head, having, either cut or painted, upon it the name of the deceased, with those of his ship and commander, and the month and year of his burial. Several of these were fifty or sixty years old, one bore the date of 1738; and another, which I found on the beach to the eastward of Hecla Cove, that of 1690, the inscription distinctly appearing in prominent relief, occasioned by the preservation of the wood by the paint, while the unpainted part had decayed around it.

The officers who remained on board the Hecla during the summer described the weather as the most beautiful, and the climate altogether the most agreeable, they had ever experienced in the polar regions Indeed, the Meteorological Journal, of which an abstract for each month is annexed to this volume, shows a temperature, both of the air and of the sea-water, to which we had before been altogether strangers within the Arctic Circle, and which goes far towards showing that the climate of Spitzbergen is a remarkably temperate one for its latitude †. It must, how-

* Perhaps the name of this bay, from the Dutch word *Treuren*, " to lament, or be mournful," may have some reference to the graves found here.

† Mr Crowe of Hammerfest, who lately passed a winter on the south-western

T

ever, be observed that this remark is principally applicable to the weather experienced *near the land*, that at sea being rendered of a totally different character by the almost continual presence of fogs; so that some of our most gloomy days upon the ice were among the finest in Hecla Cove, where, however, a good deal of rain fell in the course of the summer.

The Hecla was ready for sea on the 25th of August; but the wind blowing fresh from the northward and westward prevented our moving till the evening of the 28th, when, the weather improving, we got under way from Hecla Cove, and being favoured with a light air from the S.E., stood along the coast to the westward. On the evening of the 29th, when off Red Beach, we got on board our boat and other stores which had been left there, finding them undisturbed and in good order. The weather was beautifully fine, and the sun (to us for the first time for about four months) just dipped his lower limb into the sea at midnight, and then rose again. It was really wonderful to see that, upon this whole northern coast of Spitzbergen, where in May and June not a "hole" of clear water could be found, it would now have been equally difficult to dis-

Tuesday,
28th

Wednesday,
29th.

coast of Spitzbergen, in about latitude 78°, informed me that he had *rain at Christmas*, a phenomenon, which would indeed have astonished us at any of our former wintering stations in a much lower latitude. Perhaps the circumstance of the rein-deer wintering at Spitzbergen may also be considered a proof of a comparatively temperate climate.

cover a single mass of ice in any direction. This absence 1827.
August. of ice now enabled us to see Moffen Island, which is so low and flat that it was before entirely hidden from our view by the hummocks. On rounding Hakluyt's Headland on the 30th, we came at once into a long swell, such as occurs Thursday,
30th only in places exposed to the whole range of the ocean, and, except a small and loose stream or two, we after this saw no more ice of any kind. On the 31st we were off Friday,
31st. Prince Charles's Foreland, the middle part of which, about Cape Sietoe, appeared to be much the highest land we had seen in Spitzbergen; rising probably to an elevation of above four thousand feet.

We had favourable winds to carry us clear of Spitzbergen; September. but after the 3rd of September, and between the parallels of 70° and 60°, were detained by continual southerly and south-westerly breezes for a fortnight. On the evening of the Monday,
17th. 17th we made Shetland, and on the following day, being close off Balta Sound, and the wind blowing strong from the S.W., I anchored in the Voe at two P.M., to wait a more favourable breeze. We were here received by all that genuine hospitality for which the inhabitants of this northern part of the British dominions are so justly distin-guished, and we gladly availed ourselves of the supplies with which their kindness furnished us We here also obtained observations for our chronometers on the spot where Captain Kater and Monsieur Biot swung their pen-

T 2

dulums; and it was satisfactory, as regarded our survey of the northern shores of Spitzbergen, to find that we differed from the Ordnance-Survey only eight seconds of time.

Early on the morning of the 19th the wind suddenly shifted to the N.N.W., and almost immediately blew so strong a gale that we could not safely cast the ship until the evening, when we got under way and proceeded to the
southward; but had not proceeded farther than Fair Island, when, after a few hours' calm, we were once more met by a southerly wind Against this we continued to beat till
the morning of the 23rd, when, finding that we made but little progress, and that there was no appearance of an alteration of wind, I determined to put into Long Hope, in the Orkney Islands, to await a change in our favour, and accordingly ran in and anchored there as soon as the tide would permit.

We found lying here His Majesty's Revenue Cutter the Chichester; and Mr. Stuart, her commander, who was bound direct to Inverness, came on board as soon as we had anchored, to offer his services in any manner which might
be useful. The wind died away in the course of the night, and was succeeded on the following morning by a light air from the northward, when we immediately got under way; but had not entered the Pentland Firth, when it again fell calm and then backed to the southward, rendering it impossible to make any progress in that direction with a dull-

sailing ship. I therefore determined on returning with the Hecla to the anchorage, and then taking advantage of Mr. Stuart's offer; and accordingly left the ship at eight, A M., accompanied by Mr. Beverly, to proceed to Inverness in the Chichester, and from thence by land to London, in order to lay before His Royal Highness the Lord High Admiral, without further delay, an account of our proceedings. By the zealous exertions of Mr. Stuart, for which I feel greatly obliged to that gentleman, we arrived off Fort George the following morning, and landing at Inverness at noon, immediately set off for London, and arrived at the Admiralty on the morning of the 29th.

Owing to the continuance of southerly winds, the Hecla did not arrive in the river Thames until the 6th of October, when I was sorry, though not surprised, to learn the death of Mr George Crawford, the Greenland master, who departed this life on the 29th of September, sincerely lamented by all who knew him, as a zealous, active, and enterprising seaman, and an amiable and deserving man. Mr. Crawford had accompanied us in five successive voyages to the Polar Seas, and I truly regret the occasion which demands from me this public testimony of the value of his services and the excellence of his character.

A few days having been employed at Northfleet in repeating some of the magnetic observations necessary for completing the series of those experiments, the Hecla proceeded to Deptford. On the 17th of October His Royal Highness the Lord High Admiral was pleased to inspect the ship, together with the equipment of the boats which had been employed in the late Expedition over the ice; after which the Hecla was dismantled, and paid off on the 1st of November.

HAVING finished my Narrative of this Attempt to reach the North Pole, I may perhaps be permitted, in conclusion, to offer such remarks as have lately occurred to me, on the nature and practicability of the enterprize.

That the object is of still more difficult attainment than was before supposed, even by those persons who were the best qualified to judge of it, will, I believe, appear evident from a perusal of the foregoing pages; nor can I, after much consideration and some experience of the various difficulties which belong to it, recommend any material improvement in the plan lately adopted. Among the various schemes suggested for this purpose, it has been proposed to set out from Spitzbergen, and to make a rapid journey to the northward, with sledges, or sledge-boats, drawn wholly by dogs or rein-deer, but, however feasible

this plan may at first sight appear, I cannot say that our
late experience of the nature of the ice which they would
probably have to encounter, has been at all favourable to it.
It would, of course, be a matter of extreme imprudence to
set out on this enterprize without the means of crossing—
not merely narrow pools and "lanes"—but more extensive
spaces of open water, such as we met with between the
margin of the ice and the Spitzbergen shores; and I do
not conceive that any boat sufficiently large to be efficient
and safe for this purpose, could possibly be managed upon
the ice, were the power employed to give it motion dependent on dogs or rein-deer.   On the contrary, it was a frequent subject of remark among the officers, that reason was
a qualification scarcely less indispensable than strength and
activity, in travelling over such a road ; daily instances
occurring of our having to pass over difficult places, which
no other animal than man could have been easily prevailed
upon to attempt.   Indeed, the constant necessity of launching and hauling up the boats (which operations we had
frequently to perform eight or ten, and, on one occasion,
seventeen times in the same day) would alone render it
inexpedient, in my opinion, to depend chiefly upon other
animals ; for it would certainly require more time and
labour to get them into and out of the boats, than their
services in the intervals, or their flesh ultimately used as
food, would be worth ; especially when it is considered how

large a weight of provender must be carried for their own
subsistence *.

In case of employing rein-deer, which, from their strength,
docility, and hardy habits, appear the best suited to this
kind of travelling, there would be an evident advantage in
setting out much earlier in the year than we did; perhaps
about the end of April, when the ice is less broken up, and
the snow much harder upon its surface, than at a more
advanced part of the season. But this, it must be recol-
lected, would involve the necessity of passing the previous
winter on the northern coast of Spitzbergen, which, even
under favourable circumstances, would probably tend to
weaken in some degree the energies of the men: while, on
the other hand, it would be next to impossible to procure
there a supply of provender for a number of tame rein-deer,
sufficient even to keep them alive, much less in tolerable
condition, during a whole winter. In addition to this, it
may be observed, that any party setting out earlier must be
provided with a much greater weight of warm clothing, in
order to guard against the severity of the cold, and also
with an increased proportion of fuel for procuring water by
the melting of snow, there being no fresh water upon the
ice, in these latitudes, before the month of June.

In the kind of provisions proper to be employed in such
enterprizes—a very important consideration, where almost

* See p 6 of this Narrative.

the whole difficulty may be said to resolve itself into a
question of weight—I am not aware that any improvement
could be made upon that with which we were furnished :
for I know of none which appears to contain so much nutriment in so small a weight and compass. It may be useful,
however, to remark, as the result of absolute experience, that
our daily allowance of provisions *, although previously tried
for some days on board the ship, and then considered to
be enough, proved by no means sufficient to support the
strength of men living constantly in the open air, exposed
to wet and cold for at least twelve hours a day, seldom
enjoying the luxury of a warm meal, and having to perform
the kind of labour to which our people were subject. I
have before remarked that, previously to our return to the
ship, our strength was considerably impaired; and, indeed,
there is reason to believe that, very soon after entering upon
the ice, the physical energies of the men were gradually
diminishing; although, for the first few weeks, they did not
appear to labour under any specific complaint. This diminution of strength, which we considered to be principally
owing to the want of sufficient sustenance, became apparent,
even after a fortnight, in the lifting of the bread-bags and
other heavy weights; and I have no doubt that, in spite of
every care on the part of the officers, as well as Mr. Beverly's

* See p 59 of this Narrative

U

skilful and humane attention to their ailments, some of the
men, who had begun to fail before we quitted the ice,
would, in a week or two longer, have suffered very severely,
and become a serious incumbrance, instead of an assistance,
to our party. As far as we were able to judge, without
further trial, Mr. Beverly and myself were of opinion that,
in order to maintain the strength of men thus employed,
for several weeks together, an addition would be requisite,
of at least one third more to the provisions which we daily
issued. I need scarcely remark how much this would increase the difficulty of equipping such an Expedition.

I cannot dismiss the subject of this enterprise, without
attempting to explain, as far as I am able, how it may have
happened that the ice over which we passed was found to
answer so little to the description of that observed by the
respectable authorities quoted in a former part of this
volume *. It frequently occurred to us, in the course of
our daily journies, that this may, in some degree, have
arisen from our navigators' having generally viewed the ice
from a considerable height   The only clear and commanding view on board a ship is that from the crow's-nest; and
Phipps's most important remarks concerning the nature of
the ice to the north of Spitzbergen were made from a station several hundred feet above the sea ; and, as it is well

* Introduction.

known how much the most experienced eye may thus be
deceived, it is possible enough that the irregularities which
cost us so much time and labour may, when viewed in this
manner, have entirely escaped notice, and the whole surface
have appeared one smooth and level plain.

It is, moreover, possible that the broken state in which
we unexpectedly found the ice may have arisen, at least in
part, from an unusually wet season, preceded, perhaps, by
a winter of less than ordinary severity. Of the latter we
have no means of judging, there being no record, that I am
aware of, of the temperature of that or any other winter
passed in the higher latitudes; but, on comparing our
Meteorological Register with some others, kept during the
corresponding season, and about the same latitude *, it does
appear that, though no material difference is observable in
the mean temperature of the atmosphere, the quantity of
rain which we experienced is considerably greater than
usual, and it is well known how very rapidly ice is dissolved by a fall of rain. At all events, from whatever cause
it may have arisen, it is certain that, about the meridian
on which we proceeded northward in the boats, the sea
was in a totally different state from what Phipps experienced, as may be seen from comparing our accounts; his
ship being closely beset, near the Seven Islands, for several

* Particularly that of Mr. Scoresby during the month of July, from 1812
to 1818 inclusive, and Captain Franklin's for July and August 1818

days about the beginning of August; whereas the Hecla, in the beginning of June, sailed about in the same neighbourhood without obstruction, and, before the close of July, not a piece of ice could be seen from Little Table Island.

I may add, in conclusion, that, before the middle of August, when we left the ice in our boats, a ship might have sailed to the latitude of 82°, almost without touching a piece of ice; and it was the general opinion among us that, by the end of that month, it would probably have been no very difficult matter to reach the parallel of 83°, about the meridian of the Seven Islands

END OF THE NARRATIVE.

APPENDIX.

I.

ABSTRACT OF THE METEOROLOGICAL JOURNAL KEPT DURING
THE EXPEDITION TOWARDS THE NORTH POLE, BETWEEN
JUNE 25, and AUGUST 10, 1827,

AND ON BOARD HIS MAJESTY'S SHIP HECLA, BETWEEN
MAY 1, and SEPTEMBER 16, 1827.

Note.—THE LATITUDES AND LONGITUDES HAVING AN ASTERISK AFFIXED TO THEM, IN THE FIRST TABLE, ARE BY OBSERVATION

ABSTRACT OF THE METEOROLOGICAL JOURNAL

Day.	North Latitude at Noon.	East Longitude at Noon.	Fahrenheit's Thermometer. In Shade. Maximum.	Minimum.	Mean.	Highest in Sun.	Sea Water at surface highest.	
1827.	° ′ ″	° ′	°	°	°	°	°	
June 25	81 15 13*	21 15	36	34	35	. .	. .	. .
,, 26	81 17 0	21 17	33	32	32·5	. .	. .	. .
,, 27	81 19 0	21 21	36	33½	34·8	. .	. .	. .
,, 28	81 21 0	21 25	43	32	37	. .	. .	. .
,, 29	81 23 0*	21 33*	33	33	33	39	. .	. .
,, 30	81 24 0	21 50	35	31	33	31½	. .	. .
July 1	81 30 41*	21 12	33	29	30·7	. .	. .	. .
,, 2	81 35 50*	22 5	35	28	31	. .	. .	. .
,, 3	81 36 0	22 42	. .	. .	. .	. .	. .	. .
,, 4	81 40 0	23 55	34	33	33·7	. .	. .	. .
,, 5	81 45 15*	24 23*	34½	32	33·3	. .	32½ 39 at 400 fathoms.	. .
,, 6	81 48 0	24 20	. .	. .	. .	. .	. .	. .
,, 7	81 51 0	23 55	33½	33	33·8	. .	. .	. .
,, 8	81 54 0	24 12	35	32½	33·7	. .	32·7	. .
,, 9	81 59 0	23 46	36	34	35	. .	. .	. .
,, 10	82 3 19*	23 17*	35	33½	34	. .	32⅓	. .
,, 11	82 11 0	22 54	35	33½	34·5	37	32	. .
,, 12	82 14 28*	22 4*	36	34½	35·2	38	33½	. .
,, 13	82 17 10*	21 40	36	33½	34·3	38	32½	. .
,, 14	82 18 0	21 35	33½	32½	33	. .	. .	. .
,, 15	82 20 0	20 54	33	31	33·3	33	33¼	. .
,, 16	82 26 50*	20 32*	37½	32½	35	47	34	. .
,, 17	82 32 10*	20 32*	40	34	35·7	51	33	. .
,, 18	82 33 0	20 5	37	33½	35·5	. .	33	. .
,, 19	82 35 0	20 33	35½	31	33·2	50½	34	. .
,, 20	82 36 52*	20 5	34½	31	33·2	38	31	. .
,, 21	82 39 10*	19 52*	37	33⅓	35·8	45	33⅓	. .
,, 22	82 43 5*	19 54	34	31	32·2	38	31½	. .
,, 23	82 44 0	19 48	34½	31½	31½	35	33⅓	. .
,, 24	82 43 0	19 37	33	31	32·2	. .	. .	. .
,, 25	82 42 0	19 30	33⅓	33	33·2	. .	. .	. .
,, 26	82 40 14*	19 25*	33½	30½	31·7	37	34	. .
,, 27	82 40 0	19 30	36	30⅓	33·2	34	32½	. .
,, 28	82 38 0	19 15	33	33	33	. .	32½	. .
,, 29	82 33 7*	18 40	34½	31	31.7	. .	29½	. .
,, 30	82 20 37*	18 0	33	31	31.6	35½	30	. .
,, 31	82 11 25*	17 18*	34	30½	33	. .	31½	. .
August 1	82 11 0	17 30	33½	30	31·8	. .	. .	. .
,, 2	82 6 0*	17 46*	35½	31½	32·5	34⅓	. .	. .
,, 3	82 1 18*	17 50	37	30½	35	39	31⅓	. .
,, 4	81 57 25*	17 56*	30½	29	30·3	39	33¼	. .
,, 5	81 54 17*	18 10	35	28	31·5	42	33½	. .
,, 6	81 51 0	18 4	33½	28	30·7	34	31¼	. .
,, 7	81 46 0	17 53	34	[illegible]	33·7	. .	32⅓	. .
,, 8	81 48 0	17 58	32	32	32	. .	31½	. .
,, 9	81 37 0	18 3	33	32½	32·8	. .	31½	. .
,, 10	81 40 13*	18 29	34	32½	33·2	. .	. .	. .
			43	28	33·3	38·9	32·6	

KEPT DURING THE EXPEDITION TOWARDS THE NORTH POLE.

Prevailing Winds.		Weather, and other Remarks.
Direction.	Velocity.	
WSW.	Moderate.	Fog and rain.
SW.	Light.	Much rain.
NE. Southerly.	Moderate.	Hazy. Thick fog.
SSE.	Light.	Ditto.
Southerly.	Light.	Very clear and fine.
SSW.	Fresh.	Much snow.
SW.	Fresh.	Some snow. PM. fine.
Calm. SE.	Light.	Some snow.
Easterly.	Fresh.	Snow, sleet, and rain.
Easterly. West.	Moderate. Fresh.	Rain and fog. Overcast, with fog.
SW. South.	Light. Moderate.	Cloudy. Clear and fine.
SE.	Moderate.	Thick fog.
ESE.	Fresh.	Ditto.
ESE.	Moderate.	Rain and fog.
ESE.	Fresh.	Rain. Clear. Rain.
East.	Fresh.	Very thick fog.
E. by S. SE.	Fresh.	Fog and rain. Clear.
SE.	Moderate.	Clear.—Black bulb in ☉ 4°½ to 15½. Parhelion.
ESE.	Moderate.	Clear and fine.
ESE. SE. by E.	Moderate. Fresh.	Clear and fine. Hard rain.
SSE. WSW.	Light.	Rain. Overcast. Fog-bow coloured.
SSW. SSE.	Light. Moderate.	Clear.
SE. S. by E.	Light.	Fine.
SE.	Light.	Fog. Clear.
SE. North.	Light.	Much rain and fog.
North.	Light.	Foggy.
North. Calm.	Light.	Overcast, but clear. Some fog.
WSW. WNW.	Light.	Clear and fine. Foggy.
North.	Fresh.	Sleet.
NW. by N. W. by N.	Moderate. Fresh.	Snow—2 inches fell.
W. by N. WNW.	Fresh. Strong.	Foggy. Snow—2 inches fell.
WNW. Calm.	Strong.	Small rain. Cloudy.
SE. E. by S.	Light. Fresh.	Cloudy. Snow.
ENE. NE. by N.	Fresh. Strong.	Snow. Fog.
NE. by N.	Strong.	Overcast and misty.
NNE. NW.	Fresh. Moderate.	Fog. Cloudy. Small snow.
West.	Moderate.	Snow. Cloudy.
SW.	Light. Fresh.	Fine. Rain.
SW. by W. West.	Moderate. Light.	Cloudy, but clear. Clear.
SW. SE.	Moderate.	Clear and dry.
SE. East.	Light.	Very fine and clear.
East. E. by S.	Light. Fresh.	Ditto ditto.
SE. by E.	Fresh.	Foggy and wet.
Easterly.	Fresh.	Heavy rain.
WSW. Southerly.	Light. Moderate.	Much rain.
South.	Moderate. Strong.	Fog. Hazy. Wet.
SW.	Fresh. Moderate.	Rain and fog. Thick fog.

ABSTRACT OF THE METEOROLOGICAL JOURNAL, KEPT ON BOARD

Days.	North Latitude.		East Longitude.		Temperature of Air in Shade, registered every 2 hours.			Temperature of Sea Water at Surface, registered every 2 hours.			Daniell's Hygrometer.			
											9 A.M.		3 P.M.	
					Maximum.	Minimum.	Mean.	Maximum.	Minimum.	Mean.	Dew Point.	Air.	Dew Point.	Air.
May 1	71	28	20	59	32	26	29·3	39·5	38	38·8	......	......	......	......
,, 2	72	20	16	15	26	23·5	24·1	40	37	39·0	......	......	16	24
,, 3	72	51	11	56	28	25	26·3	39	35	37·6	19	25·5	17	27·5
,, 4	73	20	9	55	27	24	25·5	37	32	35·1	14	21	22	26·5
,, 5	73	30	7	2	27·5	24·5	25·3	30·5	28·5	29·3	20	26	22	25
,, 6	73	59	3	8	28	25·5	26·9	30	28	29·1	22	27·5	25	28
,, 7	75	5	0	9	25·5	20·5	22·9	29	28	28·7	20	22	19	22·5
,, 8	76	10	4	50	20	18	19·3	29½	28	28·8	17	18	14	20
,, 9	77	1	7	5	22·5	16	19·4	29½	28	28·7	20	22	......	......
,, 10	77	8	7	15	20·5	16·5	18·6	28½	28	28	......	......	......	......
,, 11	77	58	7	50	31·5	21	27·3	29	28	28·6	......	......	......	......
,, 12	78	18	7	55	31	30	30·5	30	29	29·2	......	......	......	......
,, 13	78	22	8	2	33·5	27·5	31·2	30	29	29·5	......	......	......	......
,, 14	79	48	10	35	32	25·5	27·9	30	29	29·5	......	......	......	......
,, 15	80	4	12	39	44	30	38·3	31	29	29·9	......	......	......	......
,, 16	80	1	13	5	40	14	25·5	29½	28	28·6	30	32	12	18·5
,, 17	79	57	13	23	24	15	17·8	29	28	28·2	......	......	10	19
,, 18	79	56	13	33	24	15½	19·3	28	28	28	......	......	10	15·5
,, 19	79	55	13	46	15	12	14·2	28½	28	28·2	10	14	......	......
,, 20					18	13	15·8	28½	28	28·2	......	......	......	......
,, 21	79	55	13	54	20	16	20·6	29	28	28·2	......	......	15	20·5
,, 22					23	16·5	19·2	29	28	28·6	15	18	......	......
,, 23	79	55	13	52	17·5	12·5	14·9	29	28	28·6	......	......	......	......
,, 24	79	55	13	55	31	14	25·2	29½	28	28·8	......	......	25	31
,, 25	79	55	13	58	32	27	30·1	30	29	29	......	......	......	......
,, 26	79	55	14	2	32	26·5	30·1	30	29	30·2	......	......	20	31
,, 27					39·5	29·5	35·3	31	29	30·5	......	......	......	......
,, 28	79	55	14	5	36	29	32·9	33	29	29·5	......	......	......	......
,, 29	79	55	14	7	43	32	36·4	39	29½	29·7	......	......	......	......
,, 30	79	55	14	9	44	35	38·7	34	30	30·3	......	......	......	......
,, 31	79	55	14	5	44	34	38·7	32	30	31·2	......	......	......	......
					44	12	26·1	40	28	30·1				

HIS MAJESTY'S SHIP HECLA AT SEA, DURING THE MONTH OF MAY, 1827.

Prevailing Winds.		Weather.	Remarks, &c.
Direction.	Velocity.		
NNE.	Moderate.	Cloudy, and snow.	
NNE.	Moderate.	Cloudy, and snow.	
NNE.	Moderate.	Squally, and snow.	
NNE.	Fresh.	Squally, and snow.	
NEasterly.	Light.	Overcast.	Several pieces of drift ice seen.
NE.	Moderate.	Cloudy.	Squally, with snow at times.
A.M. NNE. P.M. NNW.	Fresh. Moderate.	Cloudy, and snow.	A Parhelion to the right of ☉.
A.M. NW. P.M. SW.	Moderate.	Cloudy.	Snow at times.
A.M. Northerly. P.M. NW.	Fresh.	Squally, and snow.	
A.M. WNW. P.M. SW.	Fresh. Moderate.	Overcast, and snow at times.	
A.M. SE. P.M SW.	Fresh. Moderate.	Hazy, and snow.	
SEasterly.	Fresh.	Squally, with sleet and snow	
A.M. . . . . P.M. SW.	Calm. Light.	Thick fog. Cloudy.	
SWesterly.	A.M. Moderate. P.M. Strong.	Cloudy, and heavy squalls.	
A.M. SSW. P.M. SSW.	Do. Moderate.	Do. Fine, clear.	
A.M. SW. P.M. NW.	Fresh. Moderate.	Do. Cloudy, and small snow.	
A.M. NEasterly. P.M. West.	Light.	Fine and clear.	
NWesterly.	Moderate.	Fine and clear.	Parhelion on each side of ☉, angular distance 22° 28'.
West.	Fresh.	Thick, and snow.	
West.	Moderate.	Thick, and snow.	
SWesterly.	Light.	Hazy.	Snow at times.
NEasterly.	Light.	Fine, clear.	
Easterly.	Light.	A.M. Thick, hazy. P.M. Fine.	Fog hanging over the land.
Easterly.	Light.	Cloudy.	
A.M. Calm. P.M. SEasterly.	Light.	Cloudy.	
Southerly.	Light.	Overcast.	
A.M. NWesterly. P.M. Easterly.	Light.	Fine.	
NEasterly.	Light.	Cloudy.	Snow at times.
A.M. NEasterly. P.M. WNW.	Light.	Fine and clear.	Fog over land.
Easterly.	Light.	Fine and clear.	
NEasterly.	Light.	Clear.	

ABSTRACT OF THE METEOROLOGICAL JOURNAL KEPT ON BOARD

Days.	North Latitude.		East Longitude.		Temperature of Air in Shade, registered every 2 hours.			Temperature of Sea-Water at Surface, registered every 2 hours.			Daniell's Hygrometer.			
											9 A.M.		3 P.M.	
					Maximum.	Minimum.	Mean.	Maximum.	Minimum.	Mean.	Dew Pt.	Air.	Dew Pt.	Air.
	° ′		° ′		°	°	°	°	°	°	°	°	°	°
1	79	54	14	12	43	36	40·3	32	31	31·6	......	......	......	......
2	79	53	14	30	46	35	39·5	32	32	32	......	......	......	......
3	79	50	14	48	43	35	38·7	32	30	31·2	......	......	......	......
4	79	49	15	11	46	37	38·7	32	30	31	......	......	34	43.5
5	79	49	15	17	48	39	42·9	31	29½	30·4	36	43	......	......
6	79	49	15	22	42	37	39	32	30	30·6	34	39	......	......
7	79	50	15	30	42	37	40	33	29	31·2	......	......	35	41
8					43	38	40·1	32	30	30·8	34	40	35	40
9	80	17	16	19	38	31	33·5	31½	29½	30·6	......	......	......	......
10	80	34	17	32	32	31	31·9	32	31	31·5	......	......	......	......
11	80	16	17	18	32	30	31	32	30½	31·2	......	......	......	......
12	80	20	17	44	34	30	32·1	32	30½	31·2	......	......	......	......
13	80	34	19	11	32	30	31	32	30½	31·5	......	......	......	......
14	80	47	18	22	34	28	30·5	32	31	31·9	......	......	......	......
15	80	49	19	7	28	24	26·2	32	29	30·5	......	......	......	......
16	80	35	19	35	31	25	26·6	32½	31	31·6	......	......	......	......
17	80	49	20	27	34	25½	29·8	32½	31	31·3	......	......	......	......
18	80	10	17	23	36	28	33·8	32	31	31·3	......	......	......	......
19	79	59	17	16	36	32½	33·7	32	31	31·8	......	......	......	......
20					40	32	35·2	32	31	31·5	......	......	......	......
21					38	31½	36·4	32	31	31·6	......	......	......	......
22					46	33	38·1	33	31½	32	......	......	......	......
23					53	34	43·5	33½	31	32·3	......	......	......	......
24	In Hecla Cove				47	37	41	33	31½	32·2	......	......	......	......
25	79 55 8		16 53 40		44	31½	39·5	33	32	32·5	......	......	......	......
26					42	38	39·4	32½	32	32·2	......	......	......	......
27					44½	35	38·9	33	31½	32·1	......	......	......	......
28					35	35	33·9	32	31½	31·8	......	......	......	......
29					27	33	34·7	32	32	32	......	......	......	......
30					29	31	35·8	32	31	31·9	......	......	......	......
					53	24	35·8	33·5	29	31·5				

HIS MAJESTY'S SHIP HECLA, AT SEA, DURING THE MONTH OF JUNE, 1827.

Prevailing Winds.		Weather.	Remarks, &c.
Direction.	**Velocity.**		
A.M. NWesterly. P.M. Calm.	Light.	Overcast.	At 2 P.M. a shower of rain.
A.M. Calm. P.M. S.E.	. . . . . . Fresh.	Fine.	
A.M. Southerly. P.M. NWesterly.	Light.	Fine.	8·45 A.M. a slight shower for about 10 minutes.
A.M. SWesterly. P.M. Southerly.	Light.	Cloudy.	Light rain at times.
Southerly.	Light.	Cloudy.	
A.M. Northerly. P.M. Westerly.	Light.	Cloudy, and rain at times.	
Northerly.	Light.	Cloudy.	
Northerly.	Light.	Cloudy, rain at times.	
Southerly.	Moderate.	Cloudy, with sleet, rain, and snow.	
Westerly.	Moderate.	Hazy, and snow.	
WSW.	Moderate.	Thick, and snow.	
A.M. Calm. P.M. NEasterly.	. . . . . . Light.	Hazy, and snow.	
Northerly.	Light.	Thick fog, and snow.	
NNW.	Light.	Overcast, fog at times.	
Westerly.	Light.	Hazy, and small snow.	
Easterly.	Moderate.	Cloudy.	Occasional snow.
Easterly.	Moderate.	A.M. Thick fog. P.M. Fine.	
SEasterly.	Moderate.	Cloudy.	Light rain in the evening.
SEasterly.	Moderate.	Cloudy.	
NNE.	Light.	Fine, and clear.	
Northerly.	Light.	Fine.	
Northerly.	Light.	Fine, clear.	
Calm.	. . . . . .	Fine, clear.	
NNE.	Moderate.	Cloudy.	Fog hanging over the land.
NNE.	Light.	Overcast.	
Easterly.	Moderate.	Cloudy.	
A.M. Calm. P.M. NE.	. . . . . . Light.	Cloudy.	
NNW.	Light.	Foggy, and snow.	
Round the compass.	A.M. Light. P.M. Fresh.	Cloudy.	
NNE.	Moderate.	Cloudy.	

ABSTRACT OF THE METEOROLOGICAL JOURNAL KEPT ON BOARD HIS MAJESTY'S SHIP

Days	North Latitude.	East Longitude.	Temperature of Air in Shade, registered every 2 hours.			Temperature of Sea Water at Surface, registered every 2 hours.			Weather.	
			Maximum.	Minimum.	Mean.	Maximum.	Minimum.	Mean.		
July 1			38	32	35·2	33	32	32·5	Fine, clear.	. . .
2			43½	33	37·6	33	32	32·8	Fine.	. .
3			42	35	39·7	34	32	32·8	Hazy, rain, and sleet at times.	. .
4			37½	33	35·2	34	32	33·7	Cloudy.	. .
5			45	32	38·7	35	33	33·9	Fine, clear.	. .
6			45	38	42·4	35	33	34·2	Fine. Cloudy.	. .
7			44	38	40·9	35	30½	33·4	Cloudy, light rain.	. .
8			42½	38	39·8	32	30	31·1	Cloudy.	. .
9			53	37	43·2	33	32	32·3	Cloudy.	. .
10			47	37	40·5	37	32	34·6	Overcast, and fog.	. .
11			51	39	42·9	34	32½	33·4	Cloudy.	. .
12			52	42	47·9	40	31	34·9	Cloudy. Clear.	. .
13			50	40	45·8	35	33	34·6	Cloudy.	. .
14			46	39	42·2	38	38	35·9	Cloudy, slight rain.	. .
15	In Hecla Cove.		39	33	37·0	36	34	34·7	Foggy.	. .
16	79 55 8	16 48 45	50	40	46·1	40	37	38·7	Fine, clear.	. .
17			49	43	46·9	46	34	40·9	Fine, clear.	. .
18			54	47	51·1	43	37	40·4	Fine, clear.	. .
19			55	44	48·1	44	38	40·8	Cloudy.	. .
20			37	34½	36·2	39½	37	37·6	Thick fog, and rain.	. .
21			40	36	38·2	37	34	36·2	Cloudy.	. .
22			42	36	39·8	38	31	36·0	Fine, and clear.	. .
23			42	38	39·8	37	35	36·5	Cloudy.	. .
24			41	35	37·9	38	36	37·1	Cloudy.	. .
25			42	37	39·8	39	37	37·8	Cloudy.	. .
26			36	32	34·6	37	34	35·7	Cloudy.	. .
27			45	38	38·4	38	35	36·9	Cloudy.	. .
28			42	35	38·1	38	34	36·2	Cloudy.	. .
29			34	34	33·6	36	32½	34·4	Snow and sleet.	. .
30			34	33	32·8	35	33	34·1	Snow, and sleet	. .
31			38	33	35·9	37	35	35·4	Cloudy, and rain.	. .
			55	32	40·19	46½	30	35·43		

HECLA, IN HECLA COVE, SPITZBERGEN, DURING THE MONTH OF JULY, 1827.

Prevailing Winds		REMARKS, &c.
Direction	Velocity.	
NNE.	Light.	* Mean height of thermometer exposed to the ☉, registered 12 times from noon till mid. 57°.5. Sky generally clear.
Northerly.	Light.	* Mean height of ther. exposed to the ☉ from mid. till noon, registered 12 times 51°.5. Sun nearly obscured towards noon.
Easterly.	Moderate.	
NWesterly.	Moderate.	
Northerly.	Light.	
A.M. NWesterly. P.M. Easterly.	Light. Fresh	
SSE.	Fresh.	
SEasterly.	Fresh.	
SEasterly.	Fresh, and squally.	
A.M. Easterly. P.M. NWesterly.	Moderate. Light.	
SEasterly.	A.M. Fresh. P.M. Strong gales.	
A.M. SWesterly. P.M. Easterly.	Fresh. Moderate.	
SE.	Fresh.	
Easterly.	Light.	
Northerly.	Light.	
A.M. Calm. P.M. NNW.	Light.	* Mean height of thermometer exposed to the ☉ from 8 A.M. till mid. registered 15 times 75°.0. Sky generally very bright. Daniell's hygrometer shewed a mean dew point of 41°.1 in 15 observations made between 8 A.M. and midnight, the mean temperature of the air being, for the same times, 46°.5.
Round the compass.	Light.	
A.M. NWesterly. P.M. SW.	Light. Moderate.	
A.M. Calm. P.M. NNW.	Light.	
NNE.	Light.	
Easterly.	Fresh.	
A.M. ESE. P.M. West.	Strong gales. Fresh.	Mean height of ther. exposed to the ☉ registered 15 times from 5 A.M. till mid. 50.4. Sun partially clouded.
Easterly.	A.M. Light. P.M. Moderate.	
East.	Light.	Fog at times.
West.	Moderate.	Fog, rain, and snow at times.
West.	Light.	Rain and snow.
A.M. Calm. P.M. Easterly.	Moderate.	
SSE.	Moderate.	
NNE.	Strong.	
NNW.	A.M. Fresh gales. P.M. Moderate.	
SE.	Light.	

* The bulb of the thermometer covered with black wool.

Y 2

ABSTRACT OF THE METEOROLOGICAL JOURNAL KEPT ON BOARD HIS MAJESTY'S SHIP

Days	North Latitude.	East Longitude.	Temperature of Air in Shade, registered every 2 hours.			Temperature of Sea Water at Surface, registered every 2 hours.					
			Maximum.	Minimum.	Mean.	Maximum.	Minimum.	Mean.			
August 1			49·5	36	38·0	37	35	36·9	.	.	.
„ 2			43	38	40·2	40	35·5	37·8	.	.	.
„ 3			45	39	41 0	40	38	39·0	.	.	.
„ 4			47·5	37·5	42·2	42	39	40·2	.	.	.
„ 5			47	40	42·9	41	33	35·0	.	.	.
„ 6			48	40	44·0	34	32	33·2	.	.	.
„ 7			41	37	37·5	36	33	34·8	.	.	.
„ 8			46	38	42·8	42	36	38·6	.	.	.
„ 9			51	39	46·2	41	38	40·0	.	.	.
„ 10			50	39	46·6	42	38	40·0	.	.	.
„ 11			44	35	38·6	42	37	39·5	.	.	.
„ 12			37	32	34·9	39	37	38·1	.	.	.
„ 13	In Hecla Cove.		36	33·5	35·0	38	37	37·7	.	.	.
„ 14	79 55 8	16 48 43	37	32	34·2	38	36	37·5	.	.	.
„ 15			38	36	36·6	39	38	38·2	.	.	.
„ 16			42	33	37·7	38	34	36·8	.	.	.
„ 17			44	37	40·7	39	36	37·8	.	.	.
„ 18			38	32	35,7	38	35	36·8	.	.	.
„ 19			37	35	36·4	36	34	35·8	.	.	.
„ 20			37·5	35	36·6	37	34	35·5	.	.	.
„ 21			37	31·5	35·1	36	35	35·7	.	.	.
„ 22			49	35	37·2	36·5	34	35 5	.	.	.
„ 23			42	34	37·6	38	34·5	36·7	.	.	.
„ 24			42	35	39·5	37·5	37	37·0	.	.	.
„ 25			43	41	41·7	37·5	36	36.9	.	.	.
„ 26			43	34·5	40·0	38	37	37·4	.	.	.
„ 27			33·5	29	31·8	37	35	35·9	.	.	.
„ 28			31	29	30·1	36	34	35·5	.	.	.
„ 29	79 57 15	12 46 15	40	28	35,5	36	36	36·0	.	.	.
„ 30	79 46 40	10 31 0	38	36	36·7	36	31	33·5	.	.	.
„ 31	79 2 19	7 50 0	40	35	37·2	37	32	33·2	.	.	.
			51	28	38.39	42	31	36·83			

ECLA, IN HECLA COVE, SPITZBERGEN, AND AT SEA, DURING THE MONTH OF AUGUST, 1827.

Prevailing Winds.		Weather.	Remarks, &c.
Direction.	Velocity.		
Calm.	. . . . . .	Cloudy.	* At noon, thermometer exposed to the ⊙ 58°.
Round the compass.	Light.	Fine and clear.	
Round the compass.	Light.	Fine and clear.	
SEasterly.	Light.	Fine and clear.	
SEasterly.	Strong gales.	Clear.	* Mean height of thermometer exposed to the sun, registered 20 times, from 5 A.M. till mid. (generally very clear) 57°. 4.
SEasterly.	Strong.	Squally, and clear.	
Westerly.	Moderate.	Cloudy, and rain.	
Calm.	. . . . . .	A.M. Foggy. P.M. Fine and clear.	
A.M. Calm. P.M. North.	Light.	Fine, and clear.	
A.M. Calm. P.M. NW.	Light.	Fine, and clear.	
NE.	Light.	Cloudy, and rain.	
NW.	Light.	Cloudy, rain, and sleet.	
WNW.	Moderate.	Cloudy, snow, and rain.	
A.M. NW. P.M. SW. A.M. SW. P.M. NE. A.M. NE. P.M. Easterly.	Moderate. Light. Light. Fresh. Fresh. Light.	Cloudy, and snow. Fine. Fog over land. Fine, and clear. Cloudy, and snow. Thick, and snow. Fine.	* At 3 A.M. ther. exposed to the sun 63°.
SWesterly.	Light.	Cloudy.	
Westerly.	Fresh.	Hazy, rain, and snow.	
West.	Strong gales.	Cloudy, snow, and rain.	* At 9 A.M. ther. exposed to the ⊙ 59°.
West.	Moderate.	Cloudy. Snow at times.	
Westerly.	Light.	A.M. Foggy. P.M. Fine.	
SWesterly.	Light.	Fine, clear.	* Mean height of thermometer with a blackened bulb exposed to the ⊙ registered 6 times from 9 A.M. till 6 P.M. 84°. 3.
Calm.	. . . . . .	Fine, and clear.	
A.M. NW. P.M. SW.	Light.	Overcast.	
South.	Moderate.	Fine.	
Easterly.	Light.	Cloudy, and rain.	
NNW.	Moderate.	Cloudy, and snow.	
Westerly.	Moderate.	Cloudy, and snow.	
Easterly.	Light.	Fine.	
Easterly.	Moderate.	Cloudy.	
Easterly.	Moderate.	Fine.	

* The bulb of the thermometer covered with black wool.

ABSTRACT OF THE METEOROLOGICAL JOURNAL KEPT ON BOARD HIS MAJESTY'S SHIP HECLA, AT SEA, DURING A PART OF THE MONTH OF SEPTEMBER, 1827.

Days.	North Latitude.	Longitude.	Temperature of Air in shade, registered every 2 hours.			Temperature of Sea Water at Surface, registered every 2 hours.			Prevailing Winds.		Weather.
			Max.	Min.	Mean.	Max.	Min.	Mean.	Direction.	Velocity.	
Sep.	° ′ ″	° ′ ″	°	°	°	°	°	°			
1	77 29 36	8 7 9 E.	38	36	37·0	41	39	40·4	N Westerly.	Fresh.	Cloudy and rain.
2	74 40 54	6 40 54 ,,	37	34	35·8	41	39	40·1	N Westerly.	Moderate.	Cloudy, sleet, and rain.
3	72 13 0	5 59 0 ,,	40	34	36·5	45	39	42·2	WNW.	Strong.	Squally, sleet at times.
4	70 15 48	4 7 6 ,,	45½	38	43·1	47	45½	46·3	West.	Light.	Thick, and rain.
5	69 57 56	3 4 54 ,,	46	44	44·5	46	45	45·4	WNW.	Moderate.	Cloudy.
6	68 41 2	0 58 30 ,,	46	33	44·0	48	45	46·4	N Westerly.	Light.	Overcast.
7	68 11 32	0 22 42 ,,	49	46	47·0	48¼	47¼	48·0	SW.	Moderate.	Foggy.
8	67 56 56	0 33 30 ,,	51	48	49·2	49	47½	48·2	SW.	Fresh.	Hazy.
9	67 32 29	0 51 42 W.	50	48	49·6	48	47	47·8	Southerly.	Fresh.	Cloudy
10	67 5 42	2 58 30 ,,	50½	49	49·4	48½	47	47·8	SSE.	Fresh.	Thick, and rain.
11	66 55 56	3 43 2 ,,	50	48	49·2	48	47	47·5	Southerly.	Fresh.	Thick, with heavy rain.
12	66 33 26	2 27 48 ,,	49	46	48·0	48·5	46	47·7	SWesterly.	Moderate.	Cloudy.
13	64 47 11	0 47 19 ,,	48	43	46·0	51	48	48·8	WNW.	Fresh.	Squally, rain at times.
14	63 46 38	1 2 19 ,,	51	47	49·5	51·5	48	49·2	A M. SSE. P M. SWly.	Fresh. Moderate.	Thick fog, and rain.
15	63 6 2	1 26 19 ,,	51	47	49·2	50	49	49·4	WSW.	Moderate.	Overcast.
16	62 8 26	0 0 0	54	50	52·6	52	49	51·3	SWesterly.	Moderate.	Hazy, and rain.
			54	34	45·62	52	39	46·08			

II.

NOTICE RESPECTING THE CHRONOMETERS EMBARKED ON
BOARD THE HECLA, AND THE DETERMINATION
OF THE LONGITUDES

NOTICE RESPECTING THE CHRONOMETERS, &c.

THE number of Chronometers furnished by Government to the Expedition on this occasion, was six, the whole being pocket watches, of these, Messrs Parkinson and Frodsham were directed to prepare two, the dial plates of which were to have the hours from 1 to 24 marked on them, a precaution intended to provide against the possibility of incurring an error of twelve hours, when travelling over the ice towards the Pole. The rest were directed to be supplied from the Royal Observatory at Greenwich; but it so happened that, a little before the time of embarkation, the chronometers intended for the use of the Expedition were going irregularly,—a circumstance which, at this advanced state of the equipment, would have been attended with very serious inconvenience, had it not been for the liberal offer of Messrs. Parkinson and Frodsham to supply the number required, at their own risk. However, the Lords Commissioners of the Admiralty, on becoming acquainted with the circumstances of the case, immediately directed the chronometers in question to be purchased of Messrs Parkinson and Frodsham, and these, with five others, (three of which belonged to the same makers, the other two to Captain Parry and Lieutenant Foster,) were embarked on board the Hecla at Deptford, on the 24th of March, 1827, where, as in the former voyages to the Arctic Seas, they were placed in small canvas cots, lined with baize, and suspended in Captain Parry's cabin.

The rates being furnished by the makers, the error of each on mean time at Greenwich was ascertained, by comparison with the Observatory clock, on the same day, they were afterwards wound up daily at noon, by Lieutenants Foster and Crozier, and compared with a box Chronometer (No. 259) belonging to Captain Parry, considered as a standard.

The first place at which the Expedition touched, after leaving England, was Hammerfest in Lapland, where observations for the rates and errors of the chronometers on mean time at Fugleness were made, on the 20th and 27th of April, by Captain Parry and Lieutenant Foster   From these observations it was ascertained, that all the watches had in a slight degree altered their rates ; but that a more considerable change had taken place in the rates of four of them; which circumstance had, indeed, been pointed out by the daily comparisons, soon after they were put on board at Deptford.   These four were therefore rejected in the determination of the longitude of this place, which has been calculated from the observations on the 20th, and employing a mean between the rates furnished by the makers, and those obtained here.   The longitude thus deduced from the mean of seven chronometers, in which the greatest difference did not exceed four seconds of time, appears to be 23° 45′ 40.5″ East   This longitude, it may be observed, is almost identical with Captain Sabine's determination in 1823; a coincidence which must be regarded as a satisfactory corroboration of the accuracy of the longitude of Fair Haven, in Spitzbergen, on which the correctness of his measure is stated to depend.

On the arrival of the Hecla on the Western Coast of Spitzbergen on the 13th of May, the six chronometers provided for Captain Parry's use were given to the respective officers of his Expedition, to wear in their pockets , in order that, if their rates should be found to alter by this circumstance, others might be furnished from the daily comparisons with the remaining five, which were still kept in their usual places in the cabin   It is, however, highly creditable to the makers of these excellent chronometers, Messrs. Parkinson and Frodsham, that this precaution proved unnecessary, as each was found to preserve its rate extremely well, except in one instance, when it appeared, that on the 30th of May, one of them, from some unknown cause, stopped whilst in the pocket, this was replaced by another of their construction, which was found to go equally well with the rest

The next station visited by the Expedition, at which the rates of the chronometers were ascertained, was Hecla Cove, on the North Coast of Spitzbergen, where the Hecla arrived on the 19th of June , but, from unavoidable circumstances, the necessary observations were not commenced before the 21st, on which day, Captain Parry set out on his attempt to reach the North Pole,

Z

leaving four of the steadiest-going chronometers on board, by which the meridian distance of this place from Hammerfest was ascertained in the following manner

The error of each chronometer on Greenwich mean time, at noon on the 13th of May, was deduced from the mean of all the watches, by employing the data furnished at Hammerfest, and the daily comparisons of each with No. 259, previously to their being worn in the pocket as already stated. The errors thus computed, being considered the actual errors of the respective watches on Greenwich mean time at noon on the 13th of May, the longitude of Hecla Cove was determined by taking a mean between the observed rates at Hammerfest and Hecla Cove, for their actual rates in the interval between the 13th of May and 21st of June. The longitude of the Flagstaff thus determined, was 16° 52′ 45″ E , but from a subsequent determination, on the arrival of the Expedition in Balta Sound, Shetland, in September, where observations were made in the morning of the 19th, at Mr. Edmonstone's house, Buness*, it was ascertained to be 16° 48′ 45″ E , from the mean of nine chronometers in an interval of twenty-five days. This determination is considered preferable to a mean of both, in consequence of the greater number of watches employed, and the direct manner in which it was obtained

It may also be observed, that the longitudes of the different places laid down in the accompanying Chart of the North Coast of Spitzbergen, are all dependent on the longitude of Hecla Cove, considered as a first meridian ; from which their respective meridian distances were ascertained, by the going of three chronometers in short intervals of time

There being no Longitudes of Places dependent upon the going of the chronometers employed by Captain Parry, it has not been thought necessary to enter at large into the detail of their rates : it is sufficient to mention, that, under the severe trial to which these watches were subjected, the boats made Little Table Island, to a surprising degree of exactness, after an absence of fifty days, as will be seen by reference to the foregoing narrative

---

* The longitude of this spot, from the Trigonometrical Survey of Great Britain, is 0° 51′ 57 3′ W

III.

OBSERVATIONS ON THE DIP OF THE MAGNETIC NEEDLE

OBSERVATIONS ON THE DIP OF THE MAGNETIC NEEDLE

The observations contained in the following Table on the Dip of the Magnetic Needle, were made by Captain Parry and Lieutenant Foster. Those by Captain Parry were obtained with an instrument constructed by Mr. Jones, which was furnished with three rectangular needles, each four inches in length, two-tenths broad, and one-twentieth in thickness ; of these, one was used exclusively for observations on Intensity, the other two for the Dip. There was a line drawn on each of the needles in the direction of their longitudinal axes, which served as an index ; and the graduated circle was divided to every fifteen minutes of a degree, which could be read with tolerable precision to every three minutes Each of the observations in the eighth column of the Table is the mean of five readings with the face of the instrument on each side of the meridian, and the needles reversed on their axes in the two positions.

The observations by Lieutenant Foster were made with an instrument be-longing to the Board of Longitude, which was constructed by Dollond; it had also three needles, each of which was a parallelopipedon six inches long, four-tenths broad, and one-twentieth in thickness · of these, one was selected for the observations on Intensity, and, consequently, its poles were never inverted, nor its magnetism in other respects interfered with , the other two were employed for the Dip, the results of which, given in the eighth column, are the mean of six readings with the face of the instrument on each side of the vertical, and the needles reversed on their axes in the two positions, both before and after inverting their poles. Besides these observations, the Dip was also deduced by the Intensity needle, in the usual way, without reversing the poles, as well as from the times it required to perform a certain number of vertical and horizontal oscillations in the meridian, at the different places of observation

In consequence of the needles employed for Intensity by each observer, having lost part of their magnetism during the voyage, no comparison of the intensity of the force soliciting the Dipping-needle at the different stations visited on this occasion can be made.   It may, however, be useful to state (as evidencing the necessity of employing needles that have been long in use, in preference to new ones for such purposes) the amount of change that each of the needles had undergone.   That employed by Captain Parry made ten vibrations in 23.54 seconds, in March, 1827, at Northfleet; but in October following, it required 25 47 seconds to perform that number, on the same spot.   The needle employed by Lieutenant Foster exhibited a still greater change, the time of its performing ten vibrations, in March, at Northfleet, was 28 93 seconds, but in October, it was 31 33 seconds.   Thus the great changes of Intensity which the needles had themselves suffered, prevent any conclusions being drawn on the Intensity, as above stated

OBSERVATIONS ON THE DIP OF THE MAGNETIC NEEDLE.

Date.	Time.	Latitude North.	Longitude East.	Observer.	Needle.	Temperature of the Instrument.	Observed North Dip.	Mean North Dip.	REMARKS.
1827. March 26	1·30 to 3 P.M.			P	P. 2.	50	69 53·19	} 69 49·24	
,, 27	5·40 ,, 8 A.M.			P	P. 3.	48	69 45·29		
,, ,,	10·37 ,, 11·45 A.M.			F	F. 2.	48	69 54·2		In a field near the River Thames.
,, ,,	Noon ,, 1·5 P.M.	. At North fleet . .		F	F. 1.	49	69 43·2		
,, ,,	1·20 ,, 1·48 P.M.			F	F. 3.	48	69 43·5	} 69 46·8	
,, ,,	2·28 ,, 4·52 P.M.			F	F. 3.	47·2	69 46·8	. . . . .	By horizontal and vertical vibrations.
April 20	5·18 ,, 6·35 P.M.			F	F. 1.	31	77 7·3		
,, ,,	6·53 ,, 8·8 P.M.			F	F. 2.	29·5	77 20·6	} 77 0·53	
,, 21	10·8 ,, 10·35 A.M.			F	F. 3.	99·5	76 51·74		
,, ,,	4·30 ,, 5·50 P.M.	At Fagleness, Hammerfest.		F	F. 3.	28	76 39·5	. . . . .	By horizontal and vertical vibrations.
,, 20	4·30 ,, 6·30 P.M.	70 40 8	23 45 40	P	P. 2.	30·5	77 51·85		
,, ,,	6·30 ,, 7·50 P.M.			P	P. 1.	31	77 3·83	} 77 23·78	
,, 21	9 ,, 11 A.M.			P	P. 3.	29·5	77 40·18		
,, 21	10 ,, 11·30 A.M.			P	P. 2.	39	77 16·28		
July 5	7 A.M.	81 45 15	24 33 7	P	P. 2.	31	82 4·71	82 4·71	On the ice.
,, 12	8 to 9 A.M.	82 14 28	22 3 53	P	P. 2.	37·5	82 16·26	82 16·26	Ditto.
,, 21	7 ,, 8·30 A.M.	82 39 10	19 52 18	P	P. 2.	34	82 21·85	82 21·85	Ditto.
,, 26	7·15 P.M.	82 40 23	19 25 3	R	P. 2.	35	82 21·79	} 82 21·63	Ditto.
,, 27	1 to 2 A.M.			P	P. 3.	31½	82 21·47		
Aug. 14	7 ,, 9 A.M.	80 34 30	19 52 0	P	P. 2.	37	81 21·19	81 21·19	On the south-east point of Walden Island (Spitzbergen).
,, 15	8 ,, 9·30 P.M.	80 17 10	18 12 15	P	P. 2.	35	81 22·87	81 22·87	West point of Low Island (ditto).
July 3	10 ,, 10·35 A.M.			P	F. 3.	51½	80 40·16		
,, ,,	1·50 ,, 3·20 P.M.			P	F. 2.	48	80 47·9	} 80 45·91	
,, ,,	6·30 ,, 7·30 P.M.	Hecla Cove.		F	F. 1.	42·3	80 45·88		
,, 5	3·22 ,, 5·34 P.M.	79 55 8	16 48 43	F	F. 3.	66	80 49·7	. . . . .	By horizontal and vertical vibrations.
Aug. 22	4·15 ,, 5·30 P.M.			P	P. 2.	41	81 0·28	} 81 4·58	
,, ,,	3 ,, 5 P.M.			P	P. 3.	36	81 8·80		
Oct. 8	9·30 ,, 11·25 A.M.			F	P. 2.	60½	70 2·4	} 69 53·4	
,, ,,	11·30 A.M. to 0·50 P.M.			F	P. 3.	61½	69 44·4		
,, ,,	10·00 ,, 11·30 A.M.	. At North fleet . . .		C	F. 2.	61	69 28·2		In a field near the River Thames.
,, ,,	Noon ,, 1·20 P.M.			C	F. 1.	57½	69 51·3	} 69 50·1	
,, 9	9·40 ,, 10·10 A.M.			F	F. 3.	60	70 3·5		
,, ,,	1·30 P.M. to 2·50			P	F. 3.	60½	69 55·5	. . . . .	By horizontal and vertical vibrations.

IV.

OBSERVATIONS ON THE VARIATION OF THE MAGNETIC NEEDLE MADE ON SHORE, OR ON THE ICE, 1827.

Note — The initials in the Column of " Observer" are

P	Captain Parry
R	Lieutenant Ross
F	Lieutenant Foster
C	Lieutenant Crozier

OBSERVATIONS ON THE VARIATION OF THE MAGNETIC NEEDLE, MADE ON SHORE,
OR ON THE ICE, 1827.

DATE.	Time.	Latitude North.	Longitude East.	Observer.	No. of Observations.	Kater's Compass.	Westerly Variation. Observed.	Mean.	REMARKS
1827.		° ′ ″	° ′ ″			No	° ′ ″	° ′ ″	
April 21	3.50 P.M.	69 57 37	23 26	C	2	2	9 31		At Bosecop, Lapland.
„ 22	7.47 A.M.			C	5	2	10 18	9 54 30	
„ 23	6.0 „			P	5	4	10 31		
„ „	6.30 „			P	5	1	10 37		
„ „	2.0 P.M.			F	6	1	10 48		
„ „	2.15 „			F	6	1	16 0		
„ „	2.20 „			F	6	4	10 39 36		
„ „	2.30 „	70 40 8	23 45 40	F	6	4	10 9 36	10 14 12	At Fugleness, Hammerfest.
„ 24	6.0 A.M.			F	6	1	10 8		
„ „	6.15 „			F	6	1	9 45		
„ „	7.50 „			P	5	5	10 12		
„ „	8.0 „			P	5	3	9 13		
„ 27	7.40 „			P	6	5	10 31		
May 17	8.12 „	79 56 30	13 18	F	10	1	22 42	22 42 0	On ice, 300 yards N.E. of the ship.
June 2	9.28 „	79 52 40	14 34	F	6	1	21 12	21 12 0	On ice, 300 yards N. of the ship.
„ 6	6.30 „	79 49 0	15 25	F	7	1	18 51	18 51 0	Ditto ditto.
„ 8	5.11 P.M.	79 49 38	15 36	P	6	1	18 18	18 10 30	200 yards S.E. of the ship, upon the ice.
„ „	5.19 „			P	7	1	18 2 30		
„ 16	2.0 „	80 35 38	19 51 16	F	4	1	17 31	17 42 0	On shore, N.E. point of Walden Island,
„ „	2.15 „			P	6	1	17 53		Spitzbergen.
„ 29	7 A.M.	81 22 0	21 32 54	R	5	3	15 39 52	15 30 56	On the ice.
„ „	7.6 „			P	5	3	15 21		
July 5	7.0 „	81 45 15	24 23 7	P	5	3	12 33	13 15 44	Ditto.
„ „				R	5	3	13 58 28		
„ 10	6.46 „	82 3 20	23 17 16	R	5	3	13 41 11	13 41 11	Ditto.
„ 12	6.3 „	82 14 28	22 8 53	P	6	3	15 13	15 6 1	Ditto.
„ „	6.17 „			R	5	3	14 59 18		
„ 16	7.26 „	82 26 44	20 32 13	R	5	3	16 45 15	17 27 37	Ditto.
„ „	7.30 „			P	5	3	18 10		
„ 21	7 10 „	82 39 10	19 52 13	R	5	3	19 4 33	19 4 33	Ditto.
„ 26	6.0 „	82 40 23	19 25 3	P	5	3	17 57	18 9 53	Ditto.
„ „	6.3 „			R	5	3	18 22 17		
„ 31	6.40 P.M.	82 14 25	17 18 19	P	3	3	22 30	22 28 16	Ditto.
„ „	6.44 „			R	5	3	22 16 33		
Aug. 2	7.0 A.M.	82 6 0	17 45 33	R	6	3	20 46 54	20 46 54	Ditto.
„ 4	6.31 „	81 57 31	17 56 23	R	5	3	20 18 20	20 24 48	Ditto.
„ „	6.35 „			P	7	3	20 31 17		
July 30	4.0 P.M.			F	6	1	19 53		
Aug. 9	5.16 A.M.			P	6	1	18 53		
„ „	5.48 „			F	6	1	18 3		
„ 10	1.0 P.M.			C	10	1	19 9		
„ „	1.15 „			C	10	1	19 6		
„ „	5 to 6 P.M.			C	10	2	18 48		
				C	10	2	18 58		At the Observatory, Hecla Cove, Spitz-
„ 15	2 to 3 „	79 55 8	16 53 40	C	10	4	18 22	18 46 12	bergen.
				C	10	4	18 8		
				C	10	4	18 27		
				C	10	4	18 56		
„ 16	9 to 10.30 A.M.			C	10	4	19 17		
				C	10	4	19 1		
„ 20	9 to 10 „			C	10	4	18 27		
				C	10		18 2		
„ 14	11.38 P.M.	79 54 50	17 29 0	F	5	1	17 43	17 49 0	On shore, entrance to Waygatz Strait.
„ 16	0 26 „	79 36 46	17 53 55	F	5	1	17 21	17 20 0	On shore in Bear Bay, Waygatz Strait.
„ 20	11.44 A.M.	79 34 50	19 17 0	F	8	1	15 10	15 10 0	On shore, on one of Foster's Islands, do.

V.

LIEUTENANT (NOW COMMANDER) FOSTER'S ACCOUNT OF THE
OBSERVATIONS BY LIEUTENANT CROZIER AND HIMSELF,
ON THE DIURNAL VARIATION OF THE HORIZONTAL
MAGNETIC NEEDLE AT SPITZBERGEN, 1827

ACCOUNT OF THE OBSERVATIONS ON THE DIURNAL VARIATION OF THE HORIZONTAL MAGNETIC NEEDLE AT SPITZBERGEN, 1827

THE only opportunity which the present voyage afforded for observations of this nature, was at Hecla Cove, on the North Coast of Spitzbergen, where His Majesty's Ship Hecla remained during the absence of Captain Parry, in his attempt to reach the North Pole. It is to be regretted that, in consequence of the interference of other duties, these observations were not continued longer than eleven days; they were, however, carefully made by Lieutenant Crozier and myself, with an instrument the property of the Board of Longitude, constructed by Mr. Dollond, and which former experience had enabled me to contrive. It is chiefly composed of wood and ivory, without metal of any kind, the needle six inches long, and very light, is suspended within a cubical box having glass sides, by a silk fibre fifteen inches in length, passing over a pulley at the top of the box, and having an exact counterpoise of ivory for the whole weight of the needle attached to its other extremity. In the top of the box, a compound microscope is fitted directly over each end of the needle; in both these microscopes a fine wire is also fixed in the common focus of their respective glasses, so that at the time of observation, the wires are brought to coincide successively with the line drawn on the north and south ends of the needle. The reading is on opposite arcs of a circle of thirteen inches radius, divided into spaces of ten minutes, which are again subdivided into ten seconds, by means of verniers attached to the box, and moving with the microscopes.

This instrument, which was found to answer the purpose extremely well, was secured to a firm support, fixed into the ground, and was protected from the weather by a square canvas tent, placed in a situation remote from any local interference. Both ends of the needle were observed and recorded; but the *mean* of these observations only is inserted in the following Table. The zero of the scale being placed to the East of North, the higher numbers indicate the greatest westerly position of the north end of the needle, and the lower numbers the most eastern limit of the same. In deducing the amount of the maximum easterly and westerly daily change, I have assumed for the direction of the magnetic meridian, or zero of the scale, the mean of the readings at the hours when the sun bore North and South by compass, and which was found to be 2° 19′ 12″ Employing this zero, it appears that the needle is deflected more to the East than to the West of the magnetic meridian ; a circumstance, the reverse of that which took place in our observations at Port Bowen It will also be seen on looking over these observations, that the amount of the daily variation was generally about 1° 32′, varying from 2° 48′, to 0° 52′ ; and that from the mean of all the observations, the time of maximum easterly variation occurred at about half past four A M., and of the maximum westerly at about five, P M The times on each day, however, at which these phenomena have been observed to take place, have varied in the easterly position of the needle from 1ʰ to 7ʰ A M., and from 1ʰ to 9ʰ P M , in its westerly direction. It is, nevertheless, a coincidence worthy of notice, that the means of these times thus obtained, should correspond with the times of the day when the sun is East and West by compass.

Besides these observations, another series on this subject was made at the same time by Lieutenant Crozier and myself, with a needle having its directive force reduced in the ratio of 0.09 to 1 nearly, by the application of a powerful bar magnet , with a view to ascertain precisely the hours of the day, at which the needle successively arrived at its greatest easterly and westerly positions The great amount, however, of the diurnal changes in the direction of the horizontal needle that we found at this place, has rendered these observations of less importance than would otherwise have been the case, had its amount not exceeded two or three minutes of a degree. It will, therefore, be sufficient to state, that the times of maximum effect by this needle, agree on most occasions with those deduced from the above observations , and that the discrepancies in this respect, are doubtless attributable to the circumstances which I have already pointed out in the *Phil Trans* for 1826, viz., from the observations on each needle not being made simultaneously, as well as from the minuteness of some of the phenomena which affect the needle, being only observable when its directive energy is nearly neutralized.

2 A 2

OBSERVATIONS ON THE DIURNAL VARIATION OF

	A.M.											
Mean Temp.	° 43·8	° 41	° 43·7	° 43·9	° 44·6	° 45·6	° 47·4	° 19	° 51·8	° 53·3	° 53·4	° 53·5
Hour	h 1	h 2	h 3	h 4	h 5	h 6	h 7	h 8	h 9	h 10	h 11	h 12
DATE	Position of North end of Needle.	Position of North end of Needle.	Position of North end of Needle.	Position of North end of Needle.	Position of North end of Needle.	Position of North end of Needle.	Position of North end of Needle.	Position of North end of Needle.	Position of North end of Needle.	Position of North end of Needle.	Position of North end of Needle.	Position of North end of Needle.
July 30	2 18 30	2 00 55	1 33 55	1 10 42	1 42 32	1 51 55	2 3 27	1 50 32	2 17 20	2 15 47	2 6 12	2 2 55
,, 31	1 37 36	1 48 55	1 53 17	0 58 20	0 21 7	1 48 27	1 55 5	2 11 36	2 6 55	2 5 42	2 9 35	2 12 55
August 1	1 55 22	2 1 20	1 57 25	1 57 25	1 52 40	2 2 32	1 50 27	1 56 35	1 58 17	2 1 40	2 1 30	2 9 27
,, 2	2 13 27	2 21 15	1 56 5	1 37 22	1 36 00	1 48 45	2 00 35	2 2 30	2 7 00	2 25 43	2 27 30	2 28 27
,, 3	1 59 5	2 00 15	2 2 23	2 19 35	1 48 00	1 10 42	1 44 22	2 20 25	2 10 15	2 19 19	2 23 27	2 26 50
,, 4	2 1 47	1 55 15	1 57 35	1 56 37	1 59 45	1 46 45	1 52 50	1 51 35	1 58 42	2 10 20	2 20 15	2 27 59
,, 5	1 43 57	1 46 47	1 13 00	1 2 59	1 13 22	1 40 40	1 53 27	1 52 25	1 55 40	1 54 57	1 47 22	1 56 25
,, 6	2 29 10	2 00 27	1 49 2	1 57 57	1 51 37	1 49 27	2 7 22	2 32 47	1 56 50	2 18 27	2 19 32	2 19 32
,, 7	1 53 35	2 00 52	1 56 32	1 53 40	2 2 5	2 09 52	2 9 30	2 1 2	2 16 45	2 13 45	2 20 52	2 27 00
,, 8	2 27 25	2 6 47	1 42 7	1 29 7	1 35 52	1 57 5	2 7 22	1 58 45	2 12 45	2 4 49	2 15 12	2 28 22
,, 9	2 1 40	1 51 57	1 21 0	1 5 52	1 24 17	1 25 42	1 34 20	1 45 22	2 1 15	2 10 09	2 1 52	2 14 2
Mean .	2 6 11	1 59 45	1 45 55	1 35 21	1 35 12	1 45 41	1 56 48	2 3 12	2 5 37	2 11 13	2 12 23	2 17 87

THE HORIZONTAL MAGNETIC NEEDLE AT SPITZBERGEN, 1827.

					P.M.							RESULTS.		
54·1	58·9	58·8	52·7	52	51·1	50	50	48·4	47·3	45·8	45·5	Maximum Easterly.	Maximum Westerly.	Total Amount of Daily Variation
h 1	h 2	h 3	h 4	h 5	h 6	h 7	h 8	h 9	h 10	h 11	h 12			
Position of North end of Needle.	Position of North end of Needle.	Position of North end of Needle.	Position of North end of Needle.	Position of North end of Needle.	Position of North end of Needle.	Position of North end of Needle.	Position of North end of Needle.	Position of North end of Needle.	Position of North end of Needle.	Position of North end of Needle.	Position of North end of Needle.	Times A.M.	Amount of Easterly Variation	Times P.M.	Amount of Westerly Variation	Amount of Daily Variation
o ′ ″	o ′ ″	o ′ ″	o ′ ″	o ′ ″	o ′ ″	o ′ ″	o ′ ″	o ′ ″	o ′ ″	o ′ ″	o ′ ″	h	o ′ ″	h	o ′ ″	o ′ ″
2 1 5	2 39 7	2 13 20	2 34 23	2 13 32	2 56 15	3 16 12	2 41 17	2 51 15	2 49 55	2 16 00	2 26 15	4	1 8 33	7	0 57 00	2 5 30
2 31 10	3 3 17	3 8 55	3 2 31	2 47 32	2 36 42	2 43 37	2 52 57	2 56 12	2 41 22	2 27 5	2 00 25	5	1 38 5	3	0 19 13	2 17 18
2 20 17	2 28 26	2 35 30	2 42 42	2 43 5	2 45 55	2 35 50	2 42 37	2 21 47	2 33 42	2 30 15	2 28 15	7	0 25 15	7	0 30 88	1 5 23
2 20 42	2 53 25	2 31 53	2 30 00	2 37 00	2 19 25	2 50 15	2 41 03	2 29 47	2 28 17	2 29 27	2 3 32	5	0 43 12	7	0 34 13	1 17 25
2 33 12	2 36 52	2 28 50	2 19 10	2 12 12	2 23 55	2 21 7	2 18 37	2 39 45	2 11 42	2 00 52	1 58 25	6	1 8 30	9	0 21 13	1 29 3
2 41 50	2 35 52	2 31 47	2 29 42	2 28 27	2 13 00	2 15 27	2 17 7	2 31 30	2 96 55	2 35 06	2 24 50	6	0 32 27	1	0 22 28	0 55 7
2 21 35	2 28 35	3 4 55	3 14 32	2 52 27	2 13 32	2 40 10	3 11 5	2 53 52	2 59 12	3 37 37	2 55 57	4	1 16 22	4	0 55 20	2 11 42
2 31 55	2 35 10	2 26 15	2 27 00	2 29 5	2 41 42	2 31 52	2 19 35	2 40 57	2 16 47	2 19 40	2 2 47	3	0 23 16	6	1 22 33	0 72 40
2 28 25	2 20 60	2 20 7	2 26 7	2 24 49	2 29 42	2 52 37	2 31 53	2 9 5	2 34 17	2 7 52	1 48 55	1	0 25 37	7	0 33 55	0 59 2
2 36 15	2 41 45	2 31 55	2 30 52	2 53 10	2 45 00	2 51 42	2 47 7	2 10 32	2 13 40	2 41 37	2 18 45	1	0 30 8	5	0 84 58	1 24 3
2 32 35	2 41 15	2 59 55	2 53 52	2 30 55	2 14 27	2 14 27	2 32 55	2 25 20	2 17 45	2 10 40	2 0 32	1	1 13 24	4	0 34 40	1 48 0
2 27 17	3 38 42	2 37 5	2 49 57	2 39 10	2 39 8	2 43 56	2 38 20	2 36 33	2 29 27	2 23 15	2 12 32	4·27	0 55 55	5·00	0 36 25	1 32 20

VI.

LIEUTENANT (NOW COMMANDER) FOSTER'S ACCOUNT OF THE
OBSERVATIONS ON THE DIURNAL CHANGES OF INTENSITY
IN THE HORIZONTAL MAGNETIC NEEDLE,
AT SPITZBERGEN, 1827.

OBSERVATIONS ON THE DIURNAL CHANGES OF INTENSITY IN THE HORIZONTAL MAGNETIC NEEDLE, AT SPITZBERGEN, 1827.

THESE observations were also made by Lieutenant Crozier and myself, with an instrument belonging to the Board of Longitude, and made by Dollond This instrument consists of a mahogany box, the dimensions of which are thirteen inches by nine inches and a half, inside, on its bottom, is pasted a graduated circle of paper, for the purpose of measuring the extent of the arc of vibration of the needle, when suspended by a silk fibre passing through a small perforation in the top of the box, directly over its centre, there is also a square pane of glass, inserted into two of the sides of the box, through which the needle is seen and its vibrations counted. The needle is a parallelopipedon, six inches long, four tenths broad, and one twentieth in thickness; the ends are rounded, and in its centre is permanently fixed a brass arm, having a notch in its extremity made to receive a groove in the stirrup attached to the silk fibre, by which it is suspended the brass arm being of such a length that the point of suspension is so much above the centre of gravity of the needle, that its horizontality is preserved throughout all degrees of dip, a method which is considered less objectionable than the usual way of sliding the needle into a stirrup until it becomes horizontal at the different places of observation

The box was mounted upon a board, fitted with foot screws made of ivory, and the whole apparatus was placed on a firm support within a large square tent made of canvas, the frame work of which was entirely composed of wood. Previous to the commencement of the observations, the silk thread (eleven inches long) was, in the first instance, divested of torsion, by suspending a brass needle of like form, and of equal weight with that above described, after which it was removed, and the magnetized needle, having its north and south extremities in the direction of the magnetic meridian, was placed in its stead, and its centre brought directly over the centre of the circle, by means of the foot screws already mentioned. The needle being thus freely suspended, it was drawn out of the magnetic meridian somewhat more than forty degrees, by a contrivance fitted for that purpose; but its oscillations were not noted until the arc had decreased to forty degrees, at which time the observations were commenced on the times of its performing ten vibrations successively, until 200 were completed, when the terminal arc and the temperature of the instrument were registered.

The following table contains the observations; in explanation of which it may be necessary to state that the mean arcs, and mean temperatures, and the mean of the middle times of observation only, are inserted at the head of the different columns containing the times employed by the needle to perform 200 vibrations. In consequence, however, of the irregularity in the times of the day when the maximum and minimum intensities have occurred, I have appended to the Table, under the head of " Results," a few more columns in which are inserted the different times of the day that such effects have been observed to take place, together with the number of seconds required by the needle to perform 200 vibrations, under such circumstances. On looking over these columns, it will be seen that the maximum and minimum intensities have respectively occurred between the hours of $1^h 55^m$ A M and $3^h 41^m$ P M. , and between $3^h 54^m$ A M and $11^h 45^m$ P.M., without any sort of uniformity , the mean being for the time of maximum intensity $10^h 20^m$ A M. and for the minimum $12^h 17^m$ P M. The mean of these two times ($11^h 18^m$) is not very distant from the time when the sun is on the north and south magnetic meridians. It will also be seen, that the mean amount of the daily change of horizontal intensity of the needle is about $\frac{1}{12}$ part of the time of its vibration, varying, however, from $\frac{1}{27}$ to $\frac{1}{50}$ part of the same · and also that the intensity from day to day (as determined by the means of all the times of the needle performing 200 vibrations throughout the twenty-four hours) is subject to a considerable change; to exhibit which more clearly, I have converted these times into proportional intensities, by squaring the reciprocals of those times, and multiplying them by 1000000, to render them all integral, as shown in the column assigned for them in the Table

2 B

TABLE, SHOWING THE HOURLY CHANGES OF HORIZONTAL INTENSITY

A.M.

Mean Arc	25°	25°.7	25°.2	25°.3	25°.2	25°	25°.8	25°.3	26°.1	25°.9	25°.8	25°.6
Mean Temperature	47°.3	41°.7	44°.5	45°.2	45°.7	46°.1	48°	49°	52°.7	52°.0	52°.1	51°.8
Hour	h m 1·1	h m 1·55	h m 2·54	h m 3·51	h m 4·54	h m 5·51	h m 6·54	h m 7·42	h m 9·19	h m 9·58	h m 10·57	h m 11·56
DATE.	Time of performing 200 Vib.	Time of performing 200 Vib.	Time of performing 200 Vib.	Time of performing 200 Vib.	Time of performing 200 Vib.	Time of performing 200 Vib.	Time of performing 200 Vib.	Time of performing 200 Vib.	Time of performing 200 Vib.	Time of performing 200 Vib.	Time of performing 200 Vib.	Time of performing 200 Vib.
July 30	......	1235·0	1240·3	1241·8	1238·0	1237·5	1238·8	1238·8	......	1240·7	1238·5	1230·0
	......	......	......	......	......	......	......	......	......	1239·5	1231·9	1229·0
„ 31	......	1239·6	1234·3	1239·5	1264·1	1243·4	1211·5	1240·9	1237·3	......	......	......
	......	1241·5	1256·4	1263·3	1250·9	1242·5	1240·9	......	......	1232·2	1225·1	1220·1
August 1	1239·6	1237·2	1235·5	1236·6	1239·0	1237·8	1239·0	1238·8	1243·1	1237·1	1237·7	1229·9
	......	......	......	......	......	......	......	......	......	1238·6	1232·9	1237·4
„ 2	1233·4	1237·1	1231·7	1242·8	1240·5	1215·3	1241·0	1241·8	......	1240·5	1242·4	1238·0
	......	1237·3	1231·5	1216·3	1241·7	1243·4	1242·5	......	......	......	......	......
„ 3	1239·6	1237·6	1239·8	1239·5	1233·8	1235·5	1250·8	1210·0	1216·8	1248·2	1246·8	1245·3
	......	......	......	......	......	......	......	......	......	1242·7	1243·7	1242·1
„ 4	1236·9	1240·2	1240·5	1242·3	1241·9	1238·9	1243·8	1241·7	1240·5	1237·0	1238·5	1239·0
	......	1241·7	1283·2	1240·3	1238·2	1238·0	1241·2	......	......	......	......	......
„ 5	1240·0	1211·7	1239·0	1237·0	1240·4	1236·8	1232·8	1242·3	1233·7	1233·2	1233·1	1231·3
	......	......	......	......	......	......	......	......	......	1233·9	1233·0	1234·8
„ 6	1240·0	1234·6	1230·7	1232·1	1231·0	1238·4	1239·4	1234·4	1233·2	1230·7	1228·0	1226·5
	......	1235·2	1230·3	1230·2	1231·9	1230·1	1232·7	......	......	......	......	......
„ 7	1237·8	1240·7	1239·3	1241·8	1240·0	1240·3	1240·6	1240·5	......	1240·4	1241·2	1236·9
	......	......	......	......	......	......	......	......	......	1241·6	1233·7	1237·3
„ 8	1235·8	1237·7	1231·5	1235·2	1245·7	1244·3	1241·6	1240·7	1236·4	1239·8	1237·0	1236·0
	......	1234·0	1236·7	1244·0	1245·1	1242·4	1242·9	......	......	......	......	......
„ 9	1248·0	1245·0	1216·5	1250·7	1246·3	1241·3	1248·5	1246·1	1242·9	1240·8	1238·2	1239·2
	......	......	......	......	......	......	......	......	......	1240·0	1238·2	1241·2
* Mean	1239·0	1239·7	1236·6	1241·6	1242·7	1240·5	1240·8	1240·5	1239·2	1238·3	1236·8	1234·3
Prop. Intensity	6514	6517	6539	6487	6475	6498	6495	6498	6512	6521	6537	6564

* From these Means it appears that the Maximum Intensity has taken plac[e]

OF A MAGNETIZED NEEDLE AT SPITZBERGEN, 1827.

P.M.												RESULTS				
25·3	25·5	25·6	25·6	25·6	25·7	25·6	25·7	25·6	25·6	25·3			Maximum Intensity		Minimum Intensity	
52·2	52·4	52·5	52·7	50·3	52·0	49·7	50·6	49·8	18·0	47·6				Number of Seconds turned to make one Vibration		Number of Seconds taken to make one Vibration
h m 0·51	h m 1·55	h m 2·54	h m 3·41	h m 5·54	h m 6·44	h m 8·10	h m 8·56	h m 9·53	h m 10·54	h m 11·45		Times.		Times.	
Time of performing 300 Vib.	Time of performing 300 Vib.	Time of performing 300 Vib.	Time of performing 300 Vib.	Time of performing 300 Vib.	Time of performing 300 Vib.	Time of performing 300 Vib.	Time of performing 300 Vib.	Time of performing 300 Vib.	Time of performing 300 Vib.	Time of performing 300 Vib.					
s. 1230·6	s. 1227·8	s. 1223·8	s. 1223·2	s. 1227·2	s.	s.	s.	s. 1230·0	s. 1230·2	s.	1231·8	6561	2·54 P.M.	1222·6	10·54 P.M.	1242·2
1229·1	1223·7	1222·6	......	1233·3	......	1231·2	1231·6	......	1242·2	1240·8	1238·9	6515	11·56 A.M.	1229·1	8·54 A.M.	1265·5
1222·1	1226·5	1238·3	1211·0	1233·3	1234·3	......	1236·9	1240·9	1236·7	1236·7						
......	......	......	......	1233·5	......	1232·7	1240·2	1240·9	1238·5	......	1233·9	6568	0·54 P.M.	1223·3	9·49 A.M.	1245·1
1223·9	1235·4	1226·0	1232·3	1234·1	......	......	1235·8	1231·2	1231·5	......						
1223·9	1226·0	1231·4	......	......	1233·7	1234·8	......	......	......	1235·0	1235·8	6511	2·54 A.M.	1231·5	4·54 A.M.	1249·5
1233·2	1237·6	1235·6	1238·0	1243·9	1238·1	......	1235·2	1239·3	1239·7	1236·8						
......	......	......	......	1240·0	......	......	1240·0	1237·0	1237·9	......	1240·4	6499	4·54 A.M.	1233·8	6·54 A.M.	1250·8
1246·0	1236·5	1239·3	1240·8	......	1240·5	1239·5	1239·6	1242·2	1236·5	1231·6						
1238·1	1236·1	1235·8	......	......	......	......	......	......	......	......	1241·9	6484	3·41 P.M.	1236·8	6·41 P.M.	1251·7
1238·5	......	1238·0	1236·8	1247·0	1251·7	......	1247·0	1241·5	1250·2	1242·8						
......	1238·0	......	......	1247·6	......	1246·9	1245·3	1243·5	1245·5	......	1239·0	6514	11·56 A.M.	1231·3	1·55 P.M.	1251·8
1238·1	1246·0	1247·9	1241·9	1238·4	1235·4	1241·4	1239·3	1239·3	1236·7	......						
1241·1	1251·3	1247·6	......	......	......	......	......	......	......	1236·8	1231·7	6569	11·56 A.M.	1226·5	8·56 P.M.	1240·9
1229·4	1239·6	1233·7	1240·7	1240·1	1237·1	1237·3	1238·4	1236·8	1239·2	1238·3						
......	......	......	......	1236·4	......	......	1240·2	1237·9	1236·4	......	1238·3	6521	1·39 P.M.	1221·5	11·45 P.M.	1216·2
1237·0	1281·5	1237·6	1238·8	1238·3	1238·4	......	1236·6	1256·2	1235·5	1246·2						
1234·2	1235·7	1239·3	......	......	......	1236·0	......	......	......	......	1241·0	6493	1·55 A.M.	1231·0	5·54 P.M.	1251·4
1235·7	1235·2	1211·2	1239·9	1245·5	1250·1	......	1244·8	1243·5	1243·0	1239·5						
......	......	......	......	1251·4	......	1246·3	1243·8	1212·7	1241·6	......	1242·8	6474	10·57 A.M.	1238·2	3·54 A.M.	1250·7
1240·8	1211·8	1243·3	1239·2	1243·2	......	......	1243·0	1243·6	1239·7	1239·0						
1243·1	1243·1	1240·4	......	......	1245·2	1243·8	......	......	......	......						
1234·6	1235·6	1236·8	1237·1	1240·1	1240·0	1240·0	1239·9	1239·3	1239·1	1238·7		Mean	10·29 A.M.		12·17 P.M.	
6561	6550	6537	6534	6510	6504	6514	6505	6511	6518	6517						

at, or about Noon, and the Minimum about 5 o'Clock in the Morning.

VII.

TEMPERATURE AND SPECIFIC GRAVITY OF SEA-WATER BELOW THE SURFACE, 1827

During the whole of these Experiments, except those on the 14th and 15th of June, the Ship was closely beset in the Ice, within a few miles of the North Coast of Spitzbergen The Temperatures below the Surface were obtained by a Six's Thermometer, and *the same* Thermometer was used in registering that at the Surface at the time

TEMPERATURE AND SPECIFIC GRAVITY OF SEA-WATER BELOW THE SURFACE, 1827.

Day.	North Latitude.		East Longitude.		Time.		Sea Water.				Temperature.	
					H.	A.M. or P.M.	Depth in Fathoms.	Temperature.	Specific Gravity.	Temperature when weighed.	Surface Water.	Air.
1827.	°	′	°	′				°		°	°	
May 15	80	4	12	39	11	P.M.	115	32	....	.....	29·5	41
					Noon	......	101	30	1·0279	59·5	28	17
,, 16	80	1	13	5	Noon	......	At Surface		1·0278	59·5	28	17
					2	P.M.	94	29·5	....	.....	28·7	18
					4	P.M.	96	28·5	1·0278	60	28·5	18·5
,, 18	79	56	13	39	4	P.M.	66	30	....	......	28	22
					Mid.	......	72	28·5	....	......	28	15
,, 19	79	55	13	46	4	A.M.	62	29	....	......	28·5	13
					Noon	......	71	28	....	......	28	14
June 4	79	49	15	11	9	P.M.	74	29·2	....	......	30	35
					11	P.M.	73½	29·2	....	......	30	38
					1	A.M.	72	29·2	....	......	30·2	39
					3	A.M.	71	29	....	......	29·3	39
					5	A.M.	73½	29·5	....	......	31	42
					7	A.M.	76½	29·7	....	......	30·5	43
,, 5	79	49	15	17	9	A.M.	78½	29·8	....	......	31	43
					11	A.M.	80	29·8	....	......	31	44
					7	P.M.	84½	29·5	....	......	30	43
					9	P.M.	82	30	....	......	31	43
					11	P.M.	82	28·7	....	......	30	41
					1	A.M.	84	30	....	......	30	37
					3	A.M.	76	29·5	....	......	30·5	38
					5	A.M.	68	29·2	....	......	30·5	37·5
					7	A.M.	68	29·2	....	......	30·5	38
					9	A.M.	68	30	....	......	30·5	39
,, 6	79	49	15	22	11	A.M.	68	29	....	......	30·2	39
					1	P.M.	68	30	....	......	31	39
					3	P.M.	70	29·7	....	......	32	41
					7	P.M.	79	29·2	....	......	31	42
					9	P.M.	68	29·5	....	......	29·7	41
					11	P.M.	73	30	....	......	30	38
					2	A.M.	78	29·5	....	......	31	40
					4	A.M.	61	29	....	......	31·5	41
					5	A.M.	54	30	....	......	30·5	40·5
					7	A.M.	58	29·8	....	......	31	39
					9	A.M.	68	30	....	......	31·5	42
,, 7	79	50	15	30	11	A.M.	56	30	....	......	32	42
					1	P.M.	56	29	....	......	31·5	41
					3	P.M.	53	29	....	......	31	41
					5	P.M.	52	29	....	......	30	40
					7	P.M.	52½	30	....	......	33	37
					9	P.M.	53	29·5	....	......	31·5	39
					11	P.M.	52	29	....	......	31·5	38
					1	A.M.	52	29	....	......	32	40
,, 8	79	50	15	30	3	A.M.	48	28·8	....	......	30	12
					9	A.M.	55½	29·2	....	......	31·5	40
,, 14	80	47	18	22	Midt.	......	95	29·8	....	......	31	26
,, 15	80	49	19	7	7	A.M.	82	28·6	....	......	29	26
					6	P.M.	75	29	....	......	30	27

NATURAL HISTORY.

ZOOLOGY.

BY

LIEUTENANT *(NOW COMMANDER)* JAMES CLARK ROSS, R N, F L S.

THE following Zoological Catalogue comprises an enumeration of all the Animals which were met with in the course of the late voyage along the shores of Spitzbergen, amongst the Islands to the northward, and on the Ice of the Polar Sea, as far north as the latitude of $82°\frac{3}{4}$.

In the list of the Quadrupeds, the arrangement of Cuvier, in the *Règne Animal*, has been followed; the second edition of Temminck's *Manuel d'Ornithologie*, in that of the Birds; and the very excellent work of Chevalier Lamarck, *Histoire Naturelle des Animaux sans Vertèbres*, in that of the Marine Invertebrate Animals.

QUADRUPEDS.

1 Ursus Maritimus. *Polar Bear.*

Ursus Maritimus   *Cuvier, Règne Animal,* vol 1. p. 143   *Fab Faun Grœnl* p. 22.   *Supp. to Parry's First Voyage,* p. clxxxiii   *App to Franklin's Journey,* p 648   *App to Parry's Second Voyage,* p 288   *App to Parry's Third Voyage,* p 92.

Many of these animals were seen on the ice, during the progress of the ship through the " pack" to the westward and northward of Spitzbergen , and afterwards occasionally on the shores of Hecla Cove   Several were seen by the party during their journey over the ice towards the North Pole, beyond the latitude of $82°\frac{1}{2}$ N., and two females were killed.   The flesh is free from any very disagreeable taste: they proved a timely and valuable addition to our stock of provisions, and served materially to restore the strength of the party.

2. Canis Lagopus   *Arctic Fox.*

Canis Lagopus   *Cuvier, Règne Animal,* vol 1   p 155   *Fab Faun Grœnl* p 19, No. 11   *App. to Parry's Second Voyage,* p 299   *App to Parry's Third Voyage,* p. 92

Several of these animals were seen in the neighbourhood of Hecla Cove, and one was shot by Mr Foott, on the western shore of Waygatz Strait.

3. Arvicola Hudsonia.   *Hudson's Bay Lemming.*

Arvicola Hudsonia   *App to Parry's Second Voyage,* p. 308   *App to Parry's Third Voyage,* p 93   Lemmus Hudsonius   *Supp to Parry's First Voyage,* p clxxxviii   *App to Franklin's Journey,* p 661

The skeleton of one of these animals was found in a floe of ice to the northward of Spitzbergen, in latitude $81°\frac{3}{4}$ N , and distant from the nearest known land above 60 miles. The peculiar formation of the fore claws, which were quite perfect, distinctly pointed out the species, without the least doubt.

4. Cervus Tarandus   *Rein-deer.*

Cervus Tarandus.   *Cuvier, Règne Animal,* i p 254.   *Supp to Parry's First Voyage,* p. cxc.
App to Parry's Second Voyage, p 326

Very numerous along the northern shore of Spitzbergen, and near the low island of Phipps . during the stay of the ship in Hecla Cove, about seventy were killed by parties sent for the purpose, in the neighbourhood of Treurenberg Bay.

5. Phoca Fœtida.   *Rough Seal.*

Phoca Fœtida   *Fab Faun Grœnl* p. 13   *App. to Parry's Second Voyage,* p 332. *App to Parry's Third Voyage,* p. 94.
Rough Seal   *Penn Quad* 11 p 278   *Arct Zool* 1 p 160

Two young animals of this species were shot by Mr. Beverly during the journey over the ice, and were found to be excellent food , some were seen as far north as $82°\frac{3}{4}$, nearly.

6. Phoca Grœnlandica.   *Harp Seal.*

Phoca Grœnlandica.   *Cuvier, Regne Animal,* 1 p 166   *Fab. Faun Grœnl* p 11   *App. to Parry's Second Voyage,* p 336   *App to Parry s Third Voyage,* p 94

Was occasionally seen on the loose ice of the pack to the northward and westward of Spitzbergen, and also at the Seven Islands of Phipps

7 Monodon Monoceros.   *Narwhal*

Monodon Monoceros   *Cuvier, Règne Animal,* 1 p 280 *Fab Faun Grœnl* p 29   *Supp to Parry's First Voyage,* p cxcii   *App to Parry's Second Voyage,* p 336   *App to Parry's Third Voyage,* p 94

Several of these animals were seen amongst loose ice in latitude 81.40 N., on the return of the party from the attempt to reach the North Pole over the ice. They are seldom to be seen far within the edge of a "pack," and their appearance was considered by the Greenland sailors as indicative of our approach to open water, which proved to be the case much sooner than was expected.

8. DELPHINAPTERUS BELUGA. *White Whale.*

Delphinapterus Beluga. *Cuvier, Règne Animal,* 1. p 280 *App. to Parry's Second Voyage,* p 337.

Delphinus Albicans. *Fab Faun. Grœnl* p 50.

WAS frequently seen pursuing a small fish (the Merlangus Polaris) along the shores of Hecla Cove, and in the shallow water at the head of Treurenberg Bay.

9 TRICHECUS ROSMARUS. *Walrus.*

Trichecus Rosmarus *Cuvier, Règne Animal,* 1 p 167 *Fab Faun Grœnl.,* p 4 *Supp to Parry's First Voyage,* p cxci. *App to Parry's Second Voyage,* p 337.

VERY numerous along the western coast of Spitzbergen, and the Low Island of Phipps , but none were seen to the northward of Walden Island.

BIRDS.

1. Emberiza Nivalis. *Snow-bunting.*

Emberiza Nivalis. *Gmel.* 1. p 866   *Lath Ind Orn* 1 p 397   *Temm* p 319   *Fab Faun.*
Grœnl p. 117   *App to Parry's Second Voyage,* p 343   *Greenl Birds,* No 5.   *App.*
to Parry's Third Voyage, p. 98
Snow Bunting.   *Brit. Zool.* 1 p. 444.   *Arct Zool.* 11 p. 355.   *Lath. Syn.* 111 p 161.

2 Tetrao Lagopus. *Ptarmigan.*

Tetrao Lagopus.   *Gmel* 1 p 749   *Lath Ind Orn.* 11 p 639.   *Fab. Faun Grœnl* p 114.
Supp to Parry's First Voyage, p cxcvii   *App to Parry's Third Voyage,* p 99
Ptarmigan.   *Lath Syn* 1v p 741   *Arct Zool* 11 p 315.

Several of these birds were shot on the shores of Treurenberg Bay, in the autumn of 1827.

3. Charadrius Hiaticula. *Ringed Plover.*

Charadrius Hiaticula.   *Gmel* 1. p 683   *Lath Ind. Orn* 11 p 743.   *Supp. to Parry's First Voyage,* p cc.   *App to Franklin's Journey,* p 684   *App. to Parry's Second Voyage,* p. 351.
Ringed Plover   *Lath Syn* v p 201.   *Arc Zool* 11 p. 485

A single individual, shot by Mr. M Cormick in Hecla Cove, agreed with Mr. Temminck's description of the male in summer plumage, having, however, rather more white about the tail, the second pen on each side being nearly as white as the outer one · the middle feathers were not tipped with white, as in Captain Sabine's specimen.

4 Tringa Maritima   *Purple Sandpiper.*

Tringa Maritima.   *Gmel* i p 678. *Lath Ind Orn* ii. p 731. *Temm* p. 619.   *Greenl.*
        Birds, No 7   *Supp to Parry's First Voyage*, p cci.   *App to Parry's Second Voyage*,
        p 354.   *App to Parry's Third Voyage*, p 101.
Striated Sandpiper   *Arct Zool* ii p. 472   *Lath Syn* v. p 176

Abundant along the shores of Hecla Cove.

5 Sterna Arctica   *Arctic Tern.*

Sterna Arctica   *Temm* p 742. *Supp to Parry's First Voyage*, p ccii   *App. to Parry's*
        Second Voyage, p 356.   *App to Parry's Third Voyage*, p 103.

Found breeding, in great numbers, on a small islet in the centre of a large lagoon
near the south end of the Low Island of Phipps. An immature bird was
shot in latitude $81\frac{3}{4}°$ N. Several were also seen off the island of Unst, (the
northernmost of the Shetland Islands,) and two were shot in Balta Sound. These
differed, in no respect, from the Arctic specimens ; and I believe this is the first
time it has been noticed as a British species.

6. Larus Glaucus.   *Glaucous Gull.*

Larus Glaucus   *Gmel* i p 600. *Lath Ind Orn* ii p 814   *Fab. Faun Grœnl* p. 100.
        Temm p 757   *Greenl Birds*, No 19. *Supp to Parry's First Voyage*, p cciii
        App to Parry's Second Voyage, p 358   *App to Parry's Third Voyage*, p 103
Glaucous Gull   *Arct Zool* ii. p 532. *Lath. Syn* vi p. 374

Abundant along the shores of Low Island, but not seen to the northward of 81°.

7 Larus Eburneus   *Ivory Gull.*

Larus Eburneus   *Gmel* i. p 596   *Lath Ind Orn.* ii p 816   *Temm* p 769   *Greenl*
        Birds, No 21   *Supp to Parry's First Voyage*, p cciv   *App. to Parry's Third Voyage*,
        p 104.   ﹁
Ivory Gull   *Arct Zool* ii p. 529   *Lath Syn* vi. p 377.

Found as far north as the Expedition travelled, and very abundantly in the neighbourhood of Hecla Cove   An immature bird was seen at the entrance of Balta Sound.   It is mentioned by Dr Edmonstone, in the *Transactions of the Wernerian Society,* as having been shot there some years ago, though it has not yet been enumerated amongst the British birds of late authors

8 Larus Tridactylus. *Kittiwake.*

Larus Tridactylus. *Lath. Ind. Orn* ii. p 817. *Temm* p 774. *Fab Faun Grœnl* p 98 *Greenl. Birds,* No 22. *App. to Parry's Second Voyage,* p 359. *App to Parry's Third Voyage,* p 105.
Kittiwake *Arct. Zool* ii p 529 *Brit Zool.* ii p. 186 *Lath Syn* vi p 393

Was observed feeding on the Merlangus Polaris and Alpheus Polaris, as far as the expedition went to the northward ($82°\frac{3}{4}$).   Was very abundant in the autumn along the shores of Spitzbergen, and on Ross Islet, and Low Island.

9. Larus Sabini. *Fork-tailed Gull.*

Larus Sabini. *Trans Lin Soc* xii. p 520 plate 29 *Greenl Birds,* No. 23. *Supp to Parry's First Voyage,* p ccv *App to Parry's Second Voyage,* p 360.
Xema Collaris. Leach in *Ross's Voyage,* octavo edit ii p 164.

Several individuals were seen by Lieutenant Foster in Waygatz Strait, but no specimens were obtained, nor was it seen on any other part of Spitzbergen.

10. Larus Rossii (Richardson). *Cuneate-tailed Gull.*

Larus Rossii *Richardson in App to Parry's Second Voyage,* p 359

Several were seen during our travels over the ice, and as far north as the Expedition went   Lieutenant Foster also found them in Waygatz Strait, where it is probable that they breed.   No specimens were obtained.

11. Lestris Parasiticus.   *Arctic Lestris.*

Lestris Paiasiticus   *Temm* p 796.   *Greenl Birds,* No 24   *Supp to Parry's First Voyage,*
         p ccvi.   *App. to Parry's Second Voyage,* p. 361.   *App to Parry's Third Voyage,* p 105.
Larus Parasiticus   *Gmel* i p 601.   *Lath Ind Orn* ii p 819
Arctic Gull   *Arct Zool.* ii p 530.   *Brit Zool* ii p. 179   *Lath Syn* vi p 389.

ABUNDANT at Walden Island, and occasionally met with during the journey over
the ice, but not seen to the northward of 82° 2′ N.

12. Lestris Pomarinus.   *Pomarine Lestris.*

Lestris Pomarinus   *Temm.* p 793.   *Supp to Parry's First Voyage,* p ccvi   *App. to Parry s*
         Second Voyage, p 367   *App to Parry's Third Voyage,* p 105.

THE only individual seen during the voyage, flew past the boats in lat 82° N.

13. Procellaria Glacialis.   *Fulmar Petrel.*

Procellaria Glacialis   *Gmel* i p 562   *Lath Ind Orn.* ii p 823   *Temm* p. 802.   *Fab.*
         Fauna Grœnl p 86.   *Supp to Parry's First Voyage,* p. ccvi.   *App. to Parry's Third*
         Voyage, p 106.
Fulmar Petrel.   *Lath Syn* iv. p. 403   *Arct Zool* ii p 534.   *Brit. Zool.* ii. p 203

ONE of the very few birds which were found at the northernmost latitude
attained by the Expedition.

14 Anas Bernicla   *Brent Goose.*

Anas Bernicla   *Gmel* i. p. 513   *Lath Ind. Orn* ii p 844.   *Temm* p 825   *Supp to*
         Parry's First Voyage, p ccvii   *App to Franklin's Journey,* p 698.   *App to Parry's*
         Second Voyage, p 367.
Brent Goose   *Brit. Zool* ii p 151   *Arct. Zool* ii p 551.

SEEN in large flocks about Walden and Little Table Islands ; a nest with two
eggs was brought on board from Ross Islet, in lat 80° 48′ N., on the 16th of
June.   It was not seen to the northward of that place

15 ANAS MOLLISSIMA *Eider Duck*

Anas Mollissima *Gmel* i p 514 *Lath Ind Orn* ii p 815 *Fabr*. p 68 *Temm* p 848 *Supp to Parry's First Voyage,* p ccviii. *App to Parry's Second Voyage,* p 370. *App to Parry's Third Voyage,* p. 106.

Eider Duck *Brit Zool* ii p. 243. *Arct Zool* ii. p 553 *Lath. Syn* vi. p 470.

Not very numerous, but were occasionally met with along the coast of Spitzbergen and the islands to the northward. A few were shot at Hecla Cove

16. COLYMBUS SEPTENTRIONALIS. *Red-throated Diver.*

Colymbus Septentrionalis *Gmel.* i p. 586. *Lath. Ind. Orn* ii p 801. *Fabr* p 91. *Temm* p 916. *Greenl Birds,* No 16 *Supp to Parry's First Voyage,* p ccix *App. to Franklin's Journey,* p 703. *App to Parry's Second Voyage,* p 376 *App to Parry's Third Voyage,* p 106

Red-throated Diver *Brit Zool* ii. p. 169. *Arct Zool* ii p. 520. *Lath. Syn.* vi. p 314.

17. URIA BRUNNICHII. *Brunnich's Guillemot.*

Uria Brunnichii *Greenl Birds,* No 14 *Temm* p 921 *Supp to Parry's First Voyage,* p ccix *App to Parry's Second Voyage,* p 377. *App to Parry's Third Voyage,* p 106.

18 URIA GRYLLE. *Black Guillemot.*

Uria Grylle *Lath. Ind Orn* ii p 797 *Fabr* p 92 *Temm* p 925. *Greenl Birds,* No 15. *Supp to Parry's First Voyage,* p ccix *App. to Parry's Second Voyage,* p. 377. *App. to Parry's Third Voyage,* p 107.

Black Guillemot *Brit Zool* ii p 163 *Arct Zool.* ii p. 516

19. URIA ALLE. *Little Auk.*

Uria Alle. *Temm* p 928 *Supp. to Parry's First Voyage,* p. ccx *App to Parry's Third Voyage,* p 107

Alca Alle *Gmel* i p 554 *Lath. Ind Orn* ii p 795. *Fabr* p 84 *Greenl Birds,* No 13. Little Auk *Arct Zool* ii p 512. *Lath Syn* v p. 327

SEEN as far north as the party travelled, and in great numbers between the lat. of 81° and 82° on the return of the Expedition in August.

2 D

20. Mormon Fratercula. *Puffin Auk.*

Mormon Fratercula. *Temm.* p. 933 *App to Parry's Third Voyage*, p. 108.
Alca Arctica. *Gmel* i. p. 549 *Lath. Ind Orn.* ii. p. 792 *Fabr* p. 83.
Puffin Auk. *Arct. Zool* ii. p. 511. *Lath Syn.* v. p. 314

21. Alca Torda. *Razor-bill Auk.*

Alca Torda *Gmel.* i p 551 *Lath. Ind. Orn.* ii. p. 793. *Temm.* p 936. *Fabr.* p 78. *App. to Parry's Third Voyage*, p. 108.
Razor-bill Auk *Arct. Zool.* ii. p. 509 *Lath Syn.* v. p. 319.

This and the preceding species inhabit Spitzbergen, and were found in considerable numbers, breeding in the high acclivities of Walden and Little Table Islands. They were not seen to the north of those islands.

FISHES.

1 OPHIDIUM PARRII

Ophidium Parrii   *App. to Parry's Third Voyage*, p. 109.

A SINGLE individual of a species of *Ophidium*, very much resembling the *O. Parrii*, was found amongst some sea-weed on the shore of Walden Island. It differed from those of this species which were found in Baffin's Bay and Prince Regent's Inlet, in the number of rays of the pectoral fin; but this has not been considered sufficiently important to form a new species, since the very mutilated and putrid state of the only specimen which has been procured prevents any other differences from being detected. In the *O. Parrii*, the rays of the pectoral fin amount to thirty-seven, whilst, in this individual, only twenty-eight could be determined. The form of the fin, in both cases, is similar, and much larger than any of their congeners.

2. MERLANGUS POLARIS.

Merlangus Polaris.   *Supp to Parry's First Voyage*, p ccxi.   *App. to Parry's Third Voyage*, p. 110

INHABITS the Polar Sea as far north as the latitude of $82°\frac{3}{4}$ N., and is found in great abundance in small bays, where streams of fresh water run into the sea.

3. CYCLOPTERUS LIPARIS.

Cyclopterus Liparis.   *Lacepède*, ii. p 69
Liparis Communis   *Supp to Parry's First Voyage*, p ccxii.

TAKEN in a drag-net to the westward of Low Island.

4 BLENNIUS POLARIS.

Blennius Polaris   *Supp. to Parry's First Voyage*, p. ccxii

This species is very nearly allied to the *B. viviparus* and *B. Gunnellus* of authors, but differs from both in having the ventral fins of one ray each, and from the latter by the upper jaw projecting much more than the lower, and the anal, caudal, and dorsal fins being united.   The only individual which was obtained differed from Captain Sabine's description above referred to, in having eighteen rays on the pectoral fin, and only eight dark marks across the back instead of eleven   The dorsal and superior half of the caudal fins contain eighty-six rays; the anal and inferior half of the caudal about seventy rays.   It was taken in a net from a depth of eighty fathoms, in lat. 81° 6′ N

INSECT.

I am indebted to the friendship of Mr J Curtis for the following description of the only insect that was obtained during the voyage, and am most happy to have it in my power to avail myself of the authority of so eminent an ento- mologist.

" Order, HEMIPTERA, Linn , &c.   OMOPTERA, Leach
Fam APHIDÆ, Lat Leach
Genus, APHIS, Linn., &c
A Borealis, *Curtis's MSS*
Corpus magnum, atrum, hirsutum, femoribus basi ferrugineis alis magnis, subfuscis, ad
    costam atris

" At first sight this insect might be mistaken for *A Piceæ* of *Panzer*, which it resembles in size and colour   Upon a closer examination, however, it will be seen that the whole surface, excepting the wings, is covered with rather long and somewhat hoary tomentum or pubescence , and the base only of the thighs is ferruginous; whereas, in *A Piceæ*, the whole insect is naked, and the antennæ, thighs, and tibiæ are ferruginous or reddish at their base "

The circumstance of the *Aphis Borealis* having been found on floating floes of ice in the Polar Sea, at one hundred miles distance from the nearest known land, and as far north as 82°¼, renders it in a more than ordinary degree interesting Its very near resemblance to the *Aphis Piceæ*, which feeds on the silver fir (*Pinus Picea*, Linn), whence it derives its name, would induce the belief that the floating trees of fir, that are to be found so abundantly on the shores and to the northward of Spitzbergen, might possibly be the means by which this insect has been transported to the northern regions   It was never seen on the wing, and the few specimens that were obtained were in a very languid state, but revived by the heat of the hand.

MARINE INVERTEBRATE ANIMALS.

1 BEROE OVUM.

Beroe Ovum   *Fabr. Fauna Grœnl* p 361, No 355.   *Supp to Parry's First Voyage*, p ccxx.

SEEN abundantly amongst the loose ice to the northward of Spitzbergen, and as far north as the Expedition went

2. BEROE PILEUS.

Beroe Pileus.   *Lam* ii p 470   *Fabr Fauna Grœnl* p 361, No 354.   *Supp to Parry's First Voyage*, p ccxxi   *App to Parry's Third Voyage*, p 116.

INHABITS the Polar Sea, in great abundance, as far north as 82°.

3. OPHIURA FRAGILIS.

Ophiura Fragilis   *Lam* ii p 546   *Supp. to Parry's First Voyage*, p ccxxii   *App to Parry's Third Voyage*, p 116
Asterias Fragilis   *Zool Dan.* iii. p 28. Plate 98.

TAKEN very abundantly in a net to the northward of the Seven Islands of Phipps.

4 ASTERIAS PAPPOSA.

Asterias Papposa.   *Lam* ii p.559.   *Fabr. Faun. Grœnl* No. 364.   *Supp. to Parry's First Voyage*, p. ccxxii.

LAMARCK describes this animal as having "douze à quinze rayons." In the individual obtained on this occasion the number of rays varied from ten to thirteen.

5 ASTERIAS GLACIALIS.

Asterias Glacialis.   *Lam* ii p. 561. (Var B)
Asterias Angulosa.   *Mull Zool Dan* ii p 1 Plate 41

SOME very fine specimens of this beautiful species of *Asterias* were taken in a drag-net, from a depth of 80 fathoms, in lat 81° 6′ N.

6. NYMPHUM GROSSIPES.

Nymphum Grossipes. *Lam* v p 79   *Supp to Parry's First Voyage,* p ccxxv   *App to Parry's Third Voyage,* p 117
Pycnogonum Grossipes   *Mull Zool Dan.* Plate 119 fig 5—9.   *Fabr Faun. Grœnl* p 229

7. NYMPHUM HIRSUTUS.

Nymphum Hirsutus   *Supp. to Parry's First Voyage,* p ccxxvi.   *App. to Parry's Third Voyage,* p 117.

TAKEN abundantly from a depth of 80 fathoms, in the Polar Sea, to the northward of the Seven Islands of Phipps

8. IDOTEA BAFFINI.

Idotea Baffini   *Supp. to Parry's First Voyage,* p. ccxxviii Plate 1. fig 4—6   *App to Parry's Third Voyage,* p 117.

TAKEN abundantly, in a net, off the west side of Low Island.   In some of the individuals the two spines on the upper plate which include the branchiæ, are wanting; and these agree perfectly with the very accurate and beautiful plate referred to

9. CAPRELLA SCOLOPENDROIDES.

Caprella Scolopendroides   *Lam* v p 174   *App. to Parry's Third Voyage,* p. 118.
Gammarus Quadrilobatus   *Zool Dan* iii p 58, Plate 114, fig 11, 12, Female
Squilla Quadrilobata   *Zool Dan* ii p 21. Plate 56, fig 4, 5, 6, Male.
Squilla Lobata.   *Fabr. Faun Grœnl.* p 248.

THE specimens of this species, which were taken in a net to the northward of

Low Island, are of a size intermediate between those figured by Muller and those obtained, during Captain Parry's Third Voyage, at Port Bowen   The spines along the back were hardly visible without the aid of a microscope , and the second pair of legs are inserted in the anterior part of the second segment of the body, and not in the centre of it, as in the plates referred to.

10 GAMMARUS LORICATUS.   (Sabine.)

Gammarus (Gen)   *Lamarck*, v p 179

Gammarus Loricatus. *Supp to Parry's First Voyage*, p ccxxxi. Plate I, fig 7   *App to Parry's Third Voyage*, p 118

FOUND on the shores of Walden Island amongst sea-weed.

11. GAMMARUS SABINI.   (Leach.)

Gammarus Sabini   *Leach, in Ross's Voyage*, octavo edit ii p 178   *Supp to Parry's First Voyage*, p. ccxxxii Plate 1, fig 8—11   *App to Parry's Third Voyage*, p 118

TAKEN in a net from a depth of 80 fathoms, in the Polar Sea, in lat. 81° 6′ N.

12 GAMMARUS BOREUS.   (Sabine.)

Gammarus Boreus. *Supp to Parry's First Voyage*, p ccxxix   *App. to Parry's Third Voyage*, p 119.

ABUNDANT on the shores of Low Island and in Hecla Cove   A dead specimen was found on the ice in lat. 82°¼ N

13. GAMMARUS AMPULLA.

Gammarus Ampulla. *Supp. to Parry's First Voyage*, p ccxxix

Cancer Ampulla   *Phipps's Voyage, App* p 192 Plate 12, fig 2.

TAKEN from the stomach of a young seal which was shot in lat. 82°½ N   It is rather difficult to determine whether this animal belongs to the genus *Gammarus* or *Talitrus*, but this difficulty may possibly arise from the antennæ of many of the individuals being imperfect.

14 Talitrus Nugax.

Talitrus Nugax *App to Parry s Third Voyage*, p 119
Gammarus Nugax. *Supp to Parry s First Voyage*, p ccxxix
Cancer Nugax *App to Phipps's Voyage*, p 192 Plate xii. fig 3.

Taken off Low Island, and in Hecla Cove, abundantly.

15. Talitrus Edvardsii. (Sabine.)

Talitrus Edvardsii. *Supp to Parry's First Voyage*, p ccxxxii Plate ii fig 1, 4 *App to Parry's Third Voyage*, p 119

Abundant in the Polar Sea, great numbers were taken in a net from a depth of eighty fathoms, in latitude 81° 6' N., and some dead specimens were found on the loose ice to the northward of the Seven Islands, in lat. 82° N.

16 Crangon Boreas.

Crangon Boreas *Lam* v p 201 *Supp to Parry's First Voyage*, p. ccxxxv. *App to Parry's Third Voyage*, p 120
Cancer Boreas *Phipps's Voyage, App* p 194 Plate xi. fig. 1. *Zool. Dan* vol. iv. p. 14. Plate cxxii.

Very abundant in the shallow water to the westward of the Low Island of Phipps.

17. Crangon Septemcarinatus (Sabine)

Crangon Septemcarinatus *Supp to Parry's First Voyage*, p ccxxxvi Plate ii fig. 11, 13.

Considerable numbers of this animal were taken, by means of a drag net, off Red Beach, and the Low Island of Phipps, agreeing exactly with the excellent description, and plate referred to. they vary very much in size.

18. Alpheus Aculeatus.

Alpheus Aculeatus   *Supp to Parry's First Voyage*, p ccxxxvii   Plate 2, fig 9, 10.   *App to Parry's Third Voyage*, p. 120
Cancer Aculeatus.   *Fab. Faun Grœnl* p 239

Three or four individuals of this species were taken in the shallow water to the westward of Low Island, agreeing perfectly with Fabricius's description above quoted.   The plate referred to above is also very excellent.

19. Alpheus Polaris.   (Sabine.)

Alpheus Polaris   *Supp to Parry's First Voyage*, p ccxxxviii.   Plate 2, fig 5, 8

Taken in great numbers to the westward of Low Island of Phipps.   These differed from the description and plate referred to, in having generally a greater number of teeth in the upper part of the rostrum, being, in most cases, about seven above and four underneath, and also in having more spines on the middle lamella of the tail, in all other respects they agreed with the description and very beautiful engraving   Some individuals were found as far north as 82°.

20. Clio Borealis.

Clio Borealis   *Lam* vi p 286   *Leach in Ross's Voyage*, octavo ed vol. ii p 172.   *Supp to Parry's First Voyage*, p ccxxxix   *App to Parry's Third Voyage*, p 120

21 Limacina Arctica

Limacina Arctica   *Lam* vi p 290   *Leach in Ross's Voyage*, octavo edit vol ii p 172.   *Supp to Parry's First Voyage*, p ccxxxix   *App to Parry's Third Voyage*, p 120

This and the preceding species were very numerous in the Polar sea as far as $81°\frac{3}{4}$ N , towards the end of August, affording abundance of food for the numerous waterfowl which at this season are preparing to migrate with their young to the southward.

BOTANICAL APPENDIX,

BY

PROFESSOR HOOKER, LL.D., F.R.A., & L.S.

Regius Professor of Botany in the University of Glasgow

THE following List of Plants, collected during the Fourth Voyage, under Captain Parry's command, to the Arctic Regions, is very limited in the number of its species, owing to the unfavourable circumstances which compelled Captain Parry and his officers to spend almost all their time either upon the water or the ice. The greater portion were gathered by those gentlemen who remained in Spitzbergen, while the principal part of the expedition was engaged in an attempt to reach the North Pole. One species of Moss appears to be new; but, being destitute of fructification, and belonging to a tribe of that beautiful order of plants, which is remarkable for the Proteus-like forms of the individuals which compose it, I am unwilling to speak otherwise than doubtfully concerning it.

Those species that were gathered in Ross's Islet are peculiarly interesting, from the circumstance of that island constituting the most northern known land in the world.

In many instances, particularly of the Mosses and Jungermanniæ, I have inserted the names of species of which I found fragments only among the tufts of other plants, and with regard to the Hammerfest plants, I may observe that the greater portion of them belong to a collection picked out by Captain J. C. Ross from the reindeer moss which was received on board the Hecla at that place.

The Spitzbergen specimens were principally collected by Captain Ross and Mr. Halse, and Lieutenant Crozier.

WM. JACKSON HOOKER

Glasgow, December 13, 1827.

PLANTS OF SPITZBERGEN.

DICOTYLEDONES.

I RANUNCULACEÆ.

1. RANUNCULUS.

1 Ranunculus *nivalis*

α Brown in Parry's 1st Voy App p cclxiv Hooker in Parry's 2d Voy. App. p 382 3d Voy App p 121 In Linn. Trans * vol xiv. p 385, and p 361

β. Brown in Parry's 1st Voy. App p cclxiv. Hooker in Parry's 2d Voy App. p 382

HAB α Hecla Cove, Spitzbergen β Walden Island

The specimens gathered in the latter station, though subjected to pressure between paper and boards during the voyage, were still living on their being unpacked in England in the month of December, and have evidently been vegetating in that situation.

II PAPAVERACEÆ

2 PAPAVER

2 Papaver *nudicaule* Brown in Parry's 1st Voy App p cclxv. Hooker in Parry's 2d Voy. App p 384. In 3d Voy. App p 122. In Linn. Trans. vol. xiv pp 362 and 385.

HAB Hecla Cove Low Island, but stunted and small Walden Island.

The specimens from the former spot have the flowers remarkably large and beautiful; some of them broader than a half-crown-piece would cover

III CRUCIFERÆ

3 DRABA

3 Draba *alpina* Brown in Parry's 1st Voy. App. p. 265 Hooker in Parry's 2d Voy App p 385 In 3d Voy App p 122. In Linn. Trans. vol. xiv pp. 363 and 385

HAB Hecla Cove

Varying much in the colour of its flowers, from a very deep yellow to a pale dingy sulphur colour, and almost to a white. Amongst them are some which I scarcely know whether to refer to the *D pauciflora* of Brown in the 1st Voy App p cclxvii, or to *D alpina*

4 Draba *hirta* Var 4 Hooker in Parry's 2d Voy. p 386 In 3d Voy App p 122

HAB Hecla Cove

* Hooker s Account of a Collection of Arctic Plants, formed by Captain Sabine in Greenland and Spitzbergen.

4. PLATYPETALUM

5. Platypetalum *purpurascens*. Brown in Parry's 1st Voy. App. p cclxvii. Hooker in Parry's 3d Voy App. p 122.

Braya arctica. Hooker in Parry's 2d Voy. App p. 387.

HAB Hecla Cove

5 PARRYA.

6 Parrya *arctica*. Brown in Parry's 1st Voy App. p. cclxviii. Hooker in Parry's 2d Voy. App. p. 388 3d Voy App p. 123

HAB. Hecla Cove.

6 CARDAMINE

7 Cardamine *bellidifolia* Brown in Parry's 1st Voy App p. cclxx. Hooker in Parry's 2d Voy App p. 389 In 3d Voy. App p 122. In Linn. Trans. vol xiv p 386

HAB Hecla Cove. Low Island Walden Island.

IV CARYOPHYLLEÆ

7 SILENE.

8 Silene *acaulis*. Hooker in Parry's 2d Voy App p. 389 In Linn. Trans. vol xiv. p 365

HAB Hecla Cove.

8 LYCHNIS

9 Lychnis *apetala* Brown in Parry's 1st Voy. App p cclxx Hooker in Parry's 2d Voy App p 389. In 3d Voy. App p. 123 In Linn. Trans vol. xiv. pp 365 and 386

HAB Hecla Cove.

9 CERASTIUM

10. Cerastium *alpinum*

α Brown in Parry's 1st Voy. App p cclxx Hooker in Parry's 2d Voy App. p. 390 In 3d Voy App p 123 In Linn Trans. vol xiv pp 367 and 386.

β. Brown in Parry's 1st Voy App p cclxxi. Hooker in Parry's 2d Voy App. p. 390.

HAB α and β. in Hecla Cove, and on Low Island, where β becomes very dwarfish, and Walden Island, where the specimens grow to an unusually large size They have few hairs on the surface of the leaves, but have the margins strongly ciliated

10 STELLARIA.

11 Stellaria *læta* Richardson in Franklin's Journ. App. p 738. Hooker in Parry's 2d Voy. App p 390

HAB Hecla Cove Low Island

This has been found on the Rocky Mountains by Dr James.

12 Stellaria *humifusa*. Hooker in Parry's 2d Voy. App p. 391 In 3d Voy App p 124. In Linn Trans vol iv p 367

HAB Hecla Cove

11. Spergula

13 Spergula *saginoides* Hooker in Parry's 2d Voy App p. 389.

Hab. Hecla Cove

12. Arenaria.

14. Arenaria *rubella*. Hooker in Parry's 2d Voy. App. p 391. In 3d Voy. App. p. 123. In Linn. Trans vol. xiv pp 368 and 386

A *quadrivalvis* Brown in Parry's 1st Voy App. p. cclxxi.

Hab Hecla Cove Walden Island

V. SAXIFRAGEÆ.

13. Saxifraga.

15. Saxifraga *oppositifolia* Brown in Parry's 1st Voy App p cclxxiii. Hooker in Parry's 2d Voy. App p 392 In 3d Voy App p. 124 In Linn. Trans. vol xiv. pp 369 and 386

Hab Hecla Cove Low Island Walden Island

16 Saxifraga *flagellaris* Brown in Parry's 1st Voy App. p cclxxiii Hooker in Parry's 3d Voy App. p. 124. In Linn. Trans. vol xiv p 369

Hab Hecla Cove Low Island

Found on the Rocky Mountains by Dr James

17 Saxifraga *aizoides*. Hooker in Parry's 2d Voy App p 393.

Hab Hecla Cove

18 Saxifraga *rivularis* Hooker in Parry's 2d Voy App. p. 393 In 3d Voy. App. p 124. In Linn Trans vol xiv p 370

S hyperborea. ? Brown in Parry's 1st Voy. App p. cclxxiv.

Hab Hecla Cove Walden Island

19 Saxifraga *cæspitosa*

Var Surculis nullis, foliis plerumque trifidis subciliatis, caule uni-trifloro, calyce nigro-pubescente glanduloso.

S *cæspitosa*. Hooker in Parry's 2d Voy App p 393 In 3d Voy App 124 In Linn Trans vol xiv pp 370 and 386

S *uniflora* ? Brown in Parry's 1st Voy App p cclxxiv

Hab Hecla Cove. Low Island. Walden Island

Varying much in the colour of the calyx and peduncle, and in the glands, as well as in the number of flowers upon each stem or scape Some of the specimens from Walden Island have the flowers almost wholly sessile

20 Saxifraga *foliolosa* Brown in Parry's 1st Voy App p cclxxv Hooker in Parry's 2d Voy App p 393 In 3d Voy App. p 124 In Linn Trans vol xiv pp 371 and 386

Hab Hecla Cove.

21 Saxifraga *nivalis*. Brown in Parry's 1st Voy App p cclxxv Hooker in Parry's 2d Voy App p 393. In Linn Trans vol xiv pp 371 and 386

Hab Hecla Cove

Gathered on the Rocky Mountains by Dr James

22 Saxifraga *cernua* Brown in Parry's 1st Voy App p. cclxxv Hooker in Parry's 2d
Voy App p 394 In 3d Voy App p 125 In Linn Trans vol. xiv. pp 371 and 386
HAB Hecla Cove Low Island. Walden Island.

VI. ROSACEÆ

14. DRYAS

23 Dryas *octopetala*

HAB Hecla Cove

The leaves are very much cut at the margin, as in *D octopetala* , but the base is cordate, as in the foliage
of *D integrifolia D octopetala* has been found on the Rocky Mountains in a latitude as far South as 39°

15 POTENTILLA.

24. Potentilla *pulchella*. Brown in Parry's 1st Voy App p cclxxvii. Hooker in Parry's
2d Voy App p 395 In 3d Voy App p 125

HAB Hecla Cove.

25. Potentilla *nivea* Brown in Parry's 1st Voy App p. cclxxvii Hooker in Parry's 2d
Voy App p 395 In Linn Trans vol xiv pp 372 and 387

Both these species of *Potentilla* assume a very different appearance when in fruit , the stalks running out
to a much greater length, and the leaves being considerably larger

HAB Hecla Cove

VII COMPOSITÆ

16 LEONTODON

26. Leontodon *palustre*. Brown in Parry's 1st Voy App p cclxxviii. Hooker in Parry's
2d Voy. App p. 397 In 3d Voy App p 126 In Linn Trans vol xiv pp. 373 and 391
HAB Hecla Cove.

VIII ERICINEÆ

17 ANDROMEDA

27 Andromeda *tetragona* Brown in Parry's 1st Voy App p cclxxi. Hooker in Parry's
2d Voy App. p. 400 In 3d Voy App p 127 In Linn Trans. vol. xiv. p 376

HAB. Hecla Cove

IX. SCROPHULARINÆ

18. PEDICULARIS

28 Pedicularis *hirsuta*. Hooker in Parry's 2d Voy App p 402. In 3d Voy App p.
127 In Linn. Trans. vol. xiv p 377

HAB. Hecla Cove

APPENDIX.

X POLYGONEÆ

19 POLYGONUM.

29 Polygonum *viviparum* Brown in Parry's 1st Voy. App p. cclxxxi. Hooker in Parry's 2d Voy. App p 403. In 3d Voy. App p. 127 In Linn Trans vol. xiv pp 379 and 387

HAB Hecla Cove

20 OXYRIA

30 Oxyria *reniformis* Brown in Parry's 1st Voy App p cclxxxii Hooker in Parry's 2d Voy App p 403 In 3d Voy. App p 127 In Linn. Trans vol xiv. pp. 378 and 387.

HAB Hecla Cove

XI AMENTACEÆ

21 SALIX.

31 Salix *herbacea* Hooker in Parry's 2d Voy App p. 404 In 3d Voy. App p. 128.

HAB Hecla Cove. Low Island

MONOCOTYLEDONES

XII JUNCEÆ

22 LUZULA.

32 Luzula *hyperborea.* Brown in Parry's 1st Voy App p cclxxxiii Hooker in Parry's 2d Voy App. p 405 In 3d Voy. App. p 198 In Linn. Trans vol. xiv. p 380.

HAB Hecla Cove Low Island

XIII CYPERACEÆ.

23 CAREX.

33 Carex *fuliginosa* Sternb. and Hoppe Hooker in Parry's 2d Voy App p. 406. In 3d Voy App p 128 In Linn. Trans. vol xiv p. 380

C *misandra?* Brown in Parry's 1st Voy App p cclxxxiii.

HAB Hecla Cove.

24. ERIOPHORUM.

34 Eriophorum *capitatum.* Brown in Parry's 1st Voy. App p cclxxxiv. Hooker in Parry's 2d Voy App p. 407 In Linn Trans. vol xiv p. 380.

HAB Hecla Cove.

XIV GRAMINEÆ

25 Poa

35 Poa *abbreviata* Brown in Parry's 1st Voy App p. cclxxxii Hooker in Parry's 2d Voy. App. p. 408. In 3d Voy App 129.

HAB Hecla Cove Low Island

36 Poa *arctica* Brown in Parry's 1st Voy App p cclxxxiii. Hooker in Parry's 2d Voy App p 408. In 3d Voy p 129. In Linn Trans. vol. xiv. p. 380

HAB Hecla Cove found also viviparous

26 PHIPPSIA.

37 Phippsia *algida* Brown in Parry's 1st Voy App. p. cclxxxi Hooker in Parry's 3d Voy App p 129

HAB Low Island, plentiful Walden Island, and Hecla Cove

In age the larger of the two calycine valves often falls away, leaving the smaller one ; the glumes, too, are very brown at that period , and there is one specimen in the collection, which in that state has the panicle much divaricated

27 FESTUCA.

38 Festuca *brevifolia* Brown in Parry's 1st Voy. App p cclxxxix. and ccccix Hooker in Parry's 2d Voy App p 408.

HAB Hecla Cove

28. DUPONTIA

39 Dupontia *Fisheri*. Brown in Parry's 1st Voy App p ccxci Hooker in Parry's 2d Voy. App p 409

HAB Hecla Cove. Low Island

Found sometimes viviparous , entirely so in the latter station

29. HIEROCHLOE

40 Hierochloe *pauciflora* Brown in Parry's 1st Voy App p ccxciii Hooker in Parry's 2d Voy. App p 410 In 3d Voy App p 129

HAB Low Island

ACOTYLEDONES.

XV. LYCOPODINEÆ.

30 LYCOPODIUM

41. Lycopodium *Selago* Hooker in Parry's 2d Voy. App p 410 In 3d Voy App. p. 130. In Linn. Trans vol xiv p 394.

HAB Hecla Cove

XVI EQUISETACEÆ.

31 EQUISETUM

42 Equisetum *variegatum* Hooker in Parry's 2d Voy App p 411

HAB Hecla Cove.

XVII MUSCI.

32. BRYUM.

43 Bryum *palustre* Hooker in Parry's 2d Voy. App. p. 411.
HAB Walden Island Hecla Cove

44 Bryum *turgidum*. Brown in Parry's 1st Voy App p. ccxcv Hooker in Parry's 2d Voy App p 411
HAB. Hecla Cove. No fructification.

45 Bryum *crudum*. Hooker in Parry's 2d Voy App. p 411.
HAB Ross's Islet Hecla Cove.

46 Bryum *cæspititium* Hooker in Parry's 2d Voy. App p. 411. In 3d Voy. App. p. 130 In Linn. Trans vol xiv p. 388
HAB Hecla Cove

47 Bryum *turbinatum*. Hooker in Parry's 2d Voy App. p 412.
HAB. Hecla Cove Barren.

48 Bryum ? folus ovato-rotundatis laxe imbricatis valde concavis acutis insigniter reticulatis, nervo ante apicem evanescente
HAB Hecla Cove
There is no fruit on this plant, which has entirely the habit of a *Bryum*, and will rank near to *B. turbinatum* but the structure of its leaves is different from any that I am acquainted with

33 CINCLIDIUM

49 Cinclidium *stygium* Hooker in Parry's 2d Voy App p. 413
HAB Hecla Cove Barren

34 HYPNUM.

50 Hypnum *nitens*. Brown in Parry's 1st Voy. App p. ccxcv Hooker in Parry's 2d Voy App p 414
HAB Hecla Cove

51 Hypnum *aduncum*. Brown in Parry's 1st Voy. App p. ccxcv. Hooker in Parry's 2d Voy App p 414
HAB Hecla Cove. Ross's Islet

52 Hypnum *cupressiforme*. Hooker in Parry's 2d Voy App p. 414
HAB Ross's Islet

53 Hypnum *uncinatum* ?
HAB Hecla Cove

35 TRICHOSTOMUM.

54. Trichostomum *lanuginosum*. Brown in Parry's 1st Voy. App. p ccxcvii. Hooker in Parry's 2d Voy App p 416.
HAB Ross's Islet Walden and Low Islands

36 DICRANUM.

55. Dicranum *virens*   Hooker in Parry's 2d Voy. App p. 416.
HAB. Hecla Cove   Low Island   Walden Island

56. Dicranum *fuscescens*   Hooker in Parry's 2d Voy. App. p. 416.
HAB Little Table Island.

37 WEISSIA

57 Weissia *crispula.*   Hooker in Parry's 2d Voy App. p 417
HAB Hecla Cove

38 POLYTRICHUM

58. Polytrichum *septentrionale.*   Hooker in Parry's 2d Voy. App p. 418.
HAB Ross s Islet

59 Polytrichum *alpinum.*   Hooker in Parry's 2d Voy. App. p 418   In 3d Voy. App.
p 130   In Linn Trans vol xiv p 388.
HAB Hecla Cove   Walden Island

39 SPLACHNUM

60. Splachnum *Adamsianum*   Hornsch in Hor. Physic. Berol p. 57. t xii
   S. paradoxum? Br. in Parry's 1st Voy App p cccii
HAB Hecla Cove

This moss perfectly accords with my authentic specimens of *S Adamsianum,* where likewise the operculum has the appearance of being an uninterrupted continuation of the capsule, destitute of suture, and only distinguishable by its paler colour

Dr Richardson has found the same plant on his second journey, and is of opinion also that it is the same as the *S Adamsianum* of Hornschuch

Amongst specimens of this moss gathered by Captain J C Ross, in the same tuft, and I think without doubt belonging to the same plant, are stems upon longer stalks, bearing capsules without operculum; others, in which the separation between capsule and operculum is marked by a distinct suture, and some, finally, from which the operculum has fallen away, leaving exhibited the peristome, the teeth of which are united almost to the summit in fours   I should, therefore, be disposed to consider the former state as a variety or monstrosity, depending upon climate, in the same way, perhaps, as the *Bryum cæspititium* in very alpine situations, or in extremely northern latitudes, is found destitute of an inner peristome, becoming the *Ptychostomum* of authors? I may add, that, in dissecting the variety which possesses no distinct operculum, I can find, as may be expected, no trace whatever of peristome, although the capsules contain ripe seeds

40 VOITIA.

61. Voitia *hyperborea.*   Brown in Parry's 1st Voy. App. p. ccciv.   Hooker in Parry's 2d
Voy App p 419
HAB Hecla Cove.

2 F 2

XVIII. HEPATICÆ.

41. JUNGERMANNIA.

62 Jungermannia *minuta*   Brown in Parry's 1st Voy. App. p cccv   Hooker in Parry's 2d Voy. App. p. 420.
   HAB Ross s Islet

63 Jungermannia *scalaris*   Hooker in Parry's 2d Voy App. p. 420
   HAB. Walden Island

XIX LICHENES

42 GYROPHORA.

64 Gyrophora *tesselata* Hooker in Parry's 2d Voy. App. p 421. In 3d Voy. App p. 130.
   HAB Ross s Islet   Walden Island

65 Gyrophora *erosa*. Hooker in Parry's 2d Voy App p 421   In 3d Voy. App p 130.
   HAB Low Island   Little Table Island

66 Gyrophora *deusta*   Hooker in Parry's 2d Voy. App p 421
   HAB Ross s Islet

43 LECANORA.

67 Lecanora *tartarea*   Hooker in Parry's 2d Voy App. p. 422.
   HAB Hecla Cove   Walden Island

68 Lecanora *elegans*. Brown in Parry's 1st Voy. App p cccv   Hooker in Parry's 2d Voy. App p 422   In 3d Voy App. p 130.
   HAB Hecla Cove   Walden Island   Ross s Islet. Low Island

44 PARMELIA

69 Parmelia *saxatilis*   Hooker in Parry's 2d Voy App. p 422
   HAB Walden Island

45 CETRARIA

70. Cetraria *nivalis*   Brown in Parry s 1st Voy App p cccvi   Hooker in Parry's 2d Voy App. p 423   In 3d Voy App p 131.
   HAB Hecla Cove   Low and Walden Islands   Ross s Islet

71 Cetraria *cucullata*. Brown in Parry's 1st Voy App p. cccvi   Hooker in Parry's 2d Voy App p 423
   HAB Walden Island

72 Cetraria *islandica*   Brown in Parry's 1st Voy App p cccvi. Hooker in Parry's 2d Voy App p 123. In 3d Voy App p 131.
   HAB Hecla Cove   Little Table and Low Islands   Ross s Islet

46 PELTIDIA.

73 Peltidea *aphthosa*. Brown in Parry's 1st Voy App p. cccvi. Hooker in Parry's 2d Voy. App. p 423.

HAB Hecla Cove

74 Peltidea *canina*.

HAB Hecla Cove

47 CENOMYCE

75. Cenomyce *alcicornis*. Brown in Parry's 1st Voy App p. cccvii. Hooker in Parry's 2d Voy App p. 424 In 3d Voy App. p 131

HAB Walden, and Little Table Islands

76 Cenomyce *pyxidata*. Brown in Parry's 1st Voy App p cccvii. Hooker in Parry's 2d Voy App p 424 In 3d Voy App p 131.

HAB Ross's Islet Little Table Island

77. Cenomyce *gracilis* Hooker in Parry's 1st Voy App p. 424 In 3d Voy. App p. 131

HAB Low Island Little Table and Walden Islands Ross s Islet

78. Cenomyce *rangiferina* Hooker in Parry's 1st Voy App. p 424. In 3d Voy. App p. 131

HAB Hecla Cove.

79 Cenomyce *vermicularis*. Hooker in Parry's 2d Voy App. p 425 In 3d Voy App. p. 131

Cerania *vermicularis*. Brown in Parry's 1st Voy App p cccvii

HAB Low Island

48 ISIDIUM

80 Isidium *oculatum*. Hooker in Parry's 2d Voy App. p 425

HAB Walden Island

49. STEREOCAULON

81 Stereocaulon *paschale* Brown in Parry's 1st Voy App p cccvii. Hooker in Parry's 2d Voy App p. 425

HAB Little Table Island, and Ross s Islet

•

50 SPHÆROPHORON.

82. Sphærophoron *fragile*. Hooker in Parry's 2d Voy. App p 425.

HAB Walden Island Ross's Islet

51 ALECTORIA.

83 Alectoria *jubata* β *chalybeiformis*. Hooker in Parry's 2d Voy. App p 425.

HAB Little Table and Low Islands Ross s Islet

52 CORNICULARIA

84 Cornicularia *aculeata* β *spadicea*. Hooker in Parry's 2d Voy App p. 125

HAP Low Island

85 Cornicularia *ochroleuca*. Brown in Parry's 1st Voy App p cccvi Hooker in Parry's 2d Voy. App p 426

Hab. Low Island β Ross s Islet

86 Cornicularia *lanata* Brown in Parry's 1st Voy. App. p. cccvi Hooker in Parry's 2d Voy App. p 426

Hab Ross s Islet

XX. ALGÆ.

53. Ulva.

87. Ulva *crispa* Linn.

Hab. Ross s Islet.

54 Ptilota.

88 Ptilota *plumosa* Hooker in Parry's 2d Voy. App p 427.

Hab Ross s Islet Hammerfest

" Found on the shores of *Ross s Islet* abundantly, and also along the shores of Low Island, and on the beach above high-water mark in a *bleached* state, amongst the larger sea-weed (Tangle)

Protococcus *nivalis*, or Red Snow

Protococcus *nivalis*. Agardh Syst. Algarum, p 13. Grev Scot. Crypt Flora, vol iv t 231.

Palmella *nivalis* Hooker in Parry's 2d Voy App p 429

Palmella —See notices respecting it by Hooker in the Edinburgh Journal of Science, vol i. p 383, vol ii p 185, and vol iv. p 167

Uredo *nivalis* Bauer in Brande's Quarterly Journal of Science and the Arts, vol vii. p 222, t vii

Lepraria Kermesina. Wrangel in Vet Acad Handl 1823, p 71, t iii

Algarum species B in Ross's Voy ed 2 vol ii App p 195.

Terre rouge de la Neige Saussure's Voy vol ii. p 44

Red Snow, relation of some experiments on the Fungi which constitute its colouring matter Bauer in Phil. Trans 1820, p. 165, t xvii.

Hab Among snow upon the ice, nearly as far as the Arctic expedition extended, viz to lat 82 ½ north

Since the discovery of this minute, yet highly curious vegetable production by our Arctic navigators, living and vegetating *in snow*, and penetrating that element to a great depth in the high northern latitudes, the attention of botanists in Europe has been devoted to the subject, and many valuable disquisitions, and some exquisitely beautiful figures, illustrative of its history and structure, have appeared Thus has its true nature been clearly ascertained, and I think there can be no more question of its being a true vegetable, and belonging to the order Algæ, than there can be of the *Palmella cruenta* (which in the autumn and winter months especially abounds on rocks and walls in every part of Britain) being a vegetable and an Alga Snow, tinged with a red colour, has long been observed by naturalists, and its appearance accounted for, without ever investigating the nature of the substance, according to the fancy of the writer, some supposing it to have arisen from the farina of plants, others from the decomposed matter of the rocks of a red hue in the neighbourhood, while others have conjectured that the snow had fallen from the heavens imbued with that colour,—and, indeed, the very sudden appearance of this phenomenon in countries where it had not been observed before, would almost seem to favour this latter supposition Thus Agardh tells us that a relation is given in the Italian

Giornale di Fisica for November and December, 1818, of *Red Snow* that fell upon the Italian Alps and the Apennines. In March 1808, for instance, the whole country about Cadova, Belluno, and Feltri, was, in one single night, covered to the depth of twenty centimètres with a *rose-coloured snow*; but both before and after it, pure snow fell, so that the red formed a layer between the white. At the same time, a similar phenomenon was witnessed on the mountains of Valtelin, Brescia, Carinthia, and Tyrol. Another fall is mentioned, as occurring between the 5th and 6th days of March, 1808, at Tolmazzo in the Friuli, and one yet more remarkable in the night between the 14th and 15th of March, 1813, in Calabria, Abruzzo in Tuscany, and at Bologna, and upon the whole chain of the Apennines. On the 15th of April, in the same year, *Red Snow* was said to fall on the mountain of Tonal in Italy. In South America, Humboldt informs us of the statement he heard, that at Paramo of Guanacos, where the road from Bogota to Popayan passes at a height of 2300 toises above the level of the sea, *red hail* had been seen to fall. In these cases we must conclude either that the vegetable did exist, though unobserved, previous to the supposed period of its falling, or, what is highly probable and quite consistent with what we know of other nearly allied vegetable productions, that its growth and appearance are very rapid.

De Saussure seems to have been the first who speaks of having seen the *Red Snow* upon Mount Breven in Switzerland, in 1760, and he afterwards observed it to be so common upon the Alps, that he was surprised that other naturalists had not remarked it, especially the accurate Scheuchzer. Mr Ramond saw it on the Pyrenées, and Sommerfeldt in Norway. That which was brought by Captain Ross from Baffin's Bay, in 75°, 54' N. latitude, first excited the attention of our naturalists, and gave rise to the admirable observations of Bauer, Brown, and Wollaston. It was again collected and brought home during the Second Voyage, under the command of Captain Parry, when it was found not only growing on *snow*, but *attached to stones and mosses*, clothing them with a thin gelatinous crust. This circumstance made its vegetable origin appear still more probable, and from the careful examination of excellent specimens, gathered during that expedition, I was induced to refer it to the genus Palmella*, from which, however, I acknowledge that it differed, in having the granules of fructification *external*, not imbedded in the gelatinous substance of the frond.

The attention of continental botanists now began to be excited, and in Sweden, the native country of Linnæus, still yielding her ample proportion of naturalists of deep observation and research, Baron Wrangel and the celebrated Agardh published some admirable memoirs upon the subject, which tended to confirm the opinion that Brown and Bauer had advanced, as to the real nature and origin of the Red Snow, and their discoveries I have noticed in the volumes of Brewster's Journal of Science. The Treatise of Agardh is indeed fully given in the fourth volume of that Journal, and that author clearly proves, by a comparison of the *Lepraria Kermesina* of Baron Wrangel (which the latter found in the province of Nerike) with the *Red Snow* received from Dr Wollaston, that the two plants were the same,—thus identifying it as a native plant of Sweden. Agardh, however, overlooked the gelatinous structure of the plant, and described it as a new genus (of which he took the character from the granules of fructification alone), under the name which we have here adopted, of *Protococcus*.

Upon the continent of North America, during the first overland Arctic Expedition, Dr Richardson remarked the *Protococcus*, forming a red substance upon the stones at Fort Enterprise, which tinged the snow in spring, and which Captain Franklin recognised as being the same which constituted the *Red Snow* he had seen in Spitzbergen at the same period that Captain Ross observed it in Baffin's Bay.

In 1825, I showed Captain Parry's specimens of *Red Snow*, attached to stones, to the late Captain Carmichael of Appin. Upon his return to the Highlands, whilst botanizing in the little island of Lismore, upon the coast of Argyleshire, his experienced eye enabled him to detect the same substance growing abundantly near water, upon half-decayed vegetable matter, sticks, reeds, and leaves, &c., and in still greater perfection on calcareous rocks, which are occasionally flooded by the neighbouring lakes.

* See the observations on *Palmella nivalis* in Parry's 2d Voy. App. pp. 428 &c.

From these specimens, Dr Greville made his beautiful figures in the Scottish Cryptogamic Flora, which he has accompanied by a very elaborate history and description

It only remains for me to say, that, during the present voyage of Captain Parry, this highly interesting plant has been found in greater abundance perhaps than on any former occasion, and in a situation still more remarkable, for it was upon the *floes of ice*, extending nearly to the utmost limit of the journey, and there too in such abundance, and so completely imbedded in the snow, that distinct red lines were left by the tracks of the boats or sledges on the surface, thus vegetating in the most northern regions to which man has yet been able to penetrate, and flourishing most in an element (or rather a state of an element) in which no other vegetable, that we are acquainted with, can exist.

The plates illustrative of this vegetable are —

1 An exquisitely beautiful representation by Mr Bauer in Brande s Quarterly Journal of Science and the Arts, vol. vii t vii The pedicles to the globules, which are there represented in the highly magnified figures, I have never been able to discover

2 Mr Bauer s figures in the Philosophical Transactions for 1820, t 17 These, however, are chiefly intended to illustrate the mode in which that gentleman succeeded in cultivating the Red Snow in phials

3 Baron Wrangel, as quoted by Dr Greville, in Vet Acad Handl. 1823, p 71, t 3, in which the gelatinous structure or frond is omitted

4 Two representations in Dr Nees' valuable work, entitled " Robert Brown s Vermischte Botanische Schriften They are copied, the one from Mr Bauer s figure in Brande s Journal, the other from Baron Wrangel s plate, above mentioned

5. Dr Greville s excellent figures, from British specimens, in the fourth volume of his Scottish Cryptogamic Flora, t 231. These perfectly accord with the result of my own observations, made both on Scottish and Arctic plants

Fucus *Digitatus* *Linn*

HAB Found on some parts of the beach of Low Island, and near the entrance of Hecla Cove, it formed a line three or four feet deep, and for an extent of two or three miles Amongst this mass Captain Ross thinks the *Dulse (Halymenia palmata)* were found, but specimens were not brought home

PLANTS OF HAMMERFEST.

DICOTYLEDONES

1. CARYOPHYLLEE.

1. Arenaria *peploides*   *Linn*

2. LEGUMINOSÆ

2 Pisum *maritimum*.   *Linn.*

3 COMPOSITE

3 Antennaria *dioica*   *Br.*

4 CAPRIFOLIACEÆ

4 Linnea *borealis*.   *Linn.*

5. ERICINEÆ

5 Azalea *procumbens*   *Linn.*
6 Arbutus *alpina*   *Linn*

6 VACCINIÆ.

7 Vaccinium *Vitis-Idea*.   *Linn.*
8 V. *uliginosum*   *Linn.*

7 EMPETREÆ

9 Empetrum *nigrum*   *Linn.*

8, PRIMULACEÆ.

10 Diapensia *lapponica*

9. AMENTACEÆ

11. Pinus *sylvestris*   *Linn.*
12 Juniperus *communis*   *Linn*   Alpine variety

MONOCOTYLEDONES.

10 JUNCEÆ.

13. Juncus *trifidus*   *Linn*

11. CYPERACEÆ

14 Eriophorum *angustifolium*.   *Huds*

12. GRAMINEÆ.

15. Aira *cæspitosa*   *Linn.*
16 Poa *trivialis*.   *Linn.*

ACOTYLEDONES.

13 FILICLS.

17 Aspidium *filia-mas*   *Swartz*

14 LYCOPODIACÆ

18 Lycopodium *claratum*   *Suartz.*
19. L *annotinum*   *Suartz*

15 MUSCI

20 Hypnum *Schreberi*   *Linn.*
21. Trichostomum *fasciculare*   *Hedw.*
22 Dicranum *Scoparium*   *Hedw.*
23 D *longifolium*   *Hedw*
24 D *elongatum*   *Hedw*
25 Polytrichum *junipermum.*   *Hedw*
26 P. *alpinum.*   *Suartz.*

16. HEPATICÆ

27 Jungermannia *barbata*   *Hooker.*
28 J. *ciliaris.*   *Hooker*

17. LICHENES

29 Parmelia *omphalodes*   *Ach*
30 Cetraria *nivalis*   *Ach*
31 C *islandica*   *Ach*
32 Nephroma *polaris*? *Ach*   No fruit
33 Cenomyce *pyridata.*   *Ach*
34 C. *digitata.*   *Ach*
35 C *coccifera*   *Ach.*
36 C *bellidiflora*   *Ach*
37 C *ecmocyna* α. gracilis.   *Ach.*
38 C *rangiferina.*   *Ach.*

39. Stereocaulon *paschale*   *Ach.*
40 Sphærophoron *fragile*   *Ach.*

18 ALGÆ.

41 Fucus *serratus*   *Linn*
42 F *nodosus*   *Linn*
43 F *vesiculosus*? *Linn*
44 Ptilota *plumosa*   *Ag.*
45. Hutchinsia *fastigiata.*   *Ag.*

ENUMERATION

OF THE

ROCKS OF SPITZBERGEN,

AND THE NEIGHBOURING ISLES,

COLLECTED BY CAPTAIN PARRY

By ROBERT JAMESON,

Regius Professor of Natural History and Lecturer on Mineralogy in the University of Edinburgh,
F R S L & E F L S , M W S

ALTHOUGH the following notices of the rocks of Spitzbergen and some of the neighbouring isles may seem meagre, yet when we consider that they are the only ones we possess of that desolate and remote region, they cannot but be viewed with interest by the geologist

The analyses which follow were made by my young friend and former pupil Mr Reid, Lecturer on chemistry.

SPITZBERGEN.

I RED BEACH

Secondary Rocks

Red sandstone, having a marly basis, with much disseminated mica   Those varieties in which the quartz predominates are hard ; others, having an abundant marly basis, are comparatively soft, with a tendency more or less marked to the slaty structure

Among the fragments of red sandstone, there is one of quartzy greywacke.

These red rocks probably belong to a red sandstone newer than the old red sandstone

2 G 2

II. NEAR MUSSEL BAY.

Primitive Rocks.

Grey Granite.
Small granular compact Red Granite.
Red Gneiss.
Mica-slate
Hornblende-slate.
Snow-white translucent common Quartz with conchoidal fracture.
Sand from the beach, near Mussel Bay, 6th June, 1827. Gneiss-sand.

III. MUSSEL BAY.

Primitive Rocks.

Small granular greyish-white Quartz-rock, occasionally striped green with chlorite, and containing imbedded precious garnet   Some varieties, from the quantity of mica which they contain, pass into mica-slate , occasionally also imbedded crystals of common hornblende occur , and in one fragment we observed extremely minute asparagus-green crystals, which appear to be apatite.

Hornblende-slate with imbedded Iron Pyrites

IV HECLA COVE.

Primitive and Transition Rocks.

Bluish-grey Primitive Clay-slate , shining lustre and thin slaty fracture

Ash grey, greenish-grey, and greyish-white Quartz-rock, in small and fine granular distinct concretions, which latter variety occasionally is almost compact, more or less translucent   Scales of mica occasionally disseminated in the mass of the rock.   In one specimen, layers of Clay-slate in the Quartz-rock.

One specimen of grey-coloured compact quartz, with intermixed pistacite. Probably primitive.

Rose-coloured very fine granular translucent quartz rock.

Boulder of mica slate with precious garnets.   South side of Hecla Cove. Primitive

Snow-white fine granular Dolomite marble.   Primitive

According to Mr. Reid, this Dolomite contains

Carbonate of Lime	68 3
Carbonate of Magnesia . .	30 5
Siliceous matter	1.0
Loss	0 2
	100

Bluish-grey small granular foliated, slightly-translucent limestone. Primitive?

Coarse granular loosely-aggregated greyish-white translucent Quartz-rock, partially stained with reddish brown colour Transition

Reddish-coloured compact Greywacke Transition

Specimen of Greywacke Slate. Transition

Variety of Red Sandstone. Transition.

Slaty Red Sandstone Transition

Weathered Specimen, apparently of secondary Greenstone.

SOIL OF SPITZBERGEN.

Mould from Hecla Cove.

According to Mr. Reid, it is composed of the following substances:

Silica	70
Carbonate of Lime	8 5
Carbonate of Iron	3
Vegetable Debris	2 5
Water	12
Loss	4
	100

Its specific gravity is 2.750.

There was also a slight trace of Manganese.

It is remarked by Captain Parry, that the soil in this quarter is good, and covered with a tolerably abundant vegetation.

V. HECLA BAY

Transition, Secondary, and Alluvial Rocks.

Mica-slate with precious Garnets

Chlorite-slate.

Specimen of grey-coloured granular Quartz-rock, with clay-slate passing into mica-slate attached to it.

Compact Quartz, with disseminated Iron Pyrites.

From the top of the highest hill near the monument, Hecla Cove, small-granular loosely-aggregated greyish-white Quartz-rock, with attached and intermixed Brown Clay Iron Ore.

Small-granular augite Greenstone. Mr. Beverly, in the narrative, alluding to this rock, says, " At about a quarter of a mile from the base of the high land, immense masses of a very coarse granular rock (augite Greenstone) lie scattered about, and appear to have been precipitated from the upper stratum of the mountain They are composed of ferruginous sand and hornblende (augite), in such a state of decomposition as to crumble into powder under the hammer."

Alluvial bluish-grey vesicular Pipe-clay. Hecla Cove.

According to Mr Reid, this clay consists of

Silica	65
Alumina	23
Oxide of Iron and Carbonate of Lime	1
Water	11
	100

VI. MARBLE POINT.

[See bottom of p 125 of the Narrative]

Transition, Tertiary, and Alluvial Rocks.

Limestone, dark-greyish black, inclining to brownish-black, compact, opaque, traversed by numerous veins of red and white calcareous spar. When rubbed emits a fetid smell

According to Mr. Reid, this Limestone contains

Carbonate of Lime	99 6
Carbonaceous matter	4.4
	100

Masses of ash-grey splintery chert, probably imbedded in the Limestone.

Masses of grey and white calcareous spar, in granular and prismatic concretions, from the Limestone.

Specimens of red-coloured Sandstone, and of slaty greenish-grey very small granular Quartz-rock.

*   *

Brown Coal. This Brown Coal, Captain Parry informs me, burns with a clear bright flame, and emits a pleasant odour It probably belongs to a tertiary deposite.

*   *   *

Greenish-grey Marl   Is decomposed Limestone.

Specimens of ochre-yellow Alluvial clay.

*   *   *   *

Vesicular Lava   This variety is sometimes named Pumice-stone.   Captain Parry says, that a great many rounded pieces of this lava are found on this part of the Coast of Spitzbergen, and generally above the inner line of drift-wood, as if they had reached the highest limit to which the sea had attained.

VII BEVERLY BAY.

Primitive Rocks.

Beautiful, rather coarse-granular red-coloured granite, composed of pale flesh-red feldspar, greyish-brown conchoidal translucent Quartz, and silver-white or pinchbeck-brown Mica.

Grey coarse-granular Granite. Feldspar grey, Quartz sometimes milk-white, translucent, with conchoidal fracture and shining lustre, Mica dark pinchbeck-brown.

Mica-slate inclining to Gneiss, with abundant imbedded precious Garnets.

Quartz-rock, white, ash-grey, and greenish-grey, from small-granular to compact, sometimes with layers of Mica, thus forming a transition to Mica-slate. Other varieties with disseminated Iron Pyrites; some with Chlorite, and the Chlorite at times so disposed as to give the mass a slaty structure.

VIII. CAPE FANSHAWE.

The small specimens from this quarter appear to be made up principally of Silicified Madreporites, Reteporites, Orthoceratites, Terebratulites, and Cardites, apparently connected with Limestone

ISLANDS.

I LOW ISLAND.

Transition Rocks.

Purplish-red small-granular translucent Quartz-rock.

Small-granular translucent greyish-white Quartz-rock. This variety has sometimes a slaty structure, or rises in plates.

Greenish-grey small-granular Quartz-rock, with slaty structure. This variety appears to pass into greenish-grey slaty Sandstone.

Reddish Sandstone, with scales of Mica   There is a transition from this into the reddish-coloured fine-granular Quartz-rock. This Sandstone appears frequently to rise in tables or plates

On the west point of this island Captain Parry observed the strata of Quartz-rock dipping at an angle of 70° to the S. E. He also found strata of Clay-slate at a distance from the shore, of blue, red, and yellow colours, and dipping in various directions   The expedition also landed on the southern point of the island, and found the strata to be clay-slate , and near to this point is a hill about one hundred and fifty feet above the sea, which is the highest part of the island. The rocks of which the hill are composed, are of reddish slaty Quartz-rock disposed in vertical strata

II WALDEN ISLAND.

Primitive Rocks.

Granite, of a flesh-red colour.

Grey-coloured granitic Gneiss, with precious Garnets.

Grey-coloured porphyritic Granite, with imbedded milk Quartz

Greyish-white small-granular translucent Quartz-rock.

Reddish-white small-granular rather loosely aggregated Quartz-rock

Very small-granular greyish-white Quartz rock, striped green with chlorite.

Grey-coloured Quartz-rock, with abundant scales of dark-brown mica.

Mr. Beverly observed the rocks on the south-eastern and lowest part of Walden Island, which we presume are of primitive gneiss, traversed by veins, from twelve to twenty inches wide, of fine granular and grey granite, the sides of which were of whitish felspar, about three inches wide   In some places the granite cliffs were six hundred feet high

III ROSS'S ISLET.

Primitive Rocks.

Grey and reddish Granitic-gneiss, very coarse-granular, occasionally porphyritic, with imbedded precious Garnets, also a flesh-red variety of the same rock   This small island is the most northern known land of the globe

Concluding Remarks

From the preceding enumeration, it appears that Spitzbergen and its neighbouring isles afford rocks belonging to five of the great classes, namely, Primitive, Transition, Secondary, Tertiary (?) and Alluvial   The only volcanic specimen in the collection is a very vesicular Lava found at Marble Point, which, however, may have been floated thither from Iceland or Jan Mayen's Isle, both of which are of volcanic formation   With the exception of disseminated Iron Pyrites and brown-clay Iron Ore in Quartz-rocks, no metalliferous compounds were met with   The only inflammable mineral in the collection is a specimen of Brown-coal, found at Marble Point, which, considering the nature of the country, is to be viewed as very interesting, and leaves us to regret that the time of the officers of the expedition was so limited, as to prevent their determining its geognostic position   The Dolomite Marble from Hecla Cove agrees in colour, size of grain, and other characters, with the statuary marble of Italy   In these islands, as in Old Greenland, and several other islands discovered by Captain Parry during his former voyages, the Precious Garnet abounds. Its occurrence in Ross's Islet, and its known distribution in other countries, shews that of all the gems it has the widest geographical range, extending in the northern hemisphere from the equator to the high latitude of the most northern known land

THE END

2 H

LONDON
Printed by W. Clowes,
Stamford street

N

40

enwich

marle Street London

LONDON
Printed by W Clowes,
Stamford street

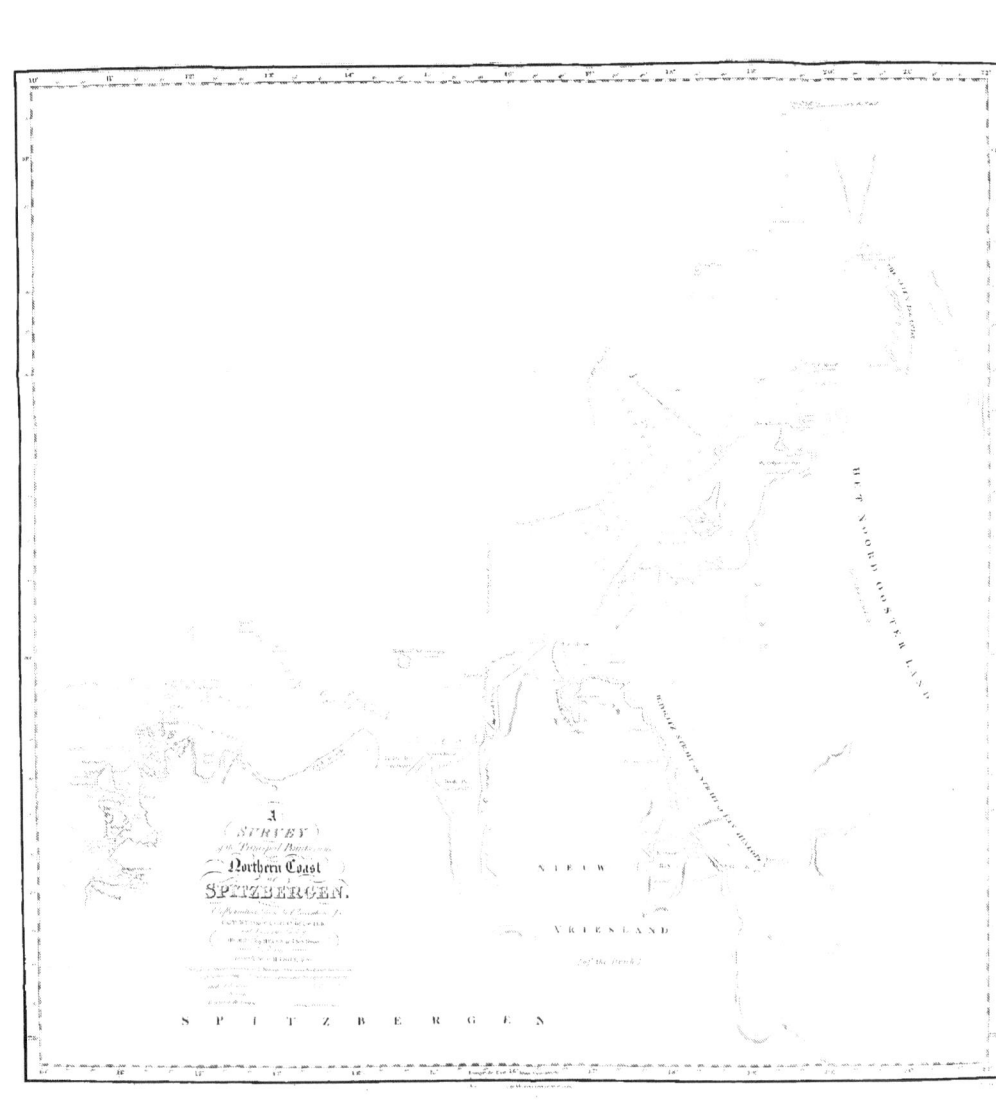

A SURVEY of the Principal Bays on the Northern Coast of SPITZBERGEN.

HET NOORD OOSTER LAND

NIEUW VRIESLAND

SPITZBERGEN

Lightning Source UK Ltd.
Milton Keynes UK
UKHW040615190220
358975UK00014B/403